Advertising, Sex, and Post-Socialism

Advertising, Sex, and Post-Socialism

Women, Media, and Femininity in the Balkans

Elza Ibroscheva

LEXINGTON BOOKS
Lanham • Boulder • New York • Toronto • Plymouth, UK

Published by Lexington Books
A wholly owned subsidiary of The Rowman & Littlefield Publishing Group, Inc.
4501 Forbes Boulevard, Suite 200, Lanham, Maryland 20706
www.rowman.com

10 Thornbury Road, Plymouth PL6 7PP, United Kingdom

Copyright © 2013 by Lexington Books

All rights reserved. No part of this book may be reproduced in any form or by any electronic or mechanical means, including information storage and retrieval systems, without written permission from the publisher, except by a reviewer who may quote passages in a review.

British Library Cataloguing in Publication Information Available

Library of Congress Cataloging-in-Publication Data

Ibroscheva, Elza, 1974–
Advertising, sex, and post-socialism : women, media, and femininity in the Balkans / Elza Ibroscheva.
pages cm
Includes bibliographical references and index.
ISBN 978-0-7391-7266-7 (cloth : alk. paper) — ISBN 978-0-7391-7267-4 (electronic)
1. Sex in advertising—Balkan Peninsula. 2. Socialism—Balkan Peninsula. 3. Post-communism—Balkan Peninsula. I. Title.
HF5827.85.i27 2013
659.1082'09496—dc23
2013010615

∞™ The paper used in this publication meets the minimum requirements of American National Standard for Information Sciences Permanence of Paper for Printed Library Materials, ANSI/NISO Z39.48-1992.

Printed in the United States of America

To my loving parents, Iulia and Nistor,
Thanks for being my beacon, my anchor, my wings

Contents

Acknowledgments		ix
Introduction		xi
1	Sex? Please, We Are Socialist: The Ideology of Femininity, Bodies, and Sex During Socialism	1
2	Advertising and the Socialist Economy: Efficiency, Necessity, and Desire	47
3	Liberating Women: The Role of Media in Defining Femininity in the Post-Socialist Transition	75
4	Of Vodka, Watermelons, and Other Sexy Fruit: Advertising and the Objectification of Women in Bulgaria	113
5	Sex and Politics: Consuming Women's Bodies	131
Conclusion		151
Bibliography		161
Index		171
About the Author		175

Acknowledgments

This book was made possible with the kind assistance of the librarians at the Bourgas Municipality Library, who were extremely helpful in not only providing me with the archival copies of the magazines and newspapers which comprised my primary data, but also in giving me numerous useful tips on other socialist publications that became relevant to my study. To them, I owe a note of gratitude for their professionalism and willingness to help in any way possible.

In addition, while the majority of the chapters were originally produced for this book, a few chapters have previously appeared in peer-reviewed journals. Chapter 2 on socialist advertising appeared first online in 2012 under the title "The Unbearable Lightness of Advertising: Culture, Media and the Rise of Advertising in Bulgaria" in *Consumption, Markets and Culture*. Chapter 4 also appeared online in 2012 under the title "Selling the Post-Communist Female Body: Portrayals of Women and Gender in Bulgarian Advertising," in *Feminist Media Studies*, and was modified to include some more recent examples of advertising campaigns. Finally, chapter 5 on women in politics appeared originally in 2009 under the title "Engendering Transition: A Critical Analysis of Portrayals of Female Politicians in the Bulgarian Press," in the *Howard Journal of Communications* (vol. 20, pp. 111–28), and has been updated to include more recent media examples. The original article was coauthored with Dr. Maria Raicheva-Stover of Washburn University, who has been a fantastic colleague and a common feminist soul.

I would also like to acknowledge the support I received from another post-socialist feminist scholar, Dr. Nadia Kaneva, whose advice and guidance through this process were always helpful and encouraging. To Nadia and Maria, *blagodaria vi ot surtse*. I would also like to thank the anonymous reviewer who provided me with invaluable feedback on the manuscript and helped me strengthen and focus my argument. Finally, I also want to acknowledge my wonderful parents, who have been an inspiration, a support network, and most able research assistants, helping me stay on track in this wonderful trip. To them, I am eternally grateful. To my husband, Sami, and my son, Adam—who was born the same time as this book project began—you have been my biggest fans and I can never thank you enough for all the love and support you have given me.

Introduction

We have all heard the old refrain "sex sells." For the longest time, it has served as a universal excuse for the sexual transgressions of the advertising industry. The motto has also fueled Madison Avenue's success in making Western advertising a global force that defines worldwide tastes and lifestyles. Successfully applied, this universal law of advertising, essentially moved by consumers' need to imagine and satisfy their sexual identities and desires, has been accepted as the one guaranteed path to generating quick profits, brand recall, and name recognition in the marketplace. And in its "magic to market desire," as Raymond Williams argued, advertising and its sexual undertones have come to define effectively the most extensive system of organized communication whose primary ethic is that of "selling."[1]

In this sense, Williams believed, advertising was a particularly unique modern phenomenon not because it focused on the human need to create and satisfy a world inhabited by fantasies and *magic*, but because its "highly organized and professional system of magical inducements and satisfactions," is "functionally very similar to magic systems in simpler societies, but rather strangely coexistent with a highly developed scientific technology."[2] What is more, this magical system is intrinsically capitalist at heart, as is implied by its very existence, placing an emphasis on consumption, not production, as well as a tendency to celebrate satisfying one's individual need for happiness through obtaining objects of desires. Ultimately, Williams contended, advertising is so intrinsic to capitalist culture that modern capitalism simply cannot function without it.

It is easy to see, then, how the notion of advertising as the moving engine of capitalist desires was also virtually absent in the culture of the Soviet bloc, where words like "individual" and "desire" were effectively erased from public discourse and skillfully replaced by a stress on collective sacrifice, and perpetual self-denial, which will allow socialist societies to achieve the ultimate superiority over the capitalist West. Therefore, it is not surprising that in socialist Eastern Europe, neither "sex" nor "selling" were topics anyone was willing to discuss publicly. In fact, the official Communist Party line professed that both sex and commercial advertising were undesirable remnants of a decadent bourgeois past, and as much, they hinder human progress by catering to the most primitive human drives—the fulfillment of desires of the flesh and desires of excessive and selfish consumption. And while Williams prophetically points out that the system of organized magic which is modern advertising sets as its primary goal the functional obscuring of man as consumer and man as user, Michael Schudson, in comparing advertising to socialist realism, claims:

> If the visual aesthetic of socialist realism is designed to dignify the simplicity of human labor in the service of the state, the aesthetic of capitalist realism— without a masterplan of purposes—glorifies pleasures and freedoms of consumer choice in defense of the virtues of private life and material ambition.[3]

During socialism, the main goal of the communist ideologues was to convince the proletariat that the "good life" is not only attainable without indulging in material goods, but in fact, is far more enjoyable and satisfying when one surrenders the private in the interest of the public, thus creating a far more superior social order to that propagated by Western capitalism. In order to make the push towards stripping citizens of their individuality and their ability to define personal pleasure through the act of buying and owning goods, the socialist ideologues faced a significant challenge in building a new socialist "man" and a new socialist "woman" whose consumer needs could be satisfied without material possessions. And for a while, the ideology of personal sacrifice along with a carefully rationed public consumption seem to have worked for the planned economy of the socialist states. But as Sutt Jhally pointed out, these repressive societies "never found a way to connect to people in any kind of pleasurable way, relegating issues of pleasure and individual expression to the non-essential and distracting aspects of social life."[4]

The denial of pleasure, whether as a means to curb individual freedoms or as a means to impose homogenizing uniformity, was a staple of the communist regime. So much so, that socialism professed to have practically transformed men and women from irrational creatures of desire into extremely efficient and emancipated beings of a higher kind. In this process of rechanneling desires and transforming needs, the communist social order has proven superior to its Western nemesis in being able to eliminate the need to cater to individual desires, fantasies, pleasures, and comforts. By focusing on restructuring class relations, communism proclaimed that all other social issues, including gender inequalities and issues of class-consciousness and consumption, would essentially disappear. As Sam Vaknin pointed out, "men and women were catapulted out of their pre-ordained social orbits into an experiment of dystopia."[5]

When the dystopia of communism ended, men and women alike were thrown back into a vortex of economic, social, and political uncertainties. More importantly, the collapse of the regimes in the East proved that the denial of freedom of choice, including the choice of expressing sexual desires and exercising one's right to shop, was virtually unsustainable. The famous feminist Gloria Steinem described this paradoxical act of liberating oneself through the act of consumption when she noted, "First, we have the revolution, and then, we all go shopping."[6] Similarly, scholars have argued that it is precisely the lack of consumer choices, many of which come as direct consequences of commercial advertising, along with the "queues, Trabants, lacks of bananas and frumpy women," that essentially led to the collapse of the popular support for the socialist project.[7] As Barbara Ehrenreich boldly proclaimed, "Soviet-style communism might have been successful at building up heavy industry and creating a minimally decent social welfare system, but centralized economies don't work so well at providing fresh fruit, pantyhose, tape cassettes, and the rest of it."[8]

Today, the freedom to choose among a variety of consumer products and the option to do so while tempted by the sexually provocative images of nude or partially clad women have become an everyday occurrence in the post-socialist transition. It is perhaps safe to say that "sex sells everything" in Eastern Europe, from alcohol, to latex paint, weapons, and auto insurance. A particularly illustrative example of this trend recently caused a media blitz, when the owners of a Polish funeral home decided to create a calendar promoting their products and services that featured photos of nude women, erotically posed on top of coffins or engaging in a provocative sexual act with what appear to be symbolically the bodies of deceased men. In addition to outraging the Catholic Church, the calendar also became an international news sensation. In defense of the advertising campaign, the owner of the funeral business said, "We could show something half-serious, colorful, beautiful; the beauty of Polish girls and the beauty of our coffins."[9] The infallible logic of using nude female bodies to push a product was perhaps best summarized in the question posited by the Reuters' reporter in the end of the story: "What could be more seductive than the merchandise of mortality?"[10] And while advertising executives in the East often cite their Western counterpart as the place where the inspiration for these hyper-sexualized images and representations is found, the "sex sells" motto has become a trivializing cliché that seems to obscure the complex relationship between culture, ideology, and expressions of power, which underscores the dramatic shift in gender relations that has taken place in post-socialist Eastern Europe.

As Katherine Sender argued, "the common sense of 'sex sells' masks the relationship between sexuality and commerce, discouraging analysis of the particular ways that sex is articulated to marketing and ignoring the limits placed on visible manifestations of sexuality in advertising and commercial media."[11]

The debate surrounding how to educate the consumer into capitalist modes of thinking about gender has been largely invisible in academia on both sides of the former ideological schism. Perhaps the reason behind avoiding this conversation is the complex ways in which ideologies of gender, markets, and identity intertwined into a web of interrelations, which serve to legitimize each other and further normalize the experience of pleasure and desire. As Sutt Jhally aptly points out:

> A critique of advertising has to start by giving people permission to recognize the pleasure, the strength, of the images of advertising, of where that power rests. From that, we can start to unfold the exact role that advertising plays in our culture from a critical perspective. There is of course a great danger involved in this move, for the recognition of pleasure becomes a distorted conception if it is not simultaneously contextualized within the context of (in this case, patriarchal) power relations. Pleasure can be used against people under the guise of freedom.[12]

The idea that pleasure is indeed synonymous with freedom has been a powerful slogan of the post-socialist transition. In its hedonistic origin, the concept of celebrating one's individual need to be happy was liberating to millions of Eastern Europeans whose lives had been defined by the homogenizing aesthetics of socialist collectivism. In essence, it also led to an almost obsessive need for visual media in general, and advertising specifically, to bring enticing and appealing messages into the public realm, a place where the communist ideology of self-control and austerity virtually obliterated any trace of displaying gratification or expression of individual joy. Advertising, it appeared, was the ideal locale for these new pleasures to appear, seamlessly writing itself within the urban landscape of the socialist cities, with explosion of colorful billboards, featuring products, places, and happy people one could only dream of prior to the collapse of the system. As Barbara Ehrenreich points out, "think of the message embodied in some of the products themselves, like blue jeans, fast (i.e., non-family) food, or rock music. These are messages about individual liberty, about sexual expression, and about a universal entitlement to comfort, pleasure—even adventure."[13]

As a young woman, coming of age during the transformative years of the collapse of communism, I remember my own first encounters with the "magic" of advertising and the joy of consumption. The vivid memory of buying my first pair of Levi's jeans is still imprinted in my mind—unimaginably expensive, yet so coveted, the jeans represented everything I imagined freedom will bring—a sense of identity that is truly mine, authored by me, put together by me, by picking and choosing what to wear and how to wear it, essentially worshiping the commodity as an expression of personal triumph over the years of restrictions and deprivation. As Djurdja Bartlett observed, Western fashion items retained the capacity for symbolic investment precisely because their availability was so scarce and so tightly controlled by the state. In her elegant study of the history of fashion and its ideological practices in the Eastern bloc, she illustratively quotes a Russian scientist's admission to an American acquaintance: "People want something that is not Soviet—anything, a shirt, a tie, a handbag, any little thing at all. It makes them feel better than other people."[14] And as many critics have acknowledged, the powerful feeling of gratification derived from the sheer act of consumption defined in this very moment what I thought self-expression and self-indulgence felt like—pleasing, rewarding, unabashedly liberating.

A similar sense of liberation was also universally felt by women who readily embraced Western concepts of female beauty standards. What was previously condemned as "bourgeois" constructions of femininity that cultivated a fashionable beauty and sexual desirability unbecoming of the socialist woman was now celebrated both as the triumph of consumption and a victory for the individualized sense of being. Here, the connection between the dearth of beauty products practically absent from the socialist market and the strict control of the state over the very little that was available, creates and explosive mix which allows women to simultaneously engage in two forbidden socialist transgressions—shopping for one's self while also trying to look good. Finally, women were allowed to cater to their own idea of physical attractiveness, aided by the influx of cosmetic products and a personalized triumph over state-imposed norms and consumer priorities. "To a certain extent, therefore, Soviet women construed the image of the commodified woman as a goal rather than a target, an image valorized by both political censure and material lack."[15] Sprinkle this with a notch of a much-needed public conservation about sex, adorned by the dazzling display of beauty pageants and readily available erotica and you have yourself a recipe for a "sexual revolution."

So what happened next? The answer to this question lies ahead in the remaining pages of this book. But to get us started, consider this illustration of how common and prevalent the sexualization of women has become as a result of the openness of the Eastern bloc to all topics sexual—Bulgarian expats and foreign residents' campaign was initiated by the online publication Vagabond to elect the cultural symbols that truly represent contemporary Bulgaria. Among emblematic cultural artifacts and humorous jabs at the peculiarities of the culture of the transition, such as abandoned Trabants in parking lots that resemble a Rainforest revival project, the following category comes in third place: "Thousands of stunning babes dressed in clothing that leaves nothing to the imagination—all whilst working as lawyers, doctors and managers. You wouldn't find that even in Venezuela!"[16] And where else, but in Eastern Europe, do you see the widely popular competitive races for young women, all dolled up and in full glamour attire, galloping through the streets of town in 9-inch stilettos in front of the ever-present eye of the camera? As one observer noted, "Eastern European women are practically born in high heels."

Growing up as a young woman, I vividly recall the grey and mundane visual landscape of communism, populated with smiling matronly-looking, hefty-set women, dressed in bland, uncomplimentary attire, beckoning to the future, while holding some complex measuring instrument or a new mechanical tool. At the same, I also recall my own mother's sense of style that she painstakingly crafted out of self-made outfits, modeled after smuggled *kroyki* (tailoring blueprints) and issues of *Burda*, which made her look her a Goddess to me. My mother's attempt to establish an identity of her own, exploring fresh opportunities the market created while deciphering the newly available codes of attractiveness and beauty, was no exception to the rule. As Beth Holmgren aptly observed, "at least in this transitional period, the market value recently tagged on women's beauty and sexual desirability still resonates with an unofficial desire, a past quest in which women did not simply consume a prescribed ideal, but exercised their own creativity and constructed their own 'unofficial' (if still convention-bound) self-image."[17] Stuck in between these two extremes, women in Eastern Europe, and particularly so young women of the transition whose growing awareness of their individual, social, and political positioning was directly impacted by the radical changes of the market revolution, were left to navigate the murky waters of the shifting definition of "womanhood" and all of its ideological and political frustrations.

The critical role that advertising plays as a compass navigating the luring world of consumption was also acknowledged by Anikó Imre in her book *Identity Games: Globalization and the Transformation of Media Cultures in the New Europe*. Imre vividly described her first encounter with the cultural landscape of the West after the fall of the Berlin Wall: "The shock over the unbearable lightness of being was overwhelming for someone unequipped with any kind of advertisement literacy—the most important skill that television teaches."[18] It is precisely this lack of advertisement literacy, which women and men in Eastern Europe experienced, I argue, that serves as a great departure point in my approach to this book—personally impacting my observations as a product of the post-communist transition and scholastically, as an academic observing and analyzing the vast media changes that have transformed and continue to determine the cultural landscape in my home country of Bulgaria and the region at large.

REGIONAL FOCUS: WHY THE BALKANS?

The Balkan region has, for reasons brilliantly outlined in Maria Todorova's *Imagining the Balkans,* been both a historic challenge and a unique cultural paradox.[19] As a geographical locale, the Balkans have been construed as a strategic bridge between the East and the West, and as such, have been noted for many decades as a region that needs to be taken seriously by its Western counterparts, if not studied in utmost detail. The interest in getting to know the Balkans did not originate in a genuine desire to become familiar with the neighborly nations to which one might turn for solace, cooperation, or protection. On the contrary, the West's desire to understand, describe, and classify the Balkans and its people has been largely motivated either out of fascination with the region's cultural notions of liberty and exoticism, or out of apprehension and fear of the unpredictable and frequently, violent behavior, of its people. As a result, the Balkan nations themselves have been marred by this tendency to be "otherized," a process of cultural subjugation which Edward Said elegantly described in his book *Orientalism*, which he described as the corporate institutions' response for dealing with the Orient: "dealing with it by making statements about it, authorizing views of it, describing it by teaching it, settling it, ruling over it: in short . . . a Western style for dominating, restructuring, and having authority over the Orient."[20] A particularly interesting notion in the discourse of the Orient as the "other" and as such, as less civilized and essentially inferior, has also been the articulation of the sexual allure of the Orient, which offered exotic tales of erotic adventure and lusciousness, often painting an extremely feminized portrait of the Orient.

In the case of the Balkans, however, as Todorova points out, this has not been the case, for the Balkans had an overtly male appeal, "the appeal of medieval knighthood, of arms, and plots."[21] "Unlike the standard orientalist discourse, which resorts to metaphors of its objects of study as female, the balkanist discourse is singularly male."[22] This observation is particularly important as it reveals the persevering power of romanticizing masculine power as a subject of national pride. At the same time, it also underlines the contradiction and the virtual impossibility of the model of socialist emancipation as viable alternative to the ingrained nature of patriarchy in the collective psyche of the Balkan nations.

What the "otherness" of the Balkans has produced as another commonly shared characteristics among the nations of the region has been a self-imposed sense of being distinct from the notion of "Europeanness," producing a paradoxical feeling of being left out, and in a sense, rejected from one's own geographical locale. As Todorova aptly describes:

> The Balkans have served as a repository of negative characteristics against which a positive and self-congratulatory image of the "European" and the "West" has been constructed. . . . The Balkans are left in Europe's thrall, anticivilization, alter ego, the dark side within.[23]

This cultural sense of being non-European, yet historically tied into the web of political and social circumstances of the continent, engendered a very complex identity, often amplified by the remnants of the Ottoman presence in the nations of the Balkans. As such, these Southeastern European countries share very little in common with their Central European neighbors, which have historically been considered much more developed and connected to the West by the sheer fact that they are far less connected to the Orient.

This notion was essentially eradicated by the attempt of the Soviet regime to homogenize the Eastern bloc through careful ideological indoctrination, all the while creating the illusion that the common goal of building socialism trumps all other signifiers of cultural identity. While I readily acknowledge that the collapse of the communist utopia of transcending national identities was the greatest proof that this cultural experiment was indeed an impossibility, I also would like to argue that despite the uniqueness of each Balkan culture, which as Todorova pointed out has been discursively constructed for the purpose of politicizing the terrain of cultural domination, in the realm of gender, a particularly virulent strain of patriarchy that is distinctly Balkan in its conceptualization of gender norms creates a powerful tangent of commonalities among the Balkan countries. And if Ivaylo Ditchev has aptly underscored the importance of recognizing distinction when he argued that, "If we want to play on words we could say that the surest sign of Balkan identity is the resistance to Balkan identity," we must also recognize that there appears to be very little argument that the cultures of the peninsula are permeated by a celebration of patriarchy, where the trope of the "Balkan man" is a universally share symbol of power across national and regional differences.[24]

In addition to distinguishing the physical boundaries of the Eastern and Central European region, we must also acknowledge that there appears to be at least in terms of formal policies imposed by the Soviet Union a familial socialist ideological notion of gender norms largely propagated by the doctrine of the equality among the sexes. This notion was adopted by all countries of the Eastern bloc, but adapted in varying degree in the localized cultural environment of each socialist state. In other words, how the Polish understood and applied the socialist ideology of gender parity was different from the way the Hungarians and the Czech understood it, and even more different from the way the Bulgarians, Romanians, Serbians, and Croats did. A similar experience is currently being observed in the case of the former socialist states of Central and Eastern Europe that recently ascended into the

European Union. Becoming full-fledged members of this highly exclusive club was a national ideology dream all of these nations shared—yet, the very fact that Hungarians, the Czech (not the Slovaks), and the Polish got there first, followed several years later by the Bulgarians and the Romanians demonstrated both the hierarchy of cultural affinity among the different tiers of "Europeanness" as well as the intrinsically common desire to receive a formal acknowledgment of having earned a place on the European map.

While I acknowledge with utmost certainty that no two countries are alike, I occasionally tend to use the terms Eastern Europe and the Soviet bloc as a larger bracket to address cultural trends and political developments that have indeed, often perhaps in varying degree, overwhelmingly shaped the region. Part of the argument stems from the fact that despite the obvious cultural differences between the countries of the Eastern bloc, Eastern and Central European countries for a long time were conveniently clumped together into one uniform cluster, based upon the universally upheld ideologies of the socialist order. Similarly, while the Soviet Union was the locus of communist ideologies that translated across the entire region, it must be noted that the countries of the Eastern bloc did not always have a uniform response to the policies commissioned by Moscow and responded to them with varying degree of compliance.

In the case of Bulgaria, which was known as the closest satellite state to the Soviets and was often referred to as the "16th Republic" by its own leaders, the official party line rarely veered away from the one issued by the Soviet ideologues, and when it did, it did so rather hesitantly and timidly, compared to the Central European countries, for example. This, however, has not been the case with other Eastern European countries—a fact that I acknowledge on several occasions as I analyze the cultural and ideological notions that served as the axis of the communist gender régime. More importantly, from a political standpoint it is crucial to acknowledge that the Bulgarians and Romanians were among the most ideologically docile followers of Soviet doctrines. This blind devotion to the Moscow directives resulted in an extremely rigid political system of control that failed to produce a popular dissent movement of the scale of the likes in Hungary, Poland, and Czechoslovakia. When attempts to rally the intellectual elite in a revolt against the communist authorities took place, those were quickly suppressed and effectively eliminated.

A final note, which I reiterate later in the chapter on socialist advertising, must be made about the unique economic model of former Yugoslavia. The federation, dominated by the Serbian Republic, practiced a different model of economic development, free of the constraints of the five-year plan. Instead, citizens of Yugoslavia enjoyed the benefits of the free market and the opportunity to interact more openly with the West. This model also resulted in a culture of openness in talking about and dealing with matters of women's bodies and sexuality, yet, curiously, failed to shake the cultural foundation of the Balkan patriarchy.

I would also like to note that in this book, I refer to the authoritarian regimes in Eastern Europe interchangeably as communism and socialism. The terms remain in currency when discussing the changes in the region and are often used as though they are transposable. In my use of these labels, I subscribe to the possibility and open-endedness of change in the post-communist transition. Similarly, I use the East/West dichotomy simply as a heuristic device in order to illuminate differences. They are in no way absolute distinctions as variations within and similarities between continue to prevail through the region. Many feminist scholars, and particularly so in transnational film and media studies, have argued for the need to broaden the scope of critical examination by cutting across the West/non-West as well as North/South divide by offering critical interactions that include often neglected voices addressing the post-socialist second world and the global south. This argument was powerfully articulated by Katarzyna Marciniak, Aniko Imre, and Áine O'Healy, who introduced the term "transnational feminist media studies" in order to address the challenges posed by the cultural shifts and changing gender dynamics in the face of globalization.[25] The focus on the post-socialist region is particularly compelling, as this area of the world is frequently absent from discussions on global trends in feminist media studies.

THE GOAL OF THE BOOK

This book aims to explore the role of advertising and the consumption that it promotes across the Balkans, with a close focus on Bulgaria, while changing cultural perceptions of sex and femininity. The book is also an attempt at theorizing how the marketing of gender identities that has taken place in the years of the post-socialist transition has fundamentally affected the social, economic, and political positioning of women in the region. Because advertising is one of the major "factories" of cultural signification and as such, serves as the most ubiquitous vessel of global norms of gendered selves, and also because advertising serves as a literacy tool for learning the grammar rules of consumption, studying the ideologies of femininity and sex before and after the collapse of the socialist project, as well as the prevailing portrayals of femininity in advertising in the present day, provides a revealing look at the mechanisms of how post-socialist norms of desired and accepted sexual behavior are being engendered, and specifically, what role the media play in this transformative process. This is important because it addresses an area of international media and cultural studies that has been largely overlooked in media research and that can offer an illuminating critical dissection of the process of establishing and constructing gendered identities in a unique set of social, economic, and cultural conditions as witnessed in the post-socialist societies.

THEORETICAL CONSIDERATIONS

So far my argument has been that despite the unique distinction of each post-socialist nation, the Balkan nations share a common, culturally anchored place between the West and the Orient which they simultaneously despise and embrace. Yet, the bigger similarity here is found in thinking about gender as refracted through the Balkan cultural heritage of an overwhelmingly masculine outlook on the world. Furthermore, in this book the notions of gender, femininity, and masculinity must be understood both as sociological constructions as well as cultural norms. The latter is particularly relevant because it positions gender both as a term defining differences between the sexes as well as deconstructing the hierarchical nature of these relations within a social context. This is further complicated by the fact that in the Balkan region the word "gender" does not exist, linguistically speaking, since distinctions between the sexes are classified purely as biological, and not as products of power relations and structural inequalities. Nonetheless, the notions of femininity and masculinity are well defined as sociological norms and have been ingrained in both political ideologies and cultural discourses. Here, for the sake of theoretical clarity, I refer to being masculine or feminine as acting within the culturally specific and socially constructed definitions of being a man and being a woman. These, as cultural scholars, sociologists, and anthropologists have pointed out, are not value-neutral concepts, as they imply both a hierarchy of power and a domain of privilege. Although this might feel as a most intuitive way to understand and respond to gender stereotype, it is also an exercise of what Janet Spence and Camille Buckner called, "defining the undefinable."[26]

These stereotypes are also important to distinguish as part of the discussion of the Soviet conceptualization of gender because issues of masculinity and femininity were directly tied to the discourse of the Soviet revolution. Eliot Borenstein contended, "It is now a commonplace of post-Soviet society to claim that women were 'masculinized' by Soviet social policy, forced to sacrifice their 'femininity' on the altar of the workers' state."[27] A particularly fitting definition of masculinity as a social practice is articulated by Mimi Schippers, who describes it as "a social position, a set of practices, and the effects of the collective embodiment of those practices on individuals, relationships, institutional structures, and global relations of domination."[28] In media studies, the issues of gender, sexuality, and stereotypes are often conflated and situated within the theoretical framework of gender hegemony, according to which media essentially serve as purveyors of gender stereotypes and as social apparatuses for legitimizing the binary, hierarchy-producing relations between the two sexes. "The significance of masculinity and femininity in gender hegemony is that they establish symbolic meanings for the relationship between women and men that provide the legitimating rationale for social relations ensuring the ascendancy and dominance of men."[29]

Because they are compact forms of communication, advertisements and commercials are considered excellent resources to study cultural values, beliefs, and myths connected to gender. As Liesbet Van Zoonen stated, "advertisements as a cultural form, display a preoccupation with gender that is hardly matched to any other genre."[30] In addition, advertisements need to convey meaning within limited space and time and will therefore exploit symbols that are relevant and salient to society as a whole.[31] As Janice Winship argued, it is precisely the commonality and the familiarity of advertising images that makes them so powerful, particularly in articulating ideas of femininity and gender relations. "We already have both a knowledge of images of women from other discourses and an acquaintance with 'real' women in our everyday lives. The signification of an ad only has meaning in relations to this 'outside' knowledge of the ideology of femininity."[32] In the case of Bulgarian, Romanian, and Yugoslav women, the outside knowledge of mediated sexuality frequently came from discourses anchored in Western ideals of femininity, communicated mainly through advertising images in shopping catalogs and fashion magazine spreads secretly circulated during communism, often hand to hand, woman to woman, with an almost cult-like devotion. This trend continued even after the collapse of communism, aided by the wide availability of ads and Western fashion magazines stressing beauty and femininity as a most desired commodity.

The importance of advertising as defining new ways of thinking about gender is also directly connected to ideas of representation. As Sue Thornham argued, "as historical beings, we cannot be outside representation; we are constructed by and in relation to its images and discourses."[33] Visual representations, and specifically so those in advertising, are defined by the social and cultural conventions of the historic period in which they are engendered. In the post-communist transition, this was a particularly powerful force, as the collapse of the ideologically controlled gender norms during communism quickly dissipated amidst the chaos of the social and political lures of the free market. Here, the role of advertising as a "dream factory" is particularly important, as advertising is the place where fantasies of lives out of our reach are transformed into material, consumer goods that become associated with the symbolic power of the dreams they represent. For example, Raymond Williams has argued that advertising is a "magic system,"[34] and Michael Schudson[35] has taken this a step further by contending that advertising is "capitalist realist art" and that, although it does not have monopoly over the symbolic marketplace, different social group are differentially vulnerable especially during transitional stages of their lives. This form of art idealized the consumer and portrays as normative, special moments of satisfaction including sexual satisfaction. It "reminds us of beautiful moments in our own lives or it pictures marginal moments we would like to experience."[36]

The transition from a communist economic system into a capitalist free market also meant a complete transformation of the dominant ideology, both politically and culturally speaking. Judith Williamson argued that ideology creates subjects and advertising works by creating us "not only as subjects, but as particularly kind of subjects."[37] In Bulgaria, and perhaps across the entire Balkan region, that subject for women was defined both by a desire to do away with the repressive imposition of ideologically controlled and politically contrived definitions of femininity and by the longing to be a part of the imagistic fantasy created by the visuals of Western advertising, both visually and discursively. Thus, studying the visual representations of women in advertising and in other visual media, mainly in magazines and newspapers, during socialism and in the post-socialist transition appears to offer an appropriate forum to explore not only the newly transformed ideals of femininity, but also the mechanisms through which these ideals become introduced in the conditions of a consumer-based economy.

In studying gender and femininity, I apply Michel Foucault's idea of discourse as a specific system of language use; in a way, a form of knowledge that creates and articulates meanings, continuously reconstructed and deconstructed in social situations.[38] In addition, because discourses transmit and produce power, they work as tools of power. In my use of the discursive analysis, I argue that today's gendered discourses of power work heavily through media culture. In addition, I also apply critical discourse analysis using Norman Fairclough's methodological framework, which conceptualizes language as a social and historical process.[39] Fairclough's idea of the three spheres of discourse, including the process of production, the process of interpretation, and the social conditions and circumstances, in which the production and interpretation is taking place, are well fitted for the purpose of this book. Finally, my discussion of the tendency to stress sexuality in advertising as a normalizing trend that not only gives visibility to women but also empowers them through the very same sexual nature is informed by the critique of the "pornographication" of media culture offered by Brian McNair[40] and the mainstreaming of sex masterfully captured in the work of Feona Attwood.[41] Both of these media critical perspectives are indeed impossible without acknowledging that pornography must also be recognized as the arena where social norms governing sexual behavior are articulated and sanctioned. As Laura Kipnis wrote, "[a] culture's pornography becomes . . . a

xxiv   *Introduction*

very precise map of that culture's borders" creating "a detailed blueprint of culture's anxieties, investments, contradictions."[42]

ON METHODOLOGY

Because of its over-arching theoretical approach, this book raises the testy issue of methodology, identifying both strengths and limitations. I readily admit that no method is perfect in the analysis of data and all have shortfalls. Yet, the emphasis of my approach heavily weighs in favor of the qualitative traditions of critical and cultural studies, with each chapter offering a combination of textual and discourse analysis with a strong emphasis on the specific mass medium (mainly print media but also broadcast media content). I have made an effort to describe details of each methodological approach in the individual body of each chapter of the narrative. Most of the time, the analysis of linguistic elements is undertaken along with a focus upon dramatic communicative components as well as those developing predominantly from still images, but on certain occasions, also sound and music. Additionally, I also want to point out that the nature of the in-depth analysis of media texts I have conducted is also limited by my own language ability, restricting me to reading primary data collected in my home country of Bulgaria. At the same time, I have attempted to extrapolate important cultural connections and ideological points of similarities and distinctions with other countries in the Balkan region and the post-socialist nations at large. Ultimately, my goal in this exercise is using Geertzian terms to present in-depth, "thick" descriptions of the post-socialist cultural climate in the Balkans that encapsulates both in its distinction and its exemplarity the shift in gender relations reflected in and enabled by the rise and domination of advertising.

NOTES

1. Williams, Raymond, "Advertising: The Magic System,"in *Problems in Materialism and Culture*, ed. Raymond Williams (London: New Left Books, 1980), 184–85.
2. Williams, "Advertising: The Magic System," 185.
3. Schudson, Michael, *Advertising, the Uneasy Persuasion: Its Dubious Impact on American Society* (London: Routledge, 1984), 218.
4. Jhally, Sutt, "Advertising at the Edge of the Apocalypse," in *The Advertising and Consumer Culture Reader*, eds. Joseph Turow et al. (New York: Routledge, 2009), 422.
5. Vaknin, Sam, "Women in Transition: From Post-Feminism to Post-Femininity," *Central Europe Review*, 3, 22 (2001): 1, accessed June 20, 2011, http://www.ce-review.org/01/3/vaknin3.html.
6. Quoted in Ehrenreich, Barbara, "Laden with Lard" *ZETA* (July/August 1990): 46.
7. Reid, Susan, "Cold War in the Kitchen: Gender and the de-Stalinization of Consumer Taste in the Soviet Union under Khrushchev," *Slavic Review*, 61, 2 (2002): 212.
8. Ehrenreich, "Laden with Lard," 46.

9. "Oddly Enough: Polish Coffin Maker Uses Nude Models to Sell Wares," *Reuters*, November 2, 2012, http://mobile.reuters.com/article/oddlyEnoughNews/idUSBRE8A10WI20121102.

10. Ibid.

11. Sender, Katherine, "Sex Sells: Sex, Taste, and Class in Commercial Gay and Lesbian Media." *GLQ*, 9, 9 (2003): 331.

12. Jhally, Sutt, "Advertising, Gender and Sex: What's Wrong with a Little Objectification?" http://www.sutjhally.com/articles/whatswrongwithalit.

13. Ehrenreich, "Laden with Lard," 46.

14. Bartlett, Djurdja, *FashionEast: The Spectre That Haunted Socialism* (Cambridge: MIT Press, 2010), 261.

15. Holmgren, Beth, "Bug Inspectors and Beauty Queens: The Problem of Translating Feminism in Russian," in *Post-communism and the Body Politic*, ed. Ellen Berry (New York: New York University Press, 1995), 22.

16. Tankova, Diamana, "In Bad Need of A Good Image," *Vagabond*, http://old.vagabond.bg/?page=live&sub=37&open_news=1047.

17. Holmgren, "Bug Inspectors and Beauty Queens," 22.

18. Imre, Aniko, *Identity Games: Globalization and the Transformation of Media Cultures in the New Europe* (Cambridge: MIT Press, 2010), 4.

19. Todorova, Maria, *Imagining the Balkans* (New York: Oxford University Press, 1997).

20. Said, Edward, *Orientalism* (New York: Penguin, 2003/1978), 3.

21. Todorova, *Imagining the Balkans*, 4.

22. Ibid., 15.

23. Ibid., 188.

24. Ditchev, Ivaylo, "The Eros of Identity," in *Balkan as metaphor: Between globalization and fragmentation*, eds. D. I. Bjelic et al. (Cambridge: MIT Press, 2002).

25. Marciniak, Katarzyna et al. (eds.), *Transnational Feminism in Film and Media* (New York: Palgrave, 2007); Marciniak, Katarzyna et al., "Transcultural Mediations and Transnational Politics of Difference," *Feminist Media Studies*, 9, 4: (2009): 385–90; Marciniak, Katarzyna, *Alienhood, Citizenship, and the Logic of Difference* (Minneapolis: University of Minnesota Press, 2006).

26. Spence, Janet, and Buckner, Camille, "Masculinity and Femininity: Defining the Undefinable," in *Gender, Power, and Communication in Human Relationships*, eds. Pamela Kalbfleisch et al. (Hillsdale: Lawrence Erlbaum Associates, 1995), xiv.

27. Borenstein, Eliot, *Men with Women: Masculinity and Revolution in Russian Fiction, 1917–1929* (Durham and London: Duke University Press, 2000), 16.

28. Schippers, Mimi, "Recovering the Feminine Other: Masculinity, Femininity, and Gender Hegemony," *Theory and Society*, 36, 1 (2007): 86–87.

29. Ibid., 91.

30. Van Zoonen, Liesbet, *Feminist Media Studies* (London: Sage Publications, 1994), 67.

31. Van Zoonen, *Feminist Media Studies*.

32. Winship, Janet, "Sexuality for Sale," in *Culture, Media, Language*, eds. Stuart Hall et al. (London: Hutchinson, 1980), 218.

33. Sue Thornham, *Women, Feminism and Media* (Edinburgh: Edinburgh University Press, 2007), 45.

34. Williams, "Advertising: The Magic System," 185.

35. Schudson, *Advertising, the Uneasy Persuasion*.

36. Ibid., 212.

37. Williamson, Judith, *Decoding Advertisements* (London: Marion Boyars, 1978), 45.

38. Foucault, Michel, *History of Sexuality, Volume 1: An Introduction* (Penguin Books: London, 1976).

39. Fairclough, Norman, *Language and Power* (London and New York: Longman, 1989).

40. McNair, Brian, *Mediated Sex: Pornography and Postmodern Culture* (London: Arnold, 1996); *Striptease Culture: Sex, Media and the Democratization of Desire* (London and New York: Routledge, 2002).

41. Attwood, Feona, *Mainstreaming Sex: The Sexualization of Western Culture* (London: I. B. Tauris, 2009).

42. Kipnis, Laura, *Bound and Gagged: Pornography and the Politics of Fantasy in America* (New York: Grove, 1996), 14.

Chapter One

Sex? Please, We Are Socialist

The Ideology of Femininity, Bodies, and Sex During Socialism

Women's roles during the socialist regime were conceptualized in the duality of mother and worker. This duality of terms served an obvious two-fold function—on the one hand, it made the communist policy of gender emancipation look markedly superior compared to gender relations in the West, where women struggled not only to enter the work field and redefine their roles outside the home, but also to compete for equal wages and equal job opportunities with men who already occupied the market and its most coveted positions. On the other hand, women's dual roles as mothers and workers served also a most basic economic function—by being engaged outside the home and into the workforce under the veil of gender equality, women were an essential force in strengthening the competitive economic advantage of the socialist order as their labor contribution became increasingly necessary in order to meet the demands of the economic realities of the post-war period. Hence, as Tatyana Kotzeva pointed out, "the only available model to women to the exclusion of other possibilities (i.e., the exclusion of identifying as only mother or only worker/professional) was that of the working mother."[1]

However, even the image of the woman who conscientiously attends to her domestic and economic responsibilities was not to be understood as a model imposed from above, but one that she actively sought and was willing to embrace as a sign of progress and as a step outside the "dark ages" of orthodox patriarchy and traditional gender roles, which did little, if anything, to advance the social and political positioning of women prior to the socialist revolution. In fact, aligned with the Marxist vision of the economic roots of the oppression of women, capitalism, and the unequal distribution of wealth which disadvantaged women in their ability to be independent players in the market was often blamed for the lack of progress and opportunity for women prior to the socialist revolution, with dominant patriarchal gender norms receiving only a tangent mention as a challenge for women's progress towards independence. As Suzanne LaFont pointed out, "precommunist patriarchy remained intact with women shouldering the burden of economic and domestic labor."[2] Not only that, but as Katherine Verdery argued, socialism practically reconfigured female and male household roles, socializing "significant elements of reproduction even while leaving women responsible for the rest, and usurped certain patriarchal functions and responsibilities, thereby altering the relation between gendered 'domestic' and 'public' sphere familiar from nineteenth-century capitalism."[3]

In order, then, to make the desire to "emancipate" beyond the menial work associated with female domestic labor appear organic, the socialist ideologues put a heavy emphasis on the "grassroot" origin of women's willingness to move into the realm of work and public life previously reserved strictly as a male domain. In this effort, print publications, but particularly so, magazines whose main target audience was women, were instrumental in serving as the forum where those organic roots of female self-awareness and progressive thought found their voices. To trace, understand, and evaluate the conceptualization of socialist femininity, this chapter offers an ideological discourse analysis of the Bulgarian women's magazines in an attempt to decipher the processes involved in the production of relations of social power and articulation of gender norms. As Krasimira Daskalova pointed out, "women's appearances, skills, motivations, behavioral styles, and notions of what constitutes the female world, its ambiance, sensibilities, and culture are transmitted via otherwise unobtrusive statements and images."[4] The magazines examined for this chapter included *Zhenata Dnes*, *Lada*, and *Bhozur*, spanning from 1945 into 1989. In addition, ideological discourse analysis was selected as the method of analysis because it provides a contextual interface "where the social and the discursive can meet and be explicitly related to each other."[5] Finally, magazines were selected because they were critical both as vessels for socialist propaganda, and also where new ideas about femininity and gender norms can be circulated, old norms can be criticized, and authoritative opinions can be articulated to sound like the experiences of ordinary women, skillfully concealing the patronizing tone of the Communist Party.

The tone of patriarchy, however, stemmed from the very nature in which women's achievements were presented on the pages of the women's magazines themselves. To illustrate this, consider an example from *Zhenata Dnes*, Bulgaria's premier magazine devoted to women and also the organ of the Bulgarian Union of Women, featuring a photo of a group of matronly looking women who are part of a *kruzhok* (a self-learning group coming from the Russian word for circle), named "Our Motherland." The photo is accompanied by a caption that reads, "In the educational units, women are starting to show that they are becoming more and more worthy of their freedom and equality." The caption implies that for women, freedom and equality are not to be construed as human rights, but are to be treated as privileges that have to be earned, either through achieving the proper level of knowledge, comparable to that of men, or through constant and relentless hard work, meant to prove that their contribution to the economic growth of the state is equitable with that of men, and therefore, worthy of recognition.

Another interesting and poignant example of how the idea of displaying the equality of the sexes was ideologically consigned comes from the inside pages of *Zhenata Dnes*, circa January 1956. In a photo that displays the perfect socialist family, we see a mother, a father, and two daughters who appear to be engaged in leisure activities. The father, dressed formally, with his tie on, seems to be perusing over a magazine, while his two daughters curiously look on over his shoulder, as they sit on the arm rests of his chair. While the three of them occupy the main focus of the photo, the mother, off center, in the far right corner of the composition, is seen adjusting a flower vase. She is very much the epitome of the 1950s American "Father Knows Best" mom—she is dressed fashionably, wearing a pencil skirt and high heels, with her hair put in a stylish hairdo, without a single hair out of place. Even her movements, captured in the still of the moment, appear smooth and effortless. From the caption of the photo, we find out that Tsvetanka Angelova is the mother figure of the family, also the only one identified by name. Her husband and two daughters, although occupying the main focus of the photo, are there to simply illustrate that "spending an evening at home after a hard day of selfless labor at work is an absolute joy." We also learn that Angelova works as a book binder, and is the leader of her production unit, further emphasizing the visual utopia of the effortlessly cozy home setting, which comes as a most natural complement to a day filled with hard, physical labor at the factory. In a way, while we see that everyone in the family—mom, dad, and the two daughters—is enjoying an evening of leisurely activities, only dad and the girls are actually featured doing so. The mother figure, who seems to be the implicit focus of this photo, serves both an ideological and aesthetic purpose—as a symbol of the worker who has completed her performance norm at the factory, as a mother who is now also completing her domestic duties, and as a woman who is enacting an ideal of femininity, while looking good and in total control of her environment.

Interestingly, the idea of taking care of one's appearance is never quite visualized, although frequently hinted and extensively discussed in numerous advice columns. These accounts, frequently masked as scientific reports, offered rational explanations of how women's looks are to be maintained in line with the socialist ideology of rationality and efficiency. That approach was not at all uncommon. As Krasimira Daskalova noted, the use of science and scholarship to talk about women and their problems was a frequent, if not preferred method of writing when it came to convincing audiences of the objectivity, and therefore, indisputably factual base of the statements, which nevertheless were implicitly ideological in nature.[6] Daskalova described this common tendency as "the appeal to the authority of science, which is signaled by the impersonal, presumably objective tone of the discourse, abundant use of technical terms, depersonalization of the object of analysis, and presentation of the author in terms of his or her scientific degree."[7] This, in turn, led to the emergence of a unique discursive approach to talking and writing about the "women's problem" in the socialist context.

Mira Marody and Anna Giza-Poleszczuk discussed these issues in the context of the Polish women's experiences. They argued, "In the state's essentializing vision, women were workers and mothers, nothing else."[8] In addition, while the presentations of women in the Polish popular magazines focused largely on these predictable social roles, the idealized woman presented in these magazines simply failed to exhibit any sense of individualized femininity. Her physicality is always non-existent, and so are any mentions of her emotional states, anxieties, or self-reflective thoughts and behaviors.

A similar trend was also noticed in *Zhenata Dnes*' 1950s issues. While women were often discussed in the context of their public and domestic responsibilities, they rarely were featured in any notable fashion that stresses their individual appearance—when they are seen, rather than heard speaking through dialogues or interviews, they are dressed in their work uniform, often concealing their figures, and emphasizing the rather homogenizing, but rational and efficient clothing line promoted by the socialist vision of womanhood. In addition, while the images of lab-coat technicians, tractor driving women, or costume-clad opera singers or ballet dancers illustrated the magazine's feature stories, they were deliberately missing any physical body features. For example, in a 1957 article titled "One of Our Men" (the word for man and human being in the Bulgarian language is the same), featuring Auntie Penka, the council woman, as she is known, we see Penka Dunikova conversing with three of her female constituents, dressed in heavy winter coats and hats. Interestingly, in the profile of this city council member who is making a difference in her community, we only get to know her as Auntie Penka—she has no last name, or any other formal identifier (the only mention of her last name is in fact in the caption of the photo). While generally endearing, this familial way of addressing women in the socialist style of magazine writing was not uncommon—used frequently for men as well, it was meant to evoke feelings of camaraderie and brotherhood, removing the formalities of name and class identifiers, often associated with one's family name and ancestral origin.

However, when men were addressed in a less formal way, they were usually called "comrade" followed by one's first name. The word "auntie," on the other hand, in Bulgarian also indicates a nurturing and matronly woman but is in fact often used as a derogatory term to describe a woman who lacks any attractiveness or memorable physical features. Auntie Penka's profile speaks highly of her ability not only to manage and single-handedly restore to glory and full capacity the formally dilapidated public bath, but also to build and operate a public movie theater, where common gatherings of the community are organized and held on a weekly basis. Clearly, Penka Dunikova's public role has produced admirable outcomes and has earned the appreciation of her constituents. Yet, the article focuses on praising her skills as a domestic worker. Towards the very last paragraph of her profile, we read, "How and when she manages her home duties is a mystery—and a secret of hers." Indeed, the mystery of the "double burden" is undeniable, as we almost never see how women handle domestic work or their responsibilities in the home. As Marody and Giza-Poleszczuk pointed out, "a woman was not seen to have her own personality. Instead, she was described through her social context; her aspirations for self-development were transferred onto the lives of her children, and her needs were subordinated to the interests of her family, and ultimately, to the needs of society and state policy."[9]

A telling illustration of the stronghold of domesticated patriarchy and its clash with the social ideology of the equality of sexes comes from the story of Stanka, the young Communist Party functionary who just got elected to serve as the people's representative. Stanka is introduced as "young, with lively eyes, dressed in plain village clothes, sweaty from working in the field." The story tells us she has been summoned by the local party leadership in order to announce her nomination as a leader of the local party branch. She is "shy, displeased," and "murmuring" her concerns about being elected to the position. "Am I the most capable woman in the village?" she hesitantly asks. Her lack of confidence is a common story line observed in many of the socialist women's profiles featured in *Zhenata Dnes*, and appears to be even more strongly pronounced for women from the rural, agrarian areas of the country.

In a similar sense of familiarity with this young woman's story, we only find her last name in the eleventh paragraph, where her credentials are finally introduced. She admits her reservations in accepting the job—it is not her lack of confidence in her ability to handle the job responsibly. "I know I can handle the job, but I am not sure I can handle my family duties. Two kids, laundry, taking care of a husband." The official response is "you will have to split job responsibilities with your comrade. He is a communist, right? We share all duties at home!" Her husbsand, Donyo, however, is the perfect antithesis of what the Party comrade is supposed to be—he is rigid and stubborn, outright rejecting the prospects of her nomination. "The Party might allow, I don't allow!" he says. The response from the Party Functionary is surprising—instead of instructing him on the merit of shared duties and labor responsibilities in the home and in public, Donyo is accused of acting "Turkish." "Throw away your fez (a traditional Turkish hat worn by men). Look at him, a young man, member of the party, and to think this way? Can you be so stupid and so jealous, like an old Turk?"

It is interesting to note the ideological discursive parallel often drawn between the backward thinking associated with the tradition of patriarchy and the metaphor of the Turk—the Ottoman occupier, who mistreats women and suppresses their desire for self-identity. In fact, the referential use of the "Turk" as a symbol of backward thinking and Oriental oppression of women was a common device used by the writers of many of *Zhenata Dnes's* articles. Partly, the treatment of the Muslim minority population in Bulgaria (the Bulgarian Turks and the Pomak, Bulgarians who converted to Islam) as the ultimate manifestation of the undesirable treatment of women in society was an integral part of the communist approach to articulating the goal of socialist gender emancipation. As Mary Neuburger pointed out, "Balkan communists conceptualized Muslim women as more oppressed than their Christian counterparts by feudal and bourgeois-capitalist society and by the Muslim patriarchy (presumed to be more onerous that the Christian one)."[10] This becomes particularly evident in the example of the magazine articles, where "Turchin" (Turk) becomes a literary figure used to symbolize backward and oppressive treatment of women, while by virtue of its juxtaposition to the values espoused by Orthodox Christianity, the Bulgarian (Christian) man, is less likely to do so, and more likely to be convinced to change his ways.

Donyo's insecurities and possessiveness towards his wife become even more evident as he expresses his worries that his wife will be "paraded around" to conferences and regional meetings, all the while in the company of other men. His logic is infallible—if she gets used to bossing everyone around, she will also boss him around and will refuse to "serve" him at home. "What kind of man will I be without the respect and fear of my wife?" he wonders. The only time he actually lightens up is at the prospect of moving to the city, suggested by some of the party functionaries in their attempt to win his consent. His reaction, however, is equally stubborn and backwards in its essence: "If I were elected, I would take her [my wife] with me in a heartbeat, but I am not following my wife around like a hound!" Donyo's unawareness of his own backward thinking is particularly striking, yet not unusual for Bulgaria's male rural population. For the Communist Party, the goal of publicizing these types of stories was not only to promote the growing role of women in public life, but also to disparage the old mores of gender oppression often associated with the Oriental mentality and the Ottoman domination over the Bulgarian population. At the same time, however, the equally oppressive, home-grown patriarchal social structure and its stifling gender norms were left intact, particularly so in the domestic sphere, creating a clear paradox between norms and expectations.

While the socialist ideology stressed the important contribution women made to the family and the party, the two roles were not entirely independent of each other. In fact, although not a requirement, most of the profiled young female party functionaries usually came from a long-standing tradition of involvement with the Communist Party. In the case of Stanka, for example, we see the typical description of her life before being assigned her new political role; in fact, her family is described as having an established communist pedigree. Her communist roots are critically important as they not only demonstrate her proper upbringing in the ideals of socialism, but also demonstrate that in some way, she has already proved her credentials and loyalty. As the story shows, her father-in-law, known in the village as the Bolshevik, actually takes her side, urging his son to allow his wife to take on this political post. Stanka is described in mental turmoil over her party loyalty and her family responsibilities. At the end, the local committee officially announces the approval of her nomination. Suddenly, she is encouraged and shows happiness in her eyes. While she accepts her comrades' congratulations, she is described looking her husband's way, as if to say, "Come on, Donyo, don't be stubborn and don't be mad. Let's invest our strength and our skills in service to the people and the party." Ultimately, we never see her directly confronting her jealous patriarch. In fact, the story is left open-ended, as we never find out what Donyo's final reaction was, or for that matter, what happened to their family after she accepted the post.

The sense of hesitation and uncertainty often associated with women's ascendance into political positions remained a common theme through the 1950s and 1960s in the discursive treatment of women and their roles in the pages of the magazines. For instance, uncertainty and hesitation permeate Mata Naidenova's feeling about her newly acquired set of public responsibilities, profiled in a 1957 feature story. Naidenova is portrayed as "the mother figure" of her entire village—she is responsible for the planning and construction of a bigger school, for building and staffing the new maternity ward at the hospital, as well as for planning and organizing the new cultural event center for the villagers—all responsibilities that clearly designate her competencies to a sphere of gender-biased tasks, naturally assumed to be a better fit for a woman than for a man. As a result of Naidenova's undying efforts and motivation, the village is clean, hygienic, in fact, she has been asked to share her knowledge and success story with other local leaders. Interestingly, the mother figure of the village makes no mention of her own family—a telling omission that demonstrates how the socialist ideology propagated a clear split between the public and private responsibilities of women. The final quote in the profile is particularly telling: "She is a woman, yet, she works as much as five men!" indicating that even when a woman manages to juggle numerous tasks, including leadership and domestic responsibilities, her skills are still evaluated by a masculine standard of efficiency. Here, the hierarchy of goals to which women should aspire is clear and well articulated—a woman's social existence trumps her individual worth, while her responsibilities as a wife and a mother are frequently blended with her social roles. This, in turn, stresses that being a good mother and a good wife also means being a good socialist and a responsible member of the social order.

In this vein, it can be argued that the role of a magazine like *Zhenata Dnes* was to effectively offer ideological prescriptions of what the proper woman should be, while passing those on as friendly advice. More often, however, these ideological prescriptions were very subtle, wrapped into practical recommendations and frequently combined with social critiques of the gender order. This was meant to instill a sense of trust and believability that Bulgarian women thought confirmed the idea that the socialist ideology is indeed one in which women can find their voices both as political activists and domestic caregivers.

In this sense, it was not uncommon to see articles that exposed social problems affecting gender relations and put the communist ideology of women's rights to the test. For example, a 1959 feature story titled "Seeds of Life" took on the issue of domestic violence and spousal abuse. The story details an abusive relationship between an aggressive and brutal husband and his wife. The narrative is told by Bozhana Stoyanova, the presiding officer of the local communist organization, who encounters the suffering of the young female worker, victim of abuse at the hands of her cheating husband, a photojournalist. The young woman gathered the courage to seek help from the local party leadership, which in turn, virtually "adopted" her and her young child. While almost skimming over the details of the abuse, the story focuses most of its coverage on painting a rosy picture of the young woman's new life, surrounded by comrades who provide for her and her son, "better than her husband ever did." To make the story even more instructing while further advancing the belief in the power of rehabilitation and the moral victory of the communist mores, the cheating and abusive husband is described realizing his mistakes and asking his wife to take him back. This time, however, he seeks the approval of Bozhana, who plays the role of marriage counselor, symbolizing the party's motherly role (it is important to note that the word Partia used to describe the Communist Party in the Bulgarian language is linguistically of the feminine gender). It appears his wife seems more than happy to relegate her personal decisions in the hands of the party, which is also described as her family away from family. Bozhana is hesitant to give him permission to see his wife, but ultimately is inclined to give him a second chance. This gesture of forgiveness is not only an admission of the communist idea that people can be led into a new path and correct their mistakes, but is also an indication of the lenient approach the communist ideologues took towards abusive husbands and their violent tendencies.

Mixing the idea of a woman's suffering in the hands of her spouse and the idea of the party as a substitute family unit, as well as the final decision maker on the future of the relationship, served as a great example of the manner in which the communist ideology lessened the gravity of domestic violence while strengthening the maternal role of the party itself. As Russian sexologist Igor Kon put it, "in public life, absolutely everything came under the control of the powerful, maternal Communist Party which knew better than anyone what was good for its members and which stood ever-prepared to correct mistakes by force."[11] The closing paragraph in the article reveals Bozhana's reflections on her decision: "Perhaps the photojournalist has indeed become a new man. And the little son of the factory will have his own father. But the factory collective defeated evil. Evil was defeated by the young, tender dove (referring to his wife). She prevailed with her beauty and her sense of dignity. Humanity triumphed." Bozhana's final reflections are markedly removed from what truly transpired in the recollection of the story—by her account, the wife prevailed, as if she actively pursued her well-being—while the humanistic approach of the Communist Party provides the ultimate moral compass.

This is what Katherine Verdery identified as "socialist paternalism," or the tendency of the state to transfer authority away from the family unit and onto the party, cultivating a "quasi-familial" dependency on the state.[12] In reality, the abused woman never got a hearing in court, or an opportunity to seek justice for her husband's violent behavior; instead, she relegated her right to make rational decisions about her life entirely in the hands of the Communist Party, which served both as a maternal and an ideological control force. As Janet Elise Johnson and Jean Robinson aptly pointed out, such diversions from analyzing the real sources of the problem of domestic violence in the Soviet world only contributed to what she called "the state's skeptical frame of domestic violence, widely circulating unchallenged in society."[13]

Domestic violence remained, albeit occasionally, a topic of discussion in the pages of the magazine. In a 1969 article, titled "Remnants of the barbaric past," the topic of spousal abuse is discussed from a different angle, focusing on how domestic abuse can affect all members of the family, including the children. The rubric, written by a female author, reads as a collection of different women's stories, describing them as loving mothers, exemplary citizens, and party functionaries who suffer at the hands of their violent spouses. The article offers pretty harsh language in portraying the degree of the physical terror women endured. Yet, even in this unusually brave approach, the discussion of domestic violence remains highly politicized. For example, the sources of this violent behavior are almost always associated with alcohol abuse by the husband, with backward thinking inherent in his peasant roots or triggered by the influence of his uneducated relatives. Rarely do we see the reasons for domestic abuse attributed to economic or social challenges, such as limited economic opportunities, financial difficulties, or income inequalities. In addition, the stories almost exclusively were resolved in rational, happy endings, when the woman suffering the abuse files for divorce and is supported in her decision by the party structure, symbolizing the compassionate treatment of the party-mother figure, all the while serving as an apparatus of social control. This is well illustrated in the recommendation the author of the article gives to the anonymous girl, seeking advice on how to stop her father from physically abusing her mother, while trying to preserve the family structure intact:

> If you want to have a family, you have to fight for it! In this fight, it will not be enough to simple prevent your father from hitting your mother. You have to try other ways to influence your father—advise him, threaten him, and seek societal assistance. If nothing helps, then support your mother in asking for divorce, accept this as your duty to the women of this land and your future daughters. So that the barbarian who is still hidden in the consciousness of some "contemporary men" will not be forgiven and sooner or later, will be entirely destroyed![14]

While the advice offered is certainly a strong recommendation for taking charge of one's life and rejecting being complacent with the abuse, the personal crisis of the young woman who asks for help is elevated to a sign of a national crisis, depersonalizing the individualized hurt from the abuse. The article essentially argues that women who witness abuse and don't do anything about it (such as report it or seek assistance in dealing with it) are also hurting other women, including future generations of females who might experience similarly abusive circumstances. Despite the harsh critique of the violent actions of abusive husbands and fathers, none of the articles discussing domestic violence ever mentioned taking on any legal measures against the perpetrator of the violent act, which in turn, is rarely, if ever, described as an actual criminal act. The potential of such articles is not only to maintain the existing mentality that domestic violence is just that—domestic and therefore, not a threat to the public welfare—but also to maintain the illusion that even extremely complex problems such as spousal abuse, can be resolved through a rational approach (in the case of the Marxist philosophy, divorce) that can bring meaningful relief to the woman from the pain and suffering, while also allowing her another chance at life.

Chapter 1
MANAGING THE DUAL ROLE OF MOTHER AND WORKER

A particularly important discussion for women's magazines was the balancing act between the traditional role of the mother and the newly assigned role of a socialist laborer women were supposed to perform in the economic realities of socialism. This is certainly well documented by a number of gender scholars, sociologists, and anthropologists, but the manner in which the ideological push in favor of the dual role of women was actually articulated in the public discourse, and particularly so in the media, remains unexamined. Since magazines provided an accessible and popular forum for this ideological work, stories quickly transformed into latent propaganda pieces, offering a look at the lives of socialist women who can do it all—not without difficulties and obstacle that need to be overcome, but always triumphant over the challenges of getting rid of the old way of thinking about womanhood while embracing the new path to progress and socialist success.

One of the main rhetorical tools of "normalizing" the double burden of domestic and labor responsibilities was providing rational explanation of the possibility and practicality of the double duty as a way to a more efficient lifestyle. Objective scientific proof frequently infused as evidence in support of women's active involvement in public life was a common thread in many of the magazine's articles, especially in the 1950s and 1960s. For example, a 1970 *Zhenata Dnes* full-page article advises women how to be more efficient in taking care of household chores. Most of the advice is about making each individual woman equivalent to a fully efficient machine in the kitchen—from selecting the direction in which she sweeps the floor to the number of time she opens the trash bin, to the exact sequence of movements to complete the procedure of ordering the washed dishes in the cupboard.

To make this a truly convincing scientific fact and not an ideological prescription for spending less time at home and more time at the factory, the socialist author—herself a female scientist—claims that all of these facts are backed by the research of East German scientists, who have also discovered that women spend most of their time in the kitchen on their feet not because of necessity, but because of poor physical habits in tending to their domestic duties. In other words, many of the kitchen chores, such as ironing and preparing ingredients for cooking dinner, can easily be done sitting down. This statement meanders between comedy and farce, but also reflects a real belief that efficiency and scientific precision can offer an answer to virtually every existing problem, including deep-seated, culturally ingrained norms of gender behavior that when properly corrected and attended to, can make everyone's life not only easier, but also a lot more enjoyable. The conclusion offered in this piece is cloaked in iron-clad logic—it is not the busy schedule and the double burden of factory labor and domestic work that keep the socialist woman on her feet, but a lack of simple self-determination to carefully watch her steps and take herself more seriously as an efficiency expert in order to avoid over-exhaustion.

The idea that the mechanical revolution can offer an answer to the "woman question" continued to find its place in the pages of the magazines. Not only do we see reports on the invention of new devices and kitchen appliances that make housework easier, but we also see extended discussions of how the socialist society is expected to step in and alleviate some of the domestic responsibilities women face in their function as a caregiver to the family. A great deal of attention is devoted to introducing statistics and other data to show the improvement in the quality of life for women who have chosen to take advantage of the mechanized means of completing kitchen chores. Even more so, those who have sought and used the services of the public sector in laundry, food preparation, and daycare facilities, are handsomely rewarded. The response offered by the experts on how to deal with the double burden is almost exclusively framed as directly connected to better use of public services such as laundry, daycare, ready-made meals, and taking advantage of the innovations in kitchen appliances. In all of these conversations, a discussion of preexisting social and gender norms is ostensibly absent. For example, Violeta Samardjieva, a researcher at the National Institute of the Economy, writes:

> Of course, organizing work inside the home also matters, but most important is what society is doing to secure minimal effort for work in the home, and how the national economy is organized in order to promote this idea. . . . Even though it might sound like wishful thinking, we see the real liberation of the woman from her household chores in the construction of a robot-housewife, which will carry all household responsibilities in a programmed way. The latest news of scientific discoveries from around the world show that these are not hyperboles, but real possibilities. In Sweden, for example, scientists have constructed a real robot that can execute 20 domestic duties (cleaning the carpet, dusting, washing dishes, cleaning windows).[15]

As futuristic and comical as this prediction might be, it is also a good illustration of how the socialist idea of progress and efficiency directly translated in the public and private function of the woman. The article also states that the woman and man of tomorrow have to be cultured and educated, expecting women to not only be good at performing their social and labor responsibilities, but also to strive to improve their performance by furthering their education and cultural sophistication. And to add more to this list of impossibilities, Samardjieva triumphantly pronounces, "the mechanization and automation of housework indirectly can have a positive impact on the birth growth of our nation," implying that spending less time on household chores is going to leave more time for women to attend to their reproductive responsibilities as well.[16] The article makes a particularly strong push for the possibility of a fully automated household, which would virtually eliminate the woman's duties in the kitchen—in fact, the year 1984 is mentioned as the deadline for the completion of this goal, making George Orwell's novel's title a particularly ironic counterpoint.

Zhenata Dnes's discussion of the "double burden" or as they deemed it "women's double responsibility" was also the ideal forum for entertaining ideas of how to formulate and indoctrinate the "woman question." Interestingly, that was one of the intended consequences of much of the debates triggered by women's socialist publications in general. In fact, Susan Gal and Gail Kligman argued, "while officially supporting equality between men and women, the regimes countenanced and even produced heated mass media debates about issues such as women's ideal and proper roles, the deleterious effects of divorce, the effects of labor-force segregation—such as the feminization of school-teaching and agriculture—and the fundamental importance of 'natural difference.'"[17] Thus, the idea of what "is natural" as far as any aspect of womanhood is concerned, whether it be appearance, domestic responsibilities, or public duties, permeated the discourse on women's roles and gender boundaries in the socialist ideology. For instance, in a 1968 article authored by Dr. Dimitria Vacheva, an assistant professor at the Institute of Economics, the idea of a reduced labor week for women (from six workdays to five workdays, not including night shifts) is discussed as a possible solution for the over-exhaustion registered by female workers. This was particularly troubling, the author argued, not because women were too tired to perform efficiently in other capacities, but because it led to a steady decline in fertility rates. The article is a particularly glaring example of the often-paradoxical nature in which the "woman question" swung the ideological pendulum of the communist establishment. While in general, the gender distinction between men and women was deliberately dismissed or entirely obfuscated in order to advocate the equality of sexes, every now and then, the approach switched to the entirely opposite argument, especially when the ideological prescriptions the Communist Party tries to propagate called for a return to a more traditional understanding of gender roles. This also meant reemphasizing the role of women as mothers and essentially providers of the bloodline for the continuation of the socialist experiment. Vacheva's report, heavily supported by statistical analysis and scientific arguments, contended that women's ability to perform their job duties, especially so during the night shift, is significantly compromised by their essentially being female. She states:

> The question of the human capacity for labor, and especially so that of females, becomes one of the most important social hygiene issues of our times. Women's anatomical and physiological makeup is a major contribution to this trend. Although equal in intellectual capacity, there are major physical discrep-

ancies between men and women. Because of these physical discrepancies, a woman's capacity for performing her labor duties is significantly lower than that of a man's. And with the passage of time, the muscular ability of both men and women diminishes, which makes those problems even more dire.[18]

Clearly, Vacheva's rationalization for a reduced work week is not based on the fact that women can barely manage juggling domestic, political, and economic responsibilities—on the contrary, she qualifies the pressing expectation for women's contributions as "a historical necessity," a trend that is necessary for the success of the socialist economy. In turn, the state has provided relief in the form of specifically designed nutritious meals, organized rest time, and ultimately, by designated certain professional occupations as "feminized."

The inherent contradiction in articulating a vision of socialist gender is further exemplified by a series of articles published in the 1969 to 1970 period. The texts, all authored by Maria Dinkova, a high ranking functionary of the Democratic Union of Women in Bulgaria, aimed to provide both a context and an analysis of the "woman question." The series, titled "Women today and tomorrow," addressed a wide range of issues which the party deemed essential in defining the role of the socialist woman in society—from the revolutionary rejection of old patriarchal structures driving the labor force, to women's participation in public life and politics, to their efficiency in performing domestic duties. In all of the pieces, written a lot more like the official speeches of the communist leaders and a lot less like an honest assessment of the realities of everyday life, the underlining argument appeared to be that while women have achieved an equal footing with men in terms of contribution and responsibilities for growing the socialist economy, they still remain in need of personal growth and self-development.

In order to justify this conclusion, Dinkova's take on the status of women essentially ascribed blame on external factors when looking at how far women have been able to grow in terms of their social and economic contributions. At the same time, she also pointed fingers at each individual woman for failing to grow in her own professional and individual capacity. "The 'woman question' still presents a number of problems because of the difficulties we experience overcoming the historical heritage, on the one hand, and on the other, because of a lack of social experience," she states.[19] The article continued further the argument that women were partly to blame for their failure to advance in their respective professions because they often either don't seek further professional advancement or don't position themselves in appropriate occupations in the first place. What is more, in the third report in the series titled "Can you carry two watermelons under one arm?," an expression commonly used by Bulgarians to describe the impossibility of multitasking, Dinkova exposes a series of paradoxes in her own analysis of the conditions of gender relations and the immediate repercussions for the positioning of women in society.[20] While the majority of the article focuses on the necessity to implement the "*byt* revolution"—the complete transformation of everyday life into a rational, mechanized, and carefully planned routine—Dinkova also suggests that one of the biggest obstacles in front of women in achieving their rightful position in society is not economic, social, or historic in nature, but is women themselves and their incorrect approaches to thinking about their jobs, their domestic duties, and about delegating responsibilities at work and in the household.

> If we look at the Bulgarian woman with a critical eye at this very moment, we are going to find out that she . . . is not a very good housewife. She is more an executor of hundreds of needed and less needed tasks, thinking that she can calm her consciousness if she takes on more duties and tasks upon herself. She is a lot less of an efficient organizer, who can properly distribute the workload, so that in a short time she can accomplish her tasks efficiently while spreading the work equally among all household members.[21]

It appears that the woman's inability to succeed in securing equal distribution of work, family, and domestic responsibilities is intrinsically a problem of her own making. By lacking the necessary skills to multitask, but more importantly, to delegate responsibilities to other members of the household, including her own children, she is essentially engaging in doing more work out of sheer guilt and inadequate leadership, and not because of the patriarchal structure of the family that by default absolves men from any domestic responsibilities.

Discussions of the necessity to organize the household in an efficient manner were also meant to promote a sense of time management and productivity that was exuberantly optimistic. The idea of good time management almost entirely singled out the woman as the sole party responsible for the integration of these innovative recommendations. Consider an example from a 1971 *Zhenata Dnes* article, which advised women on how to be more efficient in preparing their husbands' luggage for business travel. Under the guise of proper time management and self-directed efficiency, the text practically suggests that it is a most expected task for a woman to be responsible for packing her husband's belongings as he prepares for his trip. After a lengthy, step-by-step advice on how to fold his suits and shirts, the article concludes: "In fact, it is not necessary to burden yourself with this duty. Teach your husband or your son how to do it. Let them pack their own suitcases. If they forget to put some essential item, then they can be mad only at themselves."[22] The final message might sound empowering as it suggests that a better path to getting this chore completed is to pass the "practical wisdom" onto the spouse, yet it is also interesting to see that the text implies that anger and an accusatory tone is a natural response to a woman's failure to perform her domestic duties. The article also never mentioned how a woman should pack in case she is sent on a trip out of town, revealing the gender bias of the professional world, which automatically assumes that males are mobile and flexible while females are statically anchored in their domestic responsibilities.

It appears that the dynamics of defining gender boundaries and the role of women within those boundaries was hardly a straightforward task. As Janet Elise Johnson and Jean C. Robinson argued, both men and women negotiated around gender, often playing up different strategies in order to gain desired results. For example, women often catered towards their feminine side in order to gain more benefits in alleviating their assumed responsibilities as mothers and wives. But as the authors also pointed out, "the Communist Party-state held an almost complete monopoly over the politics of gender construction both because of the authoritarian institutions and practices of state socialism and because of the way gender was veiled by the 'woman question.'"[23]

The idea of gender indoctrination through defining the "woman question" evidently masqueraded as advice on how to best handle domestic chores responsibly and efficiently. However, it also surfaced in discussion on how to be a proper mother, who teaches her own daughters to be responsible and efficient mothers in their own time. Even in articles meant to advise women on how to play with their children, we see an opportunity to indoctrinate the ideological necessity of understanding the gendered nature of labor. Consider an article, written by Nevena Ziapkova in a 1969 issue of *Zhenata Dnes*, where she states: "Play prepares the young child for learning, and learning is necessary for work."[24] Not only does the author almost immediately associate child play with its potential to build work habits from an early age, but also suggests that child play might be the ideal venue where gender ideologies of labor and domestic responsibilities can be indoctrinated. "The skilled pedagogue smartly manages to combine play with work. For example, little girls like to play with dolls; they dress them, undress them, bathe them and feed them. We can teach them from a very young age how to sew clothes for their dolls, and later on, for themselves and their spouses."[25] The ideological potential of this pedagogical moment is beyond doubt—it not only advises women on how to be better in providing the proper parental guidance while raising their daughters, but it also implies that the woman as a mother figure serves the essential function of an agency of indoctrination for the communist ideology of gender. This idea was also reflected in the work of Johnson and Robinson who noted, "The gender politics prevalent under communism never challenged the validity of *gender* difference because it was assumed that all differences flowed 'naturally from the sexual and physical differences between women and men.'"[26]

SOCIALISM AND BEAUTY

The socialist policy of obliterating individuality for women also meant that any activity considered in some form or shape focusing too narrowly on the personal needs of women, will be condemned as unbecoming and unacceptable to the character of the new socialist woman. Inextricably, any interest a woman might show in her own physical appearance or function outside of her domestic and national labor duties, needed to be rationalized and reflected through the ideological lens of the socialist ideology of gender equality and femininity. In other words, women's physical being was not necessary controlled, with the exception of natal policy, but was carefully guided and skillfully manipulated under the guise of scientific advice and expert opinions. Often, it was also carefully constructed through the idea of the "socialist sisterhood," meant to defy distinction based on class, national origin, or level of education. As Kornelia Slavova pointed out, communism, "with its constant practices of panopticism and surveillance, [it] acted as a paternalistic agent prescribing women to work both inside and outside the family, interfering into the private sphere, and even controlling women's bodies."[27]

These paternalistic practices, though not unexpected, were fairly intrusive, particularly because they served as the main guidance under which women were supposed to lead both their private and public lives. One area where these types of paternalistic intrusions were particularly notable was the discussion of beauty. Beauty, understood as a matter of attractive physical appearance, was modeled after aesthetic theories of socialist functionality that treated matters of personal appearance as a token of one's desire to be efficient. It also promoted a notion of beauty as an intrinsic characteristic of progress, through featuring images of women dressed in white lab coats, glaring over test tubes, in their pursuit of the perfect feminine scent or the next scientific discovery in skin care. For example, a 1969 *Zhenata Dnes* article featured a photograph of a row of carefully arranged and positioned female workers from the State Perfumery *Alen Mak*—the Bulgarian word for Red Poppy—which happens to be the visual symbol of the Bulgarian Communist Party (the flower was also said to have been the favorite of the founder of the Bulgarian Communist Party Dimitar Blagoev). The article, written and photographed by a team of female reporters, emphasized the fact that of the twelve engineers, nine were female and most of them assumed central leadership roles in the process of making critical decisions about the "Science of Beauty"—from the scent itself, to the shape of the bottle that contains it, to the label that will display its name. Most of these processes and decisions are described as particularly complex, and often, confusing, "just like science itself." This qualification in particularly important because the urge to look attractive, otherwise characterized as impulsive, is not only devoid of logic and rationality, but also because it discredits the ability of most female consumers to make sense of scientific explanations.

In fact, the language used in most magazine articles emphasized physical beauty (*krasota*), rather than physical attraction (*privlichane*), signaling a deliberate attempt to diminish the potential of the recommended beauty regimen to improve one's appearance and lead towards increased sexual desire. Bringing the conversation on beauty to the level of scientific discourse served a similar goal, rationalizing the use of cosmetics not as a means of attracting attention from the opposite sex, but as a means to "better oneself," which was the duty of every socialist man and woman. Articles titled "Beauty by the Laws of Nature" and "The Science of Beauty Doesn't Have to Be a Mystery" were frequent occurrences on the pages of women's publications. This science-based discourse sanitized the idea of female sexuality by addressing it simply as a matter of individual, and by proxy, public hygiene. By stressing the medicinal nature of cosmetic products, the socialist visualization of the science of physical attraction essentially obliterated the potential of any sexual undertones associated with it. As Irene Dölling, Daphne Hahn, and Sylka Scholz stated, "when gender stereotypes are reproduced, by 'demigods in white coats,' they acquire a kind of scientific legitimacy."[28]

This very same socialist visualization in some ways resembles present day campaigns of world famous American cosmetic brands like Aveeno and Clinique. The latter, an Estée Lauder brand known for its science-like, lab-appearing counters at virtually every shopping mall across America, offers upscale cosmetic care for men and women, said to bear the seal of approval of the science field of beauty. The white lab coats the Clinique sale representatives wear, who are also exclusively female, serve as a powerful symbol of the undisputable proof that these products work. In fact, not only did the lab coats became a signature of the skin care products, but also became a visual token of the marketing campaigns the cosmetic maker launched in 1968, claiming to be the very first cosmetic company to introduce a "dermatologist-guided, allergy tested, fragrance free cosmetics brand." These taglines have guaranteed success for Clinique's brand recognition and their marketing efforts have landed them the award of being number one "most happy and trusted brands" in 2009. It is perhaps safe to argue, then, that despite the obvious similarities between *Alen Mak* and Clinique in approaching female beauty as a task for science, what also distinguishes the Clinique counter and the lab facilities of Bulgaria's cosmetic institutes is the commercial appeal of the product itself and its desirability projected by means of their commercial advertising campaigns.

A similar argument is advanced by Kristen Ghodsee in her fascinating study on women's consumption of cosmetic products during socialism and in the years following its collapse.[29] Ghodsee conducted a number of interviews with female subjects who shared their recollections and personal experiences, poignantly revealing that despite official attempts to dictate the official socialist doctrine on beauty, Bulgarian women continued to value their physical appearance and often used it as a marker of their individuality and a tool of resistance against the stifling and homogenizing prescriptions of the communist ideals. In fact, many of them acknowledged that they did not necessarily feel the supply of cosmetic products was lacking in the communist economy—on the contrary, albeit of less than perfect quality, personal care products were available and were indeed widely used by Bulgarian women and similarly, by women in other Eastern European countries. "In a society where the state actively tried to homogenize the sexes, women could resist the state by continuing to emphasize their femininity."[30] Ghodsee also pointed out that her informants definitely considered beauty to be an important goal regardless of what aesthetic prescriptions were printed on the pages of women's magazines. One of them shared, "All women want to be beautiful, and we all believed that women in the West were more beautiful than we were because they had better products and more time than we did."[31]

SOCIALIST FASHION AND FEMININITY

Another trend connected to the idea of what it means to be beautiful was the concept of physical appearance and the role of fashion in defining the feminine traits of the socialist woman. To accomplish this goal, magazines did not necessarily focus on advertising the products, although ads for cosmetics and other personal hygiene products existed, albeit lacking in enticing imagery or inviting copy. On the contrary, most advertisements, particularly those from the early days of socialism mainly focused on the practical uses of the product—to improve one's body odor, or make skin smoother, for instance—without stressing any of the potential consequences the products might have for the feeling of self-worth and physical attractiveness. However deficient advertisements might have been in delivering a visually compelling presentation of what the ideal woman should look like, advice columns and fashion spreads served as the ultimate fora where these imagined presentations of women came alive. In Bulgaria, magazines like *Zhenata Dnes*, the fashion oriented magazine *Lada*, and to some extent *Bozhur* magazine, the focus of which was more on the practical advice of how to tailor one's clothes, rather than on how to look attractive and feminine in them, provided the learning grounds where women came to terms with what is fashionable and stylish, but more so, with what is socially desirable and ideologically acceptable in terms of appearance, physical attractiveness, and style of dress and behavior.

It is not surprising, then, that the communist ideologues took every opportunity they could find to stress what the party expected of women in terms of their physicality, by providing an overwhelming amount of scientific rationale, expert advice, and ordinary women's testimony on why the "socialist way" is markedly superior to the Western concept of fashion, style, and women's physical appearance. Judd Stitziel pointed out in her insightful study of the intricate relationship between politics, fashion, and socialism in East Germany, that the project of "fashioning" the socialist woman was a particularly complex one as it created a sizeable tension between what the vision of "the new type of woman" propagated by the socialist functionaries entailed and what the representation of that very same woman by the socialist fashion cadres actually was.[32] In this sense, the fashion functionaries played a particularly important role—their job was essentially a balancing act in reconciling the stern and asexual look of the new woman as promoted by the communist ideology, while at the same, preserving her "natural femininity." This duality was particularly cumbersome, as it demanded an almost impossible task from the socialist fashion industry. Stitziel wrote, "As the new working woman learned to confidently represent herself and 'hold her own like a man' in the sphere of production, she threatened to destabilize gender boundaries. Most fashion functionaries therefore were quick to assure themselves and others that women's new roles and legal equality with men in society in the sphere of production did not necessitate the loss of femininity, classical ideas of beauty, or the so-called natural order."[33]

Socialist rationalization of fashion did not mean the end of fashion. As Christina Kaier states, "clothing under socialism would be responsive to history, not the market."[34] Clothes, therefore, were meant to fall out of use not because the market has generated some new style trends, but because the socialist way of life, or *byt*, has necessitated moving into new fashion, both functional and free of unnecessary frills and fussiness. The tension between presenting what is practical and what is beautiful has been at the core of the socialism fashion dilemma. Since no practical model of such an approach existed to serve the fashion designers of socialism, finding this balance became another important responsibility of the creators of the socialist *byt* or "everyday living," as it had the potential to direct and define not only the physical appearance and stylistic look of the socialist woman, but in a way, also her place in the new social order by promoting certain traits as positive and rejecting others as remnants of the bourgeoisie past.

In the area of dress, matters of personal expressions were rendered virtually of no use as far as the utility of fashion was concerned. The emphasis was almost exclusively on practical and comfortable clothes, which were meant to increase a sense of personal ease while working and wearing the dress as a matter of accepted social convention, and not as a means of creating a sense of individual identity. In fact, that same ideological emphasis over efficient mass production and not on the quality execution of individual pieces was what was often lacking in socialist fashion, causing a mixed reaction among women who faithfully read the fashion pages. Jill

Massino noted a similar use of fashion as an ideological tool for controlling gender and consumption in her study of gender and lifestyle consumption in Ceausescu's Romania. Massino contended that consumption played a crucial role in "reformulating and articulating gender identities, including fashioning a modern socialist citizenry."[35] In doing so, Romanian magazines focus much of their effort on addressing personal and everyday issues, from tips on health and beauty to recipes and ideas for home décor, and of course, fashion. "Fashion, in particular, served as visual evidence that Romania was progressing toward mature socialism. An article in *Moda* asserted, 'fashion is no longer considered to be frivolous matter' but instead has 'become a mandatory occupation for every woman.'"[36]

Bulgarian women's magazines, similar to the Romanian ones, widely featured fashion spreads, both as staples of the magazines but also as an opportunity to offer abundant practical tips and style advice. The goal behind this move was to introduce and implement a new functional aesthetics, which depended heavily on redefining and reconceptualizing the appearance and look of the woman. In some ways, the style and dress of women served as the contesting ground for writing the rules of the visual socialist utopia. In this utopia, the woman was officially perceived as a worker, dressed in practical uniforms, because as Djurdja Barlett pointed out, "the new states privileged class over gender" and the style of dress for women was where this ideological struggle was most visually apparent.[37]

Most of the ideas about how socialist women should dress as well as the conceptualization of socialist fashion itself, whether it is Bulgarian or Romanian, seem to find some roots in folk art, stressing the important connection between personal and national identity. Emphasizing the role of the peasant woman, who served as the main inspiration for integrating folk motives in fashion, was as Massino pointed out, a particularly interesting expression of national communism. "At the same time, because peasant styles were also in vogue in the West, these fashions were considered trendy and stylish rather than simply provincial or traditional."[38]

This is not unusual as much of the fashion directives and ideas about dress in the Balkans were adapted from the Soviet push towards modernism and socialist realism in all forms of artistic expression, including fashion. In the literature on the history of socialist fashion, the presence of folk elements is recognized as the uses of ethnic motifs, which were intended to inspire the true socialist fashion, markedly different from the pretentiousness and decorativeness of Western fashion.[39] As Bartlett pointed out, "In contrast, sparingly used ethnic decoration on the new socialist dresses accentuated their clean lines and made them look modern in a new way."[40]

Since fashion was not formally recognized by the socialist demagogues as a venue for waging ideological warfare, it is particularly interesting to study the way in which fashion was appropriated as a tool of defining gender relations, while trying to redraw the lines of accepted norms of demeanor and dress. In fact, the socialist utopia as conceptualized by the early socialist revolution rejected fashion in its whimsical, fussy, and indulgent Western form for much the same reasons it struggled with defining the role of advertising in a socialist economy. The connection among fashion, advertising, and the lifestyles they promoted existed at the nexus of the transformative changes of the Soviet revolution, which I will also discuss in the next chapter in connection to the origin of advertising, aesthetics, and socialist consumption.

GENDER AND EARLY SOCIALIST FASHION

It is difficult to talk about socialist fashion without recognizing its intrinsic connection to gender. The socialist revolution hailed among many other transformations a new way of thinking about the gendered self. In fact, gender became just as an important marker as class in serving as a sign of the abrupt departure from the bourgeoisie past. And just like the need to erase the boundaries of class division imposed by the oppressive capitalist structure, socialist functionaries, particularly those whose areas of expertise involved everyday life, embarked on a mission to redraw, and virtually erase, the divisions between genders, which they deemed just as contrived and oppressive as the capitalist class structure itself. The feminine self—as transformed by bourgeois commodities and "store-bought" beauty—was juxtaposed with the unfeminine soldier-self, expressed in the aesthetic of the new socialist woman. She wears no make-up, no fancy dresses, no wavy hair, no tight fitting attire; in short, she exhibits no sexual markers of any kind. In the area of visualizing this aesthetic, for the artist Alexander Rodchenko, who is often credited as the founder of Russian constructivism and creator of socialist advertising, thinking about femininity and the socialist women's bodies was a task of high relevance not only because in it he found inspiration for promoting his vision of the overall Soviet aesthetic, but also because in thinking about designing women's clothes he saw a practical outlet for materializing his vision of a new simple, yet highly efficient culture of form, art, and dress that epitomized a revolutionary change of the senses.

Although much of Rodchenko's work was in the area of painting, photography, and graphic design, he also wrote a number of influential essays that expressed his ideological conceptions of women's appearances and their connection to the socialist/modernist vision of functionality and simplicity in design. Many of his thoughts are well documented in Christina Kaier's influential study on the Russian constructivist movement, where she included a copy of the letter Rodchenko wrote to his wife, Varvara Stepanova, also a famous constructivist artist, describing what he saw as vulgar display of sexuality by women he observed during his 1925 trip to Paris as the head of the Soviet delegation at the International Exhibit of Decorative Arts:

> Here there are masses of theaters where the entire evening, naked women in expensive and enormous feathers walk on and off the scene in silence against the expensive backdrop and that's all, they walk through and that's it. . . . And they are silent and don't dance and don't move. But simply walk through . . . one . . . another . . . a third . . . five at once, twenty at once . . . and that's it. . . . I can't begin to describe exactly what this "nothingness" is for, what this "thing" is for, what is seen when it seems that only a man is a person, and women are not people, and you can do anything with them—that is a thing.[41]

Rodchenko's critical views of the Western aesthetic of femininity are obvious—he finds Parisian women, often held as the paragon of beauty, not only lacking in physical attraction, but also repulsive in their passivity and lack of individuality. He describes them perceived almost as inanimate objects, rather than active players, and their lack of livelihood and joviality is clearly attributed not only to contrived gender expectations but also to the social politics of the female body as an object of the capitalist economy. As Kaier aptly points out, "the power of his letters stems from their earnest grappling with a desire to participate in the commodity world of the West, as well as with the converse desire to escape to the imagined East."[42]

Rodchenko specifies at least one version of the transparent "new relation to woman" that he associates with the nonthreatening, non-eroticized East. On a visit to the Olympia dance hall, he describes seeing heavily made-up women in skimpy dresses dancing the foxtrot, and calls them "ugly and endlessly terrifying."[43] Rodchenko's observations of women also focused closely on their physical appearance, which he saw as physically unattractive, virtually barren and incapable of reproducing—a function of the female body deemed of utmost importance to the socialist economy. He described women "with long and thin hips, without breast and without teeth and with disgracefully long hands topped with red stains, women in the style of Picasso, women in the style of 'negroes' women in the style of 'hospital inmates' women in the style of the 'dregs of the city.'"[44]

In many ways, the Soviet revolutionary aesthetic of the woman was a direct consequence of the Marxist critique of capitalism's consumption and its excesses. In thinking about women's bodies, clearly the socialist ideological criticisms were the harshest when describing "the cult of the woman as a thing," associating, for example, the observed passivity of Parisian women with treating them as commodities. "They are immobile, merely decorating the world, rather than acting in it, lined up as in a store window, quantified at the cash register."[45] Later, Kaier explains, Rodchenko elaborates that these women were even worse than the things, because they were produced as if from a pattern, all exactly the same, according to misconstrued and poorly designed fashion.

While Rodchenko's ideas of socialist fashion for women were quite important, the work of his wife and artistic partner, Varvara Stepanova, and another one of their ideological comrades in the constructivist movement, Liubov Popova, were even more influential as they truly encapsulated the socialist design of female dress as well as their own feminine aesthetic through artistic rendering of socialist modernism. It is not surprising, then, that both Stepanova and Popova were instrumental in defining the vision for female socialist fashion, and through it had a direct influence on ways of thinking about the female body as a tool for forging revolutionary transformations. Recognizing that elimination of fashion as a remnant of bourgeoisie lifestyles is effectively impossible, Stepanova envisioned fashion as a transformational terrain, where new signs of an epoch can be created and a new image of proper womanhood can be defined. Her concept of female dress was the unreserved representation of socialist modernism—simple, rational, mass produced, and efficient. As Stepanova herself wrote, "Fashion that psychologically reflects a way of life, customs, and aesthetic taste gives way to programmed clothing . . . which is tested only through the process of working in it."[46]

Fashion, then, becomes valuable because it both expresses and produces liberation from gender hierarchies and provides a great venue where ideas of sexuality and gender norms could be contested, redrawn, and redefined. As Stepanova said in her commentary on the changes of women's clothes in early Soviet Russia, "The appearance of a woman over the last decade exhibits an exceptional picture of her emancipation. In these ten years women's dress has been rationalized to such an extent that it has come to represent in and of itself almost the greatest achievement in contemporary *byt*."[47]

More importantly, in addition to being highly efficient, the female dress for the new socialist woman had to be also free of the capitalist signage of sex, pleasure, and eroticism. As Djurdja Bartlett stated, "Stepanova pushed erotic drive, femininity, pleasure, and individual desire away from the dresses she designed in 1923–1924. Insisting exclusively on comfort, functionality, and purposefulness of dress, she revealed the constructivist unwillingness to accept desire and to offer new ways of organizing it."[48] A similar desire to rid the socialist form of excess was also evident in visual presentation of the goods and services early socialist advertising introduced for mass consumption. The modernist yet highly puritanical approach to advertising was indeed promoted by the very same artists in the constructivist movement, led by Rodchenko, who also dictated the fashion tastes for the new socialist man and woman.

Perhaps one exception to this vision of no-frill simplicity of fashion was the work of Liubov Popova. Unlike Stepanova, Popova's vision of women's fashion was to evoke designs that are chic and elegant, yet continually improving the rational approach to fashion statements in line with the new vision of the Soviet woman, while projecting the desirability presumably missing from existing fashion options for the Soviet woman. Popova, herself a jazz enthusiast and ballroom dancer, had a different vision of what the socialist dress should look like, as she actually saw the potential of fashion, and women's clothes in particular, to serve as an instrument of social change. Popova's desire was to infuse the socialist dress with a sense of femininity that is both rational and liberating in a more sensuous way. In fact, her best known design was the "flapper" dress she introduced as a hybrid between the socialist sensibility of the female body—a body that is both proletariat, yet gentle—and a Westernized way of gazing at it. In incorporating more sensual, yet not sexualized, primers of femininity, such as delicate arms in strong and athletic body types, Popova's desire to create a socialist fashion dress in line with the modernist ideals of the proletariat revolution somehow managed to maintain the allure of the Western emphasis on the erotic. Unfortunately, it ended in a utopian impossibility because it failed to negotiate a "golden mean" for the new fashionable socialist femininity that was deemed universally acceptable by the ideologues of the revolution.[49]

Removing the signs of exaggerated femininity in Soviet fashion suggested an attempt on the part of socialist designers to do away with the traditional gender hierarchies and move towards what they saw as a more modern, individualized, and androgynous appearance of women. In fact, as Popova's costume designs suggested, she saw very little value in distinguishing men's and women's costumes. "There was a fundamental disinclination to making any distinction between men's and women's costumes: it just came down to changing the pants to skirts."[50] In line with the socialist conceptualization of the equality of the sexes, fashion that discriminates between men and women, and stresses a heightened expression of feminine body features, such as legs, arms, chest, and buttocks was seen not only as backward and bourgeoisie but also as non-modern and regressive in its functionality and structure.

This general desire to reconfigure the fashion dress was welcome and quickly overtaken by the political motives behind the desire to rethink fashion and female dress as an expression of the social order and its gender hierarchies. In this task, Rodchenko's and Stepanova's vision of fashioning socialist women was instrumental in abolishing all connections to the capitalist market and the inequality it breeds. To put it simply, the new socialist woman had to compete against the female identity of the West, which was mediated through fashion, advertising, and consumerism. As Djurdja Bartlett pointed out:

Western fashions were charged with sexuality in new, transgressive ways, and this modernist, boyish-looking woman was both highly maintained and sexy. Her hectic, athletic looks were achieved through leisure activities such as visits to the beauty parlors and hair salons, through dieting, playing tennis, the wearing of fashionable flapper dresses, and a knowledgeable use of make-up. In contrast, Stepanova's ideal woman was supposed to lead a rational existence wearing simple and functional clothes.[51]

It is not surprising then, that fashion and female dress as expressions of gender identity became quickly politicized. The role of fashion, and by extension, of the visual images and advertisements that promoted it, was to serve as the foreground where the ideological battle for the hearts, minds, and in the case of fashion, the bodies of women would be waged. As Judd Stitziel argued, "officials sought to channel and control female desire by connecting women's rights as consumers with their roles as producers and by promoting rational 'socialist consumer habits' as an important component of citizenship."[52]

And since fashion in this sense was not just a way of promoting individual attention to style and appearance, it played a major role in the content and editorial pages of Bulgarian and Romanian magazines. For the most part, the fashion spreads and articles printed in the Bulgarian women's magazines were directly translated and reprinted from East German, Polish, Czech, or other Soviet magazines, always appropriately crediting the original source. The photo spreads, however, featured mostly Western looking models borrowed from Western fashion magazines such as *Neuer Schmitt*, *Constanze*, *Modeheft*, *Collections*, and *Jardin des Modes*. Often, the fashion spreads varied in size and style—some of them were colorful and very artistic, others, black and white and less impressive in their graphic execution. In most cases, the fashion spread was accompanied by an advice column. These columns, while consultative in intent, sounded a lot less like advice and a lot more like a prescriptive order. "The clothes must be beautiful, delicate, but at the same time simple and noble." Verbs, such as "must be," "ought to be," etcetera, prevailed in most of the sentences in the text, stressing the commanding voice of the fashion authority. This advice should be perceived as friendly and well-meaning, but should also be regarded with respect and treated as an important directive.

Interestingly, fashion spreads also differed in terms of the physical appearance and aesthetic features of the female (and occasionally male) models. Throughout the 1960s, *Zhenata Dnes* relied heavily on Western-based fashion spreads, which featured prominently models and fashion trends, outfits and accessories straight from the catwalks of Paris, Milan, and New York. This shift was also noted by Massino in her cultural history of gendered consumption in Romania, who attributed this acceptance of Western fashion as a sign of the overall thaw in Soviet politics that permeated that specific period of building socialism. As she noted, "No longer bourgeoisie frivolities, fashion and beauty now served as signs of socialist modernity, with consumerism becoming a palpable medium through which social leaders legitimated their rule."[53]

The fashion spreads tended to be extremely rich in color, dominant in their visual presentation and accentuating female models that could easily be recognized as "Western." However, when those photo spreads featured Bulgarian fashion, they tended to appear a lot less lush in their visual presentations—the models looked less made up, with less inviting physical presence; their outfits accentuated ethnic motives and folkloric traditions that were authentically Bulgarian, anchoring the fashion in the wholesome cultural customs and long-standing heritage of the Bulgarian national dress. Several fashion spreads celebrated the artistic achievements of Bulgarian fashion designers, whose models we see photographed against the visual symbols of the Bulgarian national identity—leaning against the gate of a traditional Bulgarian house, featuring traditional architectural details and settings, such as church yards, famous landscape sites, or locations. The setting was so deliberate, as if the fashion editors were trying to say "these are the fashion trends, but they are also truly Bulgarian in their cultural references and truly socialist in their functional nature."

In reviewing how Bulgarian magazines treated fashion as an ideological device, it must be noted that most of the fashion spreads in *Zhenata Dnes* came from other magazines devoted entirely to fashion. One such iconic magazine was *Lada*. *Lada* was in fact often referred to as the fashion encyclopedia of the Bulgarian woman and as such, was held in high regard by women from all walks of life. Not only that, but the magazine, backed by its own fashion house, essentially stood for the symbolic home of authentic Bulgarian "haute couture," good enough to compete on the global fashion scene. *Lada* sold widely in the rest of the socialist states and was sought after as a forum for expressing fashion ideas and testing new concepts in socialist fashion. In a fascinating insider look at the workings and the history of *Lada*, Nikoleta Popkostadinova calls the magazine the "Bulgarian Vogue," not only because it was recognized as the most influential voice in fashion, but because as Popkostadinova states, "it was fashion in every sense of the word."[54] In an attempt to document the chronology of the magazine, Popkostadinova interviewed former models that worked with the fashion editors and publishers of *Lada*, as well as the daughter of the founding editor and most commanding voice in Bulgarian fashion, Nadia Gancheva. According to her daughter, Vera Gancheva, the market for fashion magazines was limited, but nonetheless thriving. Among the three publications that dictated Bulgaria fashion, *Bozhur*, she claims, was the weakest, as it simply mimicked the approach of most East German fashion publications, which were known for a scarcity of images and overabundance of "do it yourself" fashion patterns.

Zhenata Dnes was recognized as a "powerhouse" in the magazine industry, but as Gancheva states, "it was too socially oriented, accentuating exclusively the psychological problems of women."[55]

The three magazines were complementary to each other, with *Lada* serving the elitist role of being truly fashion-forward, the place where socialist style was conceptualized, based upon a thorough analysis of the world trends in haute couture, yet remaining firmly anchored in the goals and needs of socialism. In order to achieve these goals, Nadia Gancheva was offered unfettered access to Western publications and fashion venues on demand, including last minute trips to Paris, Monte Carlo, and Milan, returning to Sofia the very same day to brainstorm ideas that will fit the interests of *Lada*'s female readers. Her daughter recalls that fashion magazines such as *Vogue*, *Depeche Mode*, *Harper's Bazaar*, and *Burda* were at her mother's disposal at any time, helping her find inspiration. At the same time, she was always striving to find a way to adapt this "high style to the practicality and pragmatism of everyday life in Bulgaria."[56]

Following closely Western fashion trends was important to the socialist ideologues, who used the ingenuity of their fashion editors to boast that socialist style can match the achievements of Western designers and excel in vision and originality. As fashion became more prominent as a topic of discussion on the pages of *Zhenata Dnes*, and *Bozhur*, it becomes evident that the discrepancies between what is being offered as a vision of a fashionable, visually appealing female appearance and what is in fact available as fashion items and accessories to be purchased, were stunning. Perhaps the best illustration of the enormous disconnect between what *Vogue* showed fashion to be and what "Bulgarian Vogue" displayed as fashion outfits that can be purchased, can be seen in comparing the front and the back cover of the 1960s and 1970s magazine issues of *Zhenata Dnes*. Almost exclusively, the cover features the photo, or an artist's rendition, of a Bulgarian woman of an easily identifiable profession—a doctor, an engineer, an architect. Occasionally, the cover of the magazine also featured a painting or any other artwork by a Bulgarian artist who was either female, or focused on a female-oriented topic (e.g., flowers, portraits of peasant Bulgarian women, etc.). That certainly isn't surprising, given that *Zhenata Dnes* by designation was not a fashion magazine per se. However, as soon as one turns to the back page, one sees a photograph of an attractive Western-looking model, wearing a haute couture dress or suit, looking invitingly into the camera, often as if to seduce the female (and perhaps the male) reader. In an almost Jekyll and Hyde fashion, we see the manifest appearance of the socialist woman versus her inner desires, what usually sits at the "back of her mind," filed away, in a dark corner—the first, explicitly wholesome and therefore, socialist, the latter, implicitly decadent, and Western.

And while this trend might have been nothing but a coincidence, it also shows the conflicted vision of how socialist fashion was supposed to integrate in the everyday life of socialist women. On the one hand, socialist fashion designers proclaimed that their models were not only comparable, but also superior to those of the West. On the other, they readily criticized what they saw as the unnecessary frilliness and pretentiousness of the Western trends, often dismissing them as either too decadent, and, therefore, unattractive, or failing to align with the Marxist aesthetic of the everyday life, lacking in utility and comfort. As Judd Stitziel aptly pointed out, "In reality, designs from Soviet-bloc countries were virtually indistinguishable from those of Western, capitalist ones. While some may have paid lip service to an alleged 'Marxist-Leninist' aesthetic, if it existed, it certainly did not possess any characteristics that unmistakably differentiated it from Western fashion."[57]

Accordingly, socialist fashion designers and writers dedicated a significant amount of time writing and commenting on Western fashion trends, acknowledging both in verbal, but even more so, in visual form, the fashion novelties and innovations of the West. And yet, they often countered these trends with their own Soviet version, completely disparaging their Western counterparts as not only impractical, but downright ridiculous. As a result, when discussing fashion trends from the global headquarters of fashion, magazines included often on the same page, directly opposite to the article, reports and stories about the lives of ordinary Western women, emphasizing the everyday struggles they have to endure in a capitalist economy. When discussing the latest fashion news from the Paris catwalks, for example, *Zhenata Dnes* would also run an article on the life of the everyday "Parisian woman." Under the guise of a fashion report about the style of French women, the article becomes an outright condemnation of capitalism and its oppression of women. The focus is shifted from the Parisian woman's attention to details to her struggle to find a balance between work—an opportunity only a few women can afford—and taking care of her children because of a lack of state-assured daycare assistance. What is even more, nestled right next to the Parisian article, is another piece titled "Don't forget that you are a Bulgarian," which glorifies the achievements of Bulgarian women and the social system at large, implicitly weaving a connection between fashion on one side, and socialist ideological triumph, on the other.

An even more damning proclamation against the excesses of Western fashion comes from a commentary printed in 1963 comparing Western fashion models to Bulgarian "kukeri"—an old tradition dating back to Bulgaria's pagan roots in which young men, usually unmarried, dress in hairy costumes adorned with large bells, wearing scary masks made out of animal skin, fur, and horns in order to chase the evil spirits away. Cherished as an important Bulgarian folk tradition, "kukeri" are also used as a linguistic term to often mock unattractive physical appearance, especially among women. In the fashion commentary in *Zhenata Dnes*, the "kukeri" reference is evoked when discussing the latest fads of the Western designers, including excessive, animal-like eyelashes, over-the-top make-up, pants made of animal fur, and skirts that look like horse's tails, glued together. The colorful collage that accompanied the piece is titled "Competing with . . . the kukeri," and mockingly describes the excessive peculiarities of Western fashion. The featured outfits are identified in the text as a pair of pants from New York and an evening dress from the collection of Yves Saint Laurent. The article essentially mocks these fashion items by stating that they can serve as great inspiration point for the designers of "kukeri" costumes and masks. The underlying satiric note implied by the editors of the magazine is that indeed, we can learn from the West, but only to make our national costumes more scary and extravagant.

Ironically, another article, focusing on the image of the contemporary woman, rejects vehemently the very images propagated in the preceding fashion spread. The article condemns women's obsessive desire to be fashionable by following the Western trends in clothing, hairstyle, and care for one's appearance. "The contemporary woman is not the one that turns men's heads. Go where life is in full throttle, that is where you will find her," the story carries on, clearly contextualizing socialist femininity not through the way a woman looks and appears in public, but through the work that she performs and the contribution she makes to the burgeoning economy of the new social order.

In a way, it seems, fashion presented a unique opportunity to learn and borrow from the West, while persistently dismissing its unnecessary insistence on overindulgence and luxury by declaring it excessive and self-centered. In response, socialist fashion offered contemporary solutions, stressing practicality and national tradition in its own way. The bottom line was clearly gendered, as the ultimate focus of all of the fashion advice was to define and control the norms of socialist femininity. While not directly imposing tastes, socialist fashion designers were waging an ideological battle for the minds and hearts of the socialist woman. As Judd Stitziel argued, "while some rejected fashion altogether as female folly, others argued that women's new and growing public roles in the sphere of production required them to be fashionably dressed as a sign of their own self-confidence and as a model of good taste for men and children."[58]

These types of ideological ambiguities, however, continued to populate the pages of women's magazines, generating some interesting anomalies. For example, alongside many of the articles that both emulated and condemned Western fashion and its portrayals of femininity were also articles that took on a rather critical look at the local fashion industry. Those articles often criticized the limited availability of ready-to-wear fashion, which tended to be so formulaic that it virtually obliterated the individualism of women and their tastes. A caricature from a 1960 issue of *Zhenata Dnes* illustrates this both humorously and poignantly. In it, two women passing each other in the street look at each other in contempt as they realize they are wearing the same model dress, obviously cut from the same pattern and the same fabric. To address the concerns of female consumers about the scarcity of choices in fabric and patterns, in 1963 *Zhenata Dnes* ran an open letter, asking the Ministry of Light Industry (which included textile production) to rethink their production strategies within the context of the planned economy. In it, the editorial board openly criticized the lack of diversity in the patterns offered in the fabric stores by stressing the fact that such practices do not align with the international fashion trends. "Isn't it time to finally stop the production of the same old 'designated' pattern that we see over and over in the shop windows for 15 years, just in different colors?," the editors ask.[59] Stopping short of attacking the strict control over the production and distribution of goods, the editorial clearly points a finger at the official economic policies of controlled supply and demand as responsible for the lack of goods that fit the interests and diverse styles of dress for women.

WOMEN, BODIES, AND SEXUALITY

Understanding women's bodies and the sexuality they exude was intrinsically connected to the goal of building the new socialist order. On the one hand, the seemingly progressive emancipation of women suggested that the female body should be treated as an autonomous realm, where matters of appearance, behavior, and sensibilities are relegated to the woman herself. On the other hand, however, the extreme manifestation of liberated sexuality expressed mainly through suggestive dress or lewd acts was condemned not only as immoral, but also as unbecoming of the new socialist man's and woman's sense of modesty. To some extent, the failure to demonstrate a more nuanced understanding of human sexuality as an expression of the physical needs of the body and the emotional demands of the female psyche is not surprising. Women's magazines were caught in the crossfire of trying to serve both as the venues where socialist doctrines were presented and serve as a place where discussion of sexuality and bodies could be "tamed" and successfully redirected for the political purposes for the regime. Therefore, the "body politics" became very much the focus of the discourse of popular magazines precisely because the socialist female body also became a political body—both an instrument of indoctrination and an instrument of control over the reproductive and ideological essence of womanhood.

These developments in gender awareness are certainly not new. The potential of the "woman question" to become one of the leading ideological milestones for the tectonic shift of consciousness the socialist revolution required was realized early enough by the leading philosophical minds who laid the foundations of the communist doctrine. In fact, Friedrich Engels wrote:

> The issue of "free love" comes to the forefront in every major revolutionary movement. For some people it represents revolutionary progress, liberation from old traditional bonds that are no longer necessary, for others, it is an easily acceptable tenet that conveniently hides all manner of free and easy relationships between men and women.[60]

And it is also not surprising that women whose role in society was equally exploited by the market pressures and the patriarchal norms of the early-twentieth-century capitalism, joined forces with working men to form a proletariat that saw no gender boundaries in their mutual expectations of a fair wage and a dignified existence. In fact, as Greta Slobin explained, gaining political power and control over labor productivity also meant gaining control over sexuality and women's bodies. "Male theorizing about socialist sexuality has been clearly on the side of revolutionary sublimation."[61]

The topic of sex and bodies, while not necessarily the focus of the revolutionary ideology, certainly occupied the attention of its ideologues as they struggle to come to terms with how this intrinsic human activity can define the norms and behaviors of the future generation of communist men and women. In this connection, Eliot Borenstein's fascinating volume on sex and violence in contemporary Russian popular culture offers an interesting insight in the early conceptual struggles surrounding the discursive origins of sex as related to the goals of the socialist revolution.[62] In fact, as he pointed out, the discussion of sex during communism was shrouded both in linguistics—the Slavic languages have two different words for sex, one for sex as a sexual activity (*seks*) and one for sex as a physiological function of the body (*pol*)—as well as in polemics. "Sexual discourse exists so that we can talk about sex without necessarily engaging in it. The two activities can (and do) exist quite independently of each other."[63]

That complex dynamics perhaps best manifests the complex role of sex in the new socialist order. Historically, the question of sex has been treated as a polarizing issue in the revolutionary vernacular. In fact, as Borenstein contends, two opposing views seem to have dominated the discourse on the matter of sex. On the one hand, the "new" sensibilities about sex should elevate the new socialist men and women above the shackles of an outdated moral code, advocating for a more liberated view of love, sex, and body. On the other hand, sexual passion was also seen as nothing more than an animalistic and fundamentally repulsive social practice, advocating a complete revolutionary chastity. These two polarizing perspectives defined the ideological camps in conceptualizing "socialist sexuality" and were particularly prominent in the works of revolutionary writers whose thoughts on the matter dominated intellectual discussions on what role sex should play in the new social order. In fact, discussions of sexuality were essential to the overthrow of bourgeois lifestyles, leading to both progressive legislation (abortion, divorce, and sex laws) and, in the early years, progressive norms (illegitimacy was no longer stigmatized, men being held legally responsible for all their children). To demonstrate their commitment to a new way of thinking about sex, as Borenstein explained, as soon as they came into power, the Bolsheviks almost immediately passed legislation to revamp the way private life and family were conceived in Russian society. "The transformation of Russian sexual life and legislation was staggering, equaled only by the proliferation of a new bourgeoning discourse surrounding sex."[64]

Shortly after the passage of such progressive legislation, however, the concept of an unbridgeable divide between the "good proletariat" and the "bad bourgeoisie" led to a divergence between what Gregory Carleton called "vulgar Marxism" and a discourse on abstinence.[65] In one of the very few published extensive studies on Soviet sexuality, Carleton discussed the ambiguous canon on sexuality produced in the 1920s, focusing on the role and appropriate behavior of women. Themes such as the combination of care and work, procreation and abortion, and proper dress and behavior were commonly brought into the conversation as markers of what sexuality is supposed to encompass in the very first place. These discussions further deepened the ideological rift between advocates of free, comradely love and advocates of a revolutionary restraint and sublimation, creating tensions that rose beyond matters of ideology. Similarly, as Eric Naiman's exploration of the early Bolshevik ideology of sex demonstrates, the importance of sex as an ideological narrative was not only recognized by the Bolsheviks but was deliberately exaggerated to serve as a rationale to mask the state's invasive intervention into the private lives of citizens.[66] Even more, as Borenstein argued, the Bolshevik's progressive legislation was interpreted by most men as a green light for avoiding family responsibilities altogether.[67] On the other hand, women, whose expectation of improved family lifestyles and social norms did not materialize, were left "bearing the brunt of the social upheaval."[68]

The increased intensity of sexual discourse almost came to a screeching halt with Stalin's ascent to power and the conservative values his leadership espoused. As a result of the overall tightening of the ideological control over all everyday activities, including the private realm of sexual behavior, Stalinist ideologues introduced a much more rigid family code, including the recriminalization of homosexuality and even banning abortion (which was later legalized once again after the "thaw" in cultural policies in the late 1950s). As a result, as Borenstein once again aptly pointed out, "the sex question was now closed."[69] With the exception of the occasional challenge posed either in terms of sexually provocative content produced abroad and distributed as entertainment locally, the socialist media and cultural industries remained fairly mute about matters of sex.

There are, of course, a few exceptions to this rule that demonstrate the diversity of local responses both on the part of the public but also on the part of the localized cultural elite in each of the member states of the socialist bloc. For example, as Ana Magó-Maghiar pointed out in her examination of the representation of sexuality in Hungarian popular culture during the 1980s, Hungary did not necessarily subscribe to the Soviet guidelines on matters of sex and experimented with popular culture content whose references to sex were clearly beyond the symbolic and the artistic.[70] Using a semiotic and thematic analysis of the sexualized joke illustrations published in the magazine *Ludas Matyi*, Ana Magó-Maghiar argues that despite the rather unusually liberated references to sexual bodies and provocative sexual behavior, there appeared to be a silent agreement between the socialist state and its male citizens that the liberated treatment of sex really came at the expense of women. "The state sought to buy the patience of the 'worker' (its constituency) by allowing to pursue his own sexual interests on the condition that he is not going to question the legitimacy of the political regime."[71]

A seeming rebellious, yet equally damning treatment of sexuality and women's bodies was also noted in the work of Biljana Žikić, who focused her analysis of socialist erotica in the former Yugoslavia.[72] Žikić aptly delineates the Yugoslav cultural policies from those of the Soviets by pointing out the politically complex relationship the two states maintained. Yugoslavia did not quite concede belonging to the Eastern bloc by maintaining a more liberal, market-oriented economic policy, which in many ways was further alleviated by the freedom of movement and labor flexibility Yugoslav citizens enjoyed. Because of this generally lax approach to controlling the borders and movement of people and labor, Yugoslavia also exhibited less of a conservative approach to the topic of sex. In fact, as Žikić argued, it is precisely this type of "openness" to the West that allowed Yugoslav popular culture to incorporate and often rely heavily on content that was not only erotic, but sometimes pornographic in nature. Žikić's analysis of *Start* magazine—the first Yugoslav magazine of a "hybrid" nature that combined the characteristics of a tabloid newspaper, featuring erotic and pornographic elements, with those of a high-brow magazine focused on progressive, emancipatory, and critical analysis of current affairs—brings to light the multifaceted use of sexual discourse in the cultural and political context of socialism. Among other things, her analysis demonstrated how sexual liberation became semantically associated with liberalization and progress, and how naked female bodies functioned as symbols of Yugoslavia's progressiveness, therefore relegating the power of sexual image not in the hands of women, but in the hands of men.

It is not surprising then that the treatment of sex and body, and the manner in which these two most obvious distinctions between men and women were found in *Zhenata Dnes* and other magazines, make the discussion of these ideas particularly relevant. In fact, the discussion of sex was seen as an expression of the progressive approach of the communist ideology treating such private subjects with a kind of transparency that also meant that the socialists had overcome the taboos imposed by the bourgeoisie discourse surrounding the topic of sexual behavior. For example, an article from 1968 titled "Are there women who are frigid?" features a discussion of the sexual relationships between women and men. The article, authored by Dr. Todor Bostandjiev, is a series of analytical statements about the nature of the lack of sexual drive among women, culminating in the following conclusive paragraph: "Yes, there are women who are frigid, but their frigidity is not genetic. Is it a frequent phenomenon for a woman to be frigid because she is not warmed by the tenderness, care, attention and love of their comrades and husbands. The warmth of love is much needed in order to be satisfied in the family bed. That is only possible if there is proper sexual education and high sexual culture. Marx was right when he said 'The relationship between a man and a woman is a yardstick for the culture of a society.'"[73]

An almost identical approach was noted in Massino's analysis of Romania's unusual frankness in addressing women's sexual needs and the issues of sexual relations.[74] As Massino points out, this "pillow talk" was clearly ideological in its intent. "Far from mimicking the racy articles found on the pages of Cosmopolitan, these pieces were designed to demystify the sexual act and help women regain their sexual desire so they can procreate."[75]

Even in this climate of openness about topics previously shunned in public debate, the topic of sex remained mainly defined in the realm of medical advice on how to keep the body healthy and therefore, capable of reproducing. These public hygienic concerns also prompted frank conversations about preventive practices that can keep one from contracting sexual disease. Both approaches were guided by the same ideological goal of maintaining a healthy socialist populace. Frances Berstein contended that the Soviet revolution also signaled an openness in discussing sexual habits and practices mainly by Soviet medical doctors, particularly, venereologists, who tried to assert their authority over matters of sexual behavior in order to create not necessarily a more sexually aware and educated opulence, but a healthier, eugenically enhanced future labor force.[76] In tone and in subject matter, these pieces did very little to promote and enhance an intimate and honest discussion about sexuality, which continued to be seen as taboo at home and elsewhere. And even though the degree of openness concerning these discussions clearly varied, most of the socialist countries adopted the approach that

Adriana Baban described in her discussion of sexuality and Romanian women:

> Under communist rule, even beauty and desire were proclaimed indecent and harmful. As a result of this puritan-like ethic, the nude body disappeared from paintings, décolletage from TV, and love scenes from movies. Eroticism among married couples was replaced by the glorification of the "woman-mother" and a communist cult of maternity. Adolescent sex education, called "sanitary education," was reduced to instruction in hygiene and physiology.[77]

This trend was certainly present on the pages of socialist women's magazines, although, as Masha Gessen stated, the media operated within what she called "the myth of the genderless-ness" of socialism, arguing that "for decades, the media bore the responsibility for enforcing the myth of the gender-undifferentiated wonder of the brave new world."[78] Hence, the only "allowed" conversations about sex were advice on maintaining one's sexual health and on occasion, on enhancing a married couple's intimacy. In both cases, the texts appeared as if extracted from the pages of an anatomy book, explaining with almost scientific precision the sexual functions of the human body. Even within the realm of what Igor Kon described as the triumph of sexology, the balance of educating the public without enticing their sexual instincts was obviously a difficult task.[79] While commenting on the difficult, if not impossible task of writing about Soviet sex, Kon recollects in an almost self-deprecating fashion: "Generally speaking, the Soviet people's sexual behavior is the best kept state secret of all time. The top army command at least knows the whereabouts and staffing of our military bases, but no one has an inkling of our sex lives."[80]

Regardless of how sanitized the popular sexual discourse appeared to be, the topic made casual appearances on the pages of *Zhehata Dnes*. Gregory Carleton pointed out, "Making sex a public issue served a purpose. . . . The more sex was made 'public,' the more people were victimized."[81] On most occasions, the articles focused on potential causes for problems with sexual intercourse and infertility. More often than not, articles focusing on the matter of sexual behavior were cleverly disguised as a sociological analysis, laced through with the moralizing tone of a communist manifesto. As Eric Naiman argued, the very purpose of early socialist publications was to attract as wide a readership as possible into the net of party propaganda.[82]

This model was copied by Bulgarian publications, well past the early stages of the communist overtake. For example, a 1972 article titled "Stop Julieta, Stop," written by Pavlina Popova, was a damning proclamation against premarital sexual relationships. Throughout the text, written as a conversation with "Julieta"—the collective image of the recklessly romantic young woman, who is wooed by the mythical Romeo into premarital sex—Popova never flinches at the opportunity to illustrate the dangerous consequences of what she sees as irresponsible sexual behavior. Losing one's sense of moral worth and jeopardizing the potential to bear children were condemned in the strongest possible language. "In your selfish strife to get their [men's] attention, you are distancing them from yourself. Because you increase their appetite, you create a type of a competitive spirit, you teach them to quickly conquer and easily triumph. And their triumph is your demise. . . . You and only you can save yourself from it!"[83] Here, Popova placed the responsibility of proper sexual behavior exclusively on women as the only guardians of proper moral norms. She also directly implicated women in being the deliberate provocateurs of men's irresponsible sexual acts. While doing that, Popova went a step further—she assigned the "blame" of the recklessness of premarital sex entirely on the woman, whose desire to seek pleasure and satisfy her own misconstrued notion of romantic love provokes men to act irresponsibly, mischaracterizing sex as a meaningless act of fulfilling carnal desires, lacking an emotional attachment and productive outcomes.

This reversal of roles in the sexual relationship is a great example of the communist intrumentalization of sex that focused closely on women's reproductive capacities while restricting any means of erotic expression. It is also illustrated by the different perception—both social and individual—on the matter of premarital sex. Adriana Baban pointed out that contemporary adult women were raised with traditional, patriarchal norms regarding virginal purity, condemning premarital sex as immoral and a sin.[84] In the communist mores, however, premarital sex certainly did not carry the same repercussions for men. What is more, mothers often perceived premarital sex as a legitimate sexual contact for their young sons, projecting its potential consequence as gaining valuable sexual experience, or as Baban quoted Romanian mothers who partook in her research, "this way, they won't be entrapped by the first woman they see."[85] On the other hand, for young girls, the gendered hypocrisy was glaring, illustrating yet again the intrinsic contradiction between the state's liberal sociopolitical measures to make sex "normal and acceptable" while at the same time, promoting an anti-bourgeoisie lack of eroticism and adherence to patriarchal perceptions of premarital sex.

Popova's article was counterpointed by other pieces in the magazine, presenting a different perspective on the issue of premarital sex. In a 1974 article titled "Facts That Worriy Us," Dr. Marin Muzlekov shares his thoughts and observations about young women's negative experiences with premarital sexual relationships resulting in abortion. Symbolically, the issue of abortion served as the litmus test on the progressiveness of socialist sexuality. Because the state supported its general availability (except in the case of Poland, and, with some modification, in Romania), abortion was seen as a measure of the forward-leaning gender ideology of the socialist revolution. Yet, it was also used as another opportunity to condemn what was interpreted as women's inappropriate and irresponsible treatment of their own bodies. The article is particularly interesting in that it prefaces the doctor's impressions about the need for sexual education by explaining the new regulations passed by the Ministry of People's Health, instituting that all women wishing to have abortion must first submit a request explaining their personal circumstances. Outside the invasive role of the state in surveying the private lives of young women in Bulgaria, the article is also an interesting example of how women's sexual behavior was not only sanctioned by the process of selecting who would be and who wouldn't be awarded the right to terminate unwanted pregnancy, but also of how these women's experiences were used as an opportunity to preach sexually proper behavior for the socialist youth.

The article focuses exclusively on the stories of young women who have had their lives negatively affected by an unplanned pregnancy, all of which were results of premarital affairs. It follows the personal accounts of five young women, identified only by their initials, who share a lot more than the unhappy ending brought by their irresponsible attitude towards sex. All of the girls are from working class backgrounds, claiming humble origins and good family roots. However, the focus of each story is quickly shifted to the purported sexual encounter that has produced the unwanted pregnancy. For example, one of the girls reported being raped by a random companion after a night of drinking, while another had premarital sex with her college student boyfriend, mindless of how a pregnancy can affect both their chances to obtain their degrees and assume their "rightful place in society." Dr. Muzlekov clearly places the blame of such poor life choices on the lack of education, which he squarely describes as an essential function of the family unit that can also be improved by the youth socialist organization and the school system itself. Placing the blame on external factors, rather than on internal deficiencies is further exemplified by another curious statement. "There is another bitter fact," the doctor states. "There is not enough being done to foster the feeling of national pride among the youth. That is why many young women find themselves attracted to foreigners: students, tourists, and others, often resulting in very sad outcomes. There are more than just a few disappointed young girls, who had sexual relations with foreigners, who come to ask the committee for permission to abort their pregnancies."[86] The technique of relocating responsibility and blame was just another skilled tactic on the part of the socialist ideologues to redirect the attention away from the social circumstances that can explain the peak in abortions among young, unwed women. It also helped deflect suspicion and potential criticism away from the inept party's strategy to institute a moral code of sexual behavior while masquerading as a champion of free love and women's rights.

The socialist policy of discouraging premarital sex as socially undesirable was replicated in the practice of presenting premarital sex as an unfit practice for the immature bodies of young men and women. Premarital sex, it was argued, could potentially not only affect their social success, but can literally, as socialist scientists and doctors proved, damage their delicate, undeveloped bodies and psyches. Such statements were frequently positioned in the strictly defined realm of physiological science, but had to be further solidified with numerous anecdotes, illustrating how young people's bodies can potentially be damaged in the process of succumbing to the temptation of early sex.

A good illustration of this approach can be seen in a 1974 piece titled "Sexology: A Belated Conversation." Written by another medical expert, the article focuses exclusively on how detrimental premarital sex could be for both young women and men, arguing that early sexual encounters can possibly delay and improperly redirect the growth of the adolescent organism, leading to a series of dangerous complications later on in life. The article clearly argues in support of avoiding premarital sex purely as a bodily function that could potentially damage the "spirit" of the young man or woman, but it also discusses in a similarly convincing scientific tone the idea of abstinence, essentially dispelling "the long-standing, provincial misconception" that abstinence can damage a young's men sexual drive and scar him for life in his future sexual encounters. The ultimate outcome of this personal advice disguised as scientifically informed narrative is this—just like sex itself, the mixed-message approach of the communist ideologues in their attempt to demystify the sexual act itself while continuing to create an aura of complexity around it, failed to provide the clarity needed to justify the social-moral code socialism advocated.

It is not surprising then that the social-moral regulation that appeared as a conversation rather than as stated imposition of rules wielded the kind of results the communist ideologues were hoping for. As Igor Kon pointed out, "This philosophy was well enshrined both in the stereotype of peasant thinking, nourished on a diet of anti-sexual morality, and in the ideas of the left radical intelligentsia, on the possibility of, and the need for, remaking human nature."[87] What Kon seems to miss in this poignant commentary, however, is that the responsibility for the ideological instrumentalization of sexual morale fitted for the socialist times was implicitly shifted on the shoulders of women, whose role as the purveyors of proper norms as mothers of future socialist sons and daughters really called for "the remaking" of women's nature, not human nature. As a result, instead of changing public perceptions and attitudes about sex, women experienced what Katrin Sieg called "impoverishment and alienation of sexual relations subordinated to the state propaganda of population growth."[88] Not only that, but despite the heavy load of moral responsibility women were supposed to carry, they were also expected to partake in fulfilling male desires and needs, leading once again to the hypocrisy of the socialist ideology of sex, aptly stated by Ann Oakley, "Sexuality was bad for women and that only 'bad' women were sexual."[89]

The communist desire to initiate, control, and direct the discourse on sex in socialist Bulgaria also translated in the larger effort to dictate the acceptable standards of physical appearance for their populace. Thus, magazine articles varied in their discussions of the body, ranging from historical analyses of standards of beauty, to fashion tips on how to dress the "overweight," the "elderly," and the "working" woman. In this wide range of body-related themes, one body that was conspicuously absent was the sexual female body. A similar trend was also documented in other parts of the socialist bloc, for example, in Eastern Germany—a trend skillfully captured by Judd Stitziel in her analysis of the inherent connection between socialist fashion and gender ideology.[90] The female body presented the ultimate battleground where the aesthetics of the West and the new socialist ideologies came clashing, visually juxtaposing each other in terms of the way women dressed themselves in public, but also in the standards of acceptable body appearance that the two opposing ideologies celebrated. Stitziel described, "in contrast to capitalism's objectification of women and its worship of the young and slender body, under socialism all women supposedly enjoyed the right to clothing appropriate to their bodies."[91]

As a result of this proclaimed celebration of the many sizes of beauty women can enjoy, the socialist ideology coined a number of endearing, yet, equally dismissive expressions used to address women whose weight was considered outside the norm. Ranging from "full-figured" to "chubby" to "stronger," women whose bodies did not fit the mold were both invited to join the fashion world, where "to be round is no misfortune," while simultaneously singling them out for having special needs that regular fashion simply can't address, and shouldn't in the first place.[92] Therefore, the fashion magazines, as well as all other magazines catering to women's interests, abounded in tips and advice on how to "hide full-figured women's disadvantages" in terms of their physical appearance so they can appear attractive, without being tasteless. This obviously was a difficult task, but for the fashion writer whose job was to masterfully sell an ideological imposition—in this case, how women should look—without ever looking too propagandistic, the art of offering advice was always best understood through the indisputable words of science.

Thus, the pages of the magazines almost on a regular basis offered advice on how to create optical illusions through carefully selecting the fabric's pattern in order to hide a chubby figure, or how to best combine a color palette for an outfit, based on the theory of perception, helping one appear slender, without looking boorish. A 1968 article titled "Fashion and the Chubby Woman" offers an interesting insight. The article starts by pointing out that women who are overweight often feel neglected by the fashion trends, and therefore, left with the wrong impression that fashion is only appropriate for the young and the slender. "This type of thinking in incorrect," the article boldly proclaimed, continuing to point out that "chubbiness" is not age-prone, and that even "the overweight woman can be decently dressed, if she followed the rules for aesthetic and harmonic dress."[93] Already, the tone and the words of the fashion advice signal what lies ahead—rather than a heart-warming advice for accepting one's self and maintaining an identity that is not ruled by external appearance, the article continued in the most rigorous tone to offer a series of prescriptions bordering on commands, concealed as professional tips to increase one's confidence. From the beginning paragraph, women are advised that they "should know the weaknesses of their figures and dress accordingly," clearly contradicting the encouragement felt in the first two sentences. As the column progresses, it focuses almost exclusively on what "chubby women *should not* dress like" and "what defects of their bodies" they should cover, rather than on celebrating their bodies, promoting a sense of self-acceptance. The following advice is just one illustration:

> If the arms are short and fat, then they should be fully covered with long, narrow sleeves. Even the youngest of all should not show their knees if they are fat or somehow flawed. A rather unpleasant sight for the eyes, a fact that is often ignored, is the sight of the ugly creases on the back of a fat woman's knees. The fat, muscular legs must be dressed in dark, but not too thick, stockings, and the shoes must be of average height and width, with a slightly longer front end. Excessively high heels make the woman's body unstable and unattractive, without adding much to her height.[94]

It becomes very clear from the language used in this example that the main goal of the socialist fashion functionaries was not to make full-figured women feel accepted as "elegant and chic," but rather, to commission, albeit in a less obvious way, the slender body as the socialist ideal. As Stitziel pointed out, "Implicitly and often explicitly, the 'normal' or the 'ideal' body remained thin, even under socialism."[95] In support of this ideal, socialist fashion experts often recommended patterns that can slim the body down, accessories that can create the appearance of a slender figure, basically advocating that women should dress not according to fashion, but according to their body type, and that the body type of the "stronger" woman while on the surface remains generally acceptable, under the guise of fashion norms, is certainly less desirable, and therefore, must be carefully scrutinized and corrected.

To further illustrate the fine distinction between the "desirable" body—that of the younger, thinner woman—and that of the "accepted" body—the fuller, less shapely woman—magazines frequently featured two separate fashion spreads. One featured younger, slender bodies modeling the fashion for the ideal body type, while the other featured special spreads designated for the full-figured woman, who also appeared older, less playful, and certainly more stoic than the colorful photo spreads that were "Parisian catwalk" style. The special spreads featured less attractive models, but also, "only slightly heavier than the models with the Twiggy-like figures," clearly demonstrating that the socialist norm of the visually attractive female body was just a bit, if at all, different from what the West celebrated as their body ideal.[96]

Another body attribute, which found itself frequently mentioned on the pages of *Zhenata Dnes*, was the issue of weight. Body weight, just like age and physical appearances, was clearly singled out as a token of physicality that socialist functionaries and fashion experts could easily incorporate and skillfully weave into the master narrative guiding the standards of proper gender roles and appearance. Under the guise of health advice, women's magazines printed on a regular basis full page directions for exercises, specifically tailored for women, to help keep them in top physical condition, while at the same time implicitly encouraging them to lose weight. "Consumer magazines increasingly reminded the 'strong woman' of the only socially acceptable solution to her dilemma: 'Resolve starting tomorrow to try a little more intensively and deliberately to reduce your weight by a few pounds, which separate you from the general ideal of beauty" is just one example of the type of advice that heavier women received, stressing once again the paradoxical nature of the socialist standard of female physical beauty.[97]

Just like the double burden, the socialist woman was also enduring a double standard in physical appearance—the socially desirable and utilitarian hefty body build, which was widely popularized by communist propaganda and stood as a token for the emancipation of gender relations in the new socialist state, was juxtaposed against the physically desirable slender body of the fashion model, which encompassed what the "ideal woman" should strive to be. Such state practices made the "fuller" body an undesirable exception, while underscoring the fact that the East subscribed to the same beauty ideal as the West despite its public condemnation of it.[98] Essentially, the state forced an artificially engineered concept of egalitarian socialist fashion, accepting women of all shapes and sizes only to promote and implicitly impose a standard of beauty very much in line with the slender body ideals of the West.

Zhenata Dnes also devoted column inches to what could be construed as a scientific discussion of the importance of physical appearance for the well-being of society and the national pride of the country. In line with the socialist ideologues' obsession with eugenics—the popular view in early-twentieth-century social science promoting the idea that through careful social engineering, humanity can progress away from deficiencies towards the optimal improvement of the human body—the communist ideologues were also interested in promoting not only a stronger and physically improved version of the socialist man and woman, but also a physically more attractive one.[99] As an illustration of this trend, consider a 1971 article titled "The Physical Appearance of the Bulgarian." Given the gender specificity of the Bulgarian language, which linguistically assigns gender to all objects, it becomes automatically evident in the title of the article that the primary subject of this discussion is the Bulgarian man, not the Bulgarian woman. What is more, the article features a photo of Stefan Danailov—at the time the most recognizable face of the Bulgarian cinema who also became known as the ultimate "sex symbol" for his portrayals of a suave Bulgarian intelligence officer, a socialist James Bond. The article boasts newly found anthropological data demonstrating that Bulgarians are considered an "attractive" race by a recently published index of "attractiveness," emphasizing the importance of good looks in the socialist idea of what is considered physically desirable. The article also designates a good amount of space attacking women over the age of forty, particularly those who have allowed themselves "to grow fat" and therefore must watch what they eat in order to remain within "the accepted health and beauty norms."

This is particularly instructive as it demonstrates yet again the internal conflict inherent in socialist gender norms aiming to reconcile both the utilitarian function of the female body—as bearer of children, and therefore, proliferators of the future state—as well as its purely aesthetic function—the pleasing, shapely, and physically attractive body that can be used as a counter argument to beauty standards promoted by the West. The irony of the "double standard" also stems from the fact that as Elizabeth Waters contended, "a solidly built woman was popularly regarded as healthy, capable of childbearing and hard work, and attractive."[100] However, as Waters herself argued, the forces of economic growth and its attendant economic and cultural revolutions practically weakened this image leading to a takeover of the urban culture by the cult of the Western-looking slender body.

NOTES

1. Kotzeva, Tatyana, "Reimagining Bulgarian Women: The Marxist Legacy and Women's Self-iIdentity," in *Gender and Identity in Central and Eastern Europe*, ed. Chris Corrin (London: Frank Cass Publishers, 1999), 83–99.

2. LaFont, Suzanne, *Women in Transition: Voices from Lithuania* (Albany, NY: State University of New York Press, 2001), 205.

3. Verdery, Katherine, "From Parent-State to Family Patriarchs: Gender and Nation in Contemporary Eastern Europe," *East European Politics and Societies*, 8, 2 (1994): 232.

4. Daskalova, Krasimira, "Women's Problems, Women's Discourses in Post-Communist Bulgaria," in *Reproducing Gender: Politics, Publics and Everyday Life After Socialism*, eds. Susan Gal and Gail Kligman (Princeton: Princeton University Press, 2000), 349.

5. Van Dijk, Teun, "Ideological Discourse Analysis, *Courant*, 4 (1996): 136.

6. Daskalova, "Women's Problems."

7. Ibid., 351.

8. Marody, Mira, and Giza-Poleszczuk, Anna, "Changing Images of Identity in Poland: From the Self-sacrificing to the Self-investing Woman?," in *Reproducing Gender: Politics, Publics and Everyday Life After Socialism*, eds. Susan Gal and Gail Kligman (Princeton: Princeton University Press, 2000), 156.

9. Ibid., 167.

10. Neuburger, Mary, "Pants, Veils, and Matters of Dress: Unraveling the Fabric of Women's Lives in Communist Bulgaria," in *Style and Socialism: Modernity and Material Culture in Post-War Eastern Europe*, eds. David Rowley and Susan Reid (Oxford: Berg Publishing, 2000), 172.

11. Kon, Igor, *The Sexual Revolution in Russia: From the Age of the Czars to Today*, trans. James Riordian (New York: Free Press, 1995), 150–51.

12. Verdery, Katherine, *What Was Socialism, And What Comes Next?* (Princeton: Princeton University Press, 1996).

13. Johnson, Janet Elise, and Robinson, Jean (eds.), *Living Gender After Communism* (Bloomington: Indiana University Press, 2007), 43.

14. "Remnants of a barbaric past," *Zhenata Dnes*, 10 (1969): 9.

15. Samardjieva, Violeta, "Women and the Scientific Technical Revolution," *Zhenata Dnes*, 7 (1970): 14.

16. Ibid., 14.

17. Gall, Susan, and Kligman, Gail (eds.), *Reproducing Gender: Politics, Publics and Everyday Life After Socialism* (Princeton: Princeton University Press, 2000), 6.

18. Vacheva, Dimitria, "Things That Worry Us," *Zhenata Dnes*, 3 (1968): 7.

19. Dinkova, Maria, "Women Today and Tomorrow," *Zhenata Dnes*, 5 (1969): 5.

20. Dinkova, Maria, "Could you carry two watermelons under one arm?," *Zhenata Dnes*, 4 (1971): 5–6.

21. Ibid., 6.

22. "Travel tips for the wife," *Zhenata Dnes*, 10 (19711): 25.

23. Johnson and Robinson, *"Living Gender After Communism,"* 7.

24. Ziapkova, Nevena, "Children at Play," *Zhenata Dnes* (1969): 21.

25. Ibid., 21.

26. Johnson and Robinson, *"Living Gender After Communism,"* 7.

27. Slavova, Kornelia, "Looking at Western Feminisms Through the Double Lens of Eastern Europe and the Third World," in *Women and Citizenship in Central and Eastern Europe*, eds. Jasmina Lukic, Joanna Regulska, and Darja Zavirek (Aldershot: Ashgate, 2007), 253.

28. Dölling, Irene, Hahn, Daphne, and Scholz, Sylka, "Birth Strike in the New Federal States: Is Sterilization an Act of Resistance?," in *Reproducing Gender: Politics, Publics and Everyday Life After Socialism*, eds. Susan Gal and Gail Kligman (Princeton: Princeton University Press, 2000), 28.

29. Ghodsee, Kristen, "Potions, Lotions and Lipstick: The Gendered Consumption of Cosmetics and Perfumery in Socialist and Post-socialist Urban Bulgaria," *Women's Studies International Forum*, 30, 1, (2007): 26–39.

30. Ibid., 29.

31. Quote from ibid., 29.

32. Stitziel, Judd, *Fashioning Socialism: Clothing, Politics, and Consumer Culture in East Germany* (Oxford: Berg, 2005).

33. Ibid., 59.

34. Kaier, Christina, *Imagine No Possessions: The Socialist Objects of Russian Constructivism* (Cambridge, MA: MIT Press, 2005), 123.

35. Massino, Jill, "From Black Caviar to Blackouts: Gender, Consumption, and Lifestyle in Ceausescu's Romania,' in *Communism Unwrapped: Consumption in Cold War Eastern Europe*, eds. Paulina Bren and Mary Neuburger (Oxford: Oxford University Press, 2012), 227.

36. Ibid., 232.

37. Bartlett, Djurdja, *FashionEast: The Spectre That Haunted Socialism* (Cambridge, MA: MIT Press, 2010), 5.

38. Massino, "From Black Caviar to Blackouts," 232.

39. Bartlett, *FashionEast*.

40. Ibid., 47.
41. Quoted in Kaier, *Imagine No Possessions*, 216.
42. Ibid., 217.
43. Ibid., 218.
44. Quoted in Kaier, *Imagine No Possessions*, 218.
45. Ibid., 216.
46. Quoted in Bartlett, *FashionEast*, 18.
47. Quoted in Kaier, *Imagine No Possessions*, 124.
48. Bartlett, *FashionEast*, 22.
49. Kaier, *Imagine No Possessions*.
50. Kaier, *Imagine No Possessions*, 132.
51. Bartlett, *FashionEast*, 26.
52. Stitziel, *Fashioning Socialism*, 3.
53. Massino, "From Black Caviar to Blackouts," 230.
54. Popkostadinova, Nikoleta, "Bulgarian Vogue: Socialist or Not, Lada is the Coolest Bulgarian Fashion Magazine," accessed May 11, 2011, http://www.viceland.com/bg/v2n4/htdocs/bbjta-365.php.
55. Ibid., ¶7.
56. Quoted in Popkostadinova, "Bulgarian Vogue," 11.
57. Bartlett, *FashionEast*, 65.
58. Stitziel, *Fashioning Socialism*, 4.
59. "Open letter to the Ministry of Light Industry," *Zhenata Dnes*, 2 (1963): 14.
60. Quoted in Igor Kon, "Sexuality and Culture," in *Sex and Russian Society*, eds. Igor Kon and James Riordian (London: Pluto Press, 1993), 22.
61. Slobin, Greta, "Revolution Must Come First: Reading V. Aksenov's *Island of Crimea*," in *Nationalism and Sexualities*, eds. A. Parker, M. Russo, and P. Yaeger (London: Routledge, 1992), 249.
62. Borenstein, Eliot, *Overkill: Sex and Violence in Contemporary Russian Popular Culture* (Ithaca and London: Cornell University Press, 2008).
63. Ibid., 28.
64. Ibid., 31.
65. Carleton, Gregory, *Sexual Revolution in Bolshevik Russia* (Pittsburgh, PA: University of Pittsburgh Press, 2005).
66. Naiman, Eric, *Sex in Public: The Incarnation of Early Soviet Ideology* (Princeton: Princeton University Press, 1997).
67. Borenstein, *Overkill*.
68. Ibid., 32.
69. Ibid.
70. Magó-Maghiar, Ana, "Representations of Sexuality in Hungarian Popular Culture of the 1980s," *Medij. Istraz*, 16, 1 (2009): 73–95.
71. Ibid., 73.
72. Žikić, Biljana, "Dissidents Liked Pretty Girls: Nudity, Pornography and Quality Press in Socialism," *Medij. Istraz*, 16, 1 (2009): 53–71.
73. Bostandjiev, Todor, "Are Our Women Frigid?" *Zhenata Dnes*, 5 (1968): 17.
74. Massino, "From Black Caviar to Blackouts."
75. Ibid., 234.
76. Berstein, Frances, *The Dictatorship of Sex: Lifestyle Advice for the Soviet Masses* (DeKalb: Northern Illinois University Press, 2007).
77. Baban, Adriana, "Women's Sexuality and Reproductive Behavior in Post-Ceausescu Romani: A Psychological Approach," in *Reproducing Gender: Politics, Publics and Everyday Life After Socialism*, eds. Susan Gal and Gail Kligman (Princeton: Princeton University Press, 2000), 239.
78. Gessen, Masha, "Sex in Media and the Birth of the Sex Media in Russia," in *Post-Communism and the Body Politics*, ed. Ellen Berry (New York: New York University, 1995), 199.
79. Kon, "Sexuality and Culture."

80. Ibid., 27.
81. Carleton, *Sexual Revolution in Bolshevik Russia*, 232.
82. Naiman, *Sex in Public*.
83. Popova, Pavlina, "Stop, Julieta, Stop," *Zhenata Dnes*, 9 (1972): 15.
84. Baban, "Women's Sexuality and Reproductive Behavior."
85. Ibid., 241.
86. Muzlekov, Marin, "Facts That Worry Us," *Zhenata Dnes*, 4 (1974): 19.
87. Kon, "Sexuality and Culture," 24.
88. Sieg, Katrin, "Sex, Subjectivity, and Socialism: Feminist Discourse in East Germany," in *Post-Communism and the Body Politic*, ed. Ellen Berry (New York: New York University, 1995), 122.
89. Oakley, Ann, "Sexuality," in *Feminism and Sexuality: A Reader*, eds. S. Stevi Jackson and S. Scott (New York: Columbia University Press, 1996), 5.
90. Stitziel, *Fashioning Socialism*.
91. Ibid., 61.
92. Ibid.
93. Braikova, Vasila, "Fashion and the Chubby Woman,' *Zhenata Dnes*, 5 (1968): 17.
94. Ibid.
95. Stitziel, *Fashioning Socialism*, 61.
96. Ibid., 62.
97. Ibid.
98. Stitziel, *Fashioning Socialism*.
99. Carleton, *Sexual Revolution in Bolshevik Russia*.
100. Waters, Elizabeth, "Soviet Beauty Contests," in *Sex and Russian Society*, eds. Igor Kon and James Riordian (London: Pluto Press, 1993), 121.

Chapter Two

Advertising and the Socialist Economy

Efficiency, Necessity, and Desire

Socialism, consumption, and commercial advertising have always been caught in an ideologically uncomfortable disparity. In fact, in the 2003 award-winning film *Good-Bye Lenin*, which tells the story of the demise of communism in Eastern Germany and the fall of the Berlin Wall, a particular scene presents the perfect backdrop for this paradox. In the movie, the main character Alex, a young East German student whose involuntary participation in a protest results in his arrest, is caught in the line of irreversible transformations. Unfortunately, his arrest is witnessed by his frail mother who suffers a severe heart attack at the scene and falls in a deep coma. By the time she wakes up, East Germany is no longer and the world of communism has taken a new, unexpected turn. To protect his frail mother from suffering another, and this time, possibly a fatal shock, Alex takes on a rather ambitious task—to recreate the communist world of East Germany in the surroundings of his tiny socialist block apartment and thus, continue the illusion of "business as usual" for his communist-faithful mother. From this point on, the movie becomes a series of tragic-comedic commentaries on life under communism, but also a rather poignant look into socialist aesthetics and its impact on the people of the Eastern bloc.

One recurring theme seems particularly telling in this connection and offers a frank and rather amusing insight into the perception of advertising during the socialist rule. The scene features Alex's mother, Christiane, looking on through their apartment's window and marvelling at a giant banner advertising Coca-Cola being unfurled on the side of the adjacent building. The challenge grows for Alex as he tries to explain this "un-communist" visual transgression to his mother by claiming that East Germany won an international patent dispute, which proved that it was actually East German scientists who invented the secret formula for Coke.

While this anecdote offers a comical critique of the East's failure to come to terms with the concept of consumption and market demands, in many ways, it also offers a clever jab at the role of advertising and its conceptualization during communism, a topic largely overlooked in the historical discussion of the roles of commercial advertising during communism. Most of the studies on advertising during communism were conducted with the purpose of offering both a look into the Marxist-Leninist interpretation of the role of promotion in the planned economy, but to also criticize the system's failure to recognize the role of the market and the mass appeal of advertising as a means of promoting consumption.[1] Perhaps one of the most popular analyses of communist advertising as a mass media business was offered by Fred Siebert, Theodore Peterson, and Wilbur Schramm in their *Four Theories of the Press*, where advertising was seen as a propaganda tool for the Communist Party, and therefore, as having a damaging ideological impact on the freedom of the press.[2] More recent studies of advertising and marketing in the Soviet Union,[3] as well as the studies of the culture of consumption,[4] offer an insight into the Soviet specificities of advertising lifestyle and propagating political beliefs. However, as Patrick Patterson pointed out, "on the broader social and cultural consequences of consumption, advertising and marketing in socialist lands, the scholarly literature available in Western languages remains thin,"[5] and to date one major study has examined the historical roots of early Soviet advertising.[6]

This chapter offers a historical analysis of the evolution of the concept of advertising both as a propaganda tool and a means of encouraging consumption—through personal style and fashion—in socialist Bulgaria, from the accession of the Communist Party to power at the end of World War II and into the post-communist transition of the 1990s. In exploring the public discourse on the function and importance of advertising in the popular media, namely, in the state-owned and run Bulgarian newspapers over the last fifty years, this chapter explores the discursive approach used to define the need for advertising in the Bulgarian society. In doing so, this chapter presents an insight into the complex ways in which socialist ideologies came to term with the "inevitable" logic of the market, expressed in recognizing on one hand, the need for consumption and on the other, the necessary utility of advertising which promotes and supports this very consumption and sustains the operation of a commercially viable media system.

The chapter engages a historical analysis in search of a more hermeneutic and systematic perspective on the complex processes at work in understanding the relationship between culture, media, and advertising. Historical analysis "involves the use of historical methods by sociologists, political scientists, and other social scientists."[7] Primary sources for this study were the only two major publications of communist press in Bulgaria, namely, *Rabotchnichesko Delo* (Worker's Cause), the official newspaper of the Communist Party, and *Otechevstven Front* (Fatherland Front), the official paper of the People's movement, encompassing almost the entire Bulgarian population. In addition, the only officially sanctioned newspaper devoted to matters of culture and art, *Kultura* (Culture) was also examined in order to study the response of the professional media critics to the rise of commercial advertising. The data included original articles, think pieces, as well as letters to the editors. All newspaper issues, beginning in 1944 and continuing until 1989 were carefully studied to detect any mentions on the topic of advertising. Given that all three newspapers were usually four pages total, the analysis was accomplished by reading headlines and lead paragraphs for certain keywords, including advertising, consumption, socialist aesthetics, visual propaganda, taste and style, fashion, journalism, and media. When such keywords were detected, the articles were further examined in their entirety for notable discursive threads, noting whether they were authored or not. The textual examples were then analyzed and discussed in the order in which they were published.

In line with its approach, this study uses a narrative tracing in-depth the development of the idea of commercial advertising as the engine of a consumer-based economy and a media system that is supported by and relies on commercial profits. As Nord asserted, a "narrative is more than a description; it is a logical organization of material into a chronological sequence for the purpose of explanation."[8] Hence, the explanatory power of the historical narrative approach lies with its ability to trace the logical progression of each step.[9]

A BRIEF HISTORY OF SOVIET ADVERTISING

The development of advertising in Bulgaria, as well as most other socialist states, was inextricably connected to the development of the Soviet concept of advertising and the socialist conceptualization of production, distribution, and marketing of consumer goods. One of the major tenets upon which advertising was to be understood in the Soviet world rested upon the assumption that advertising, as well as other competitive marketing techniques, was wasteful, and therefore should be avoided and treated with hostility.[10] As James Markham pointed out, what he called "the Orthodox Communist View" propagated denial of the need for advertising as a "parasitic form of activity and a drain on the economy."[11] In fact, the large *Soviet Encyclopedia* well illustrated this hard-liner rigid rejection of advertising by defining it as a result of unrestrained market competition that artificially stimulates consumption, while forcing people to buy what they do not need and cannot afford.[12]

Although commercial advertising was not a foreign concept to pre-revolutionary Russia, as well as the rest of the Eastern European countries, it certainly underwent a major reconceptualization process, which was intricately connected to concepts of cultural policy and aesthetics, modernization, and economic growth. On the one side, as Natasha Tolstikova pointed out, "the expression 'Soviet advertising' appears to be an oxymoron."[13] Since the state was responsible for the production of consumer goods, the need for competition or for the establishing of brands of goods was unjustified, and therefore, irrational and wasteful. On the other hand, advertising was also seen as a model of promoting the development of a socialist aesthetic as well as the cultivation of a "measured" and "controlled" consumption that was to benefit both the producers and consumers of goods, which in the case of the socialist state, were virtually the same.

To understand how advertising has evolved during the years of ideological articulation of means of production, consumption, and distribution of goods, it is useful to begin at the offset of the Socialist revolution in Russia. One of the first acts signed by the new government after the October Revolution in 1917 was a Decree on the Introduction of a State Monopoly in Publicity.[14] The idea behind this act was to abolish not only private property, but also the free market.[15] This did not, however, lead to the end of commercial advertising in Russia; it merely meant that all private advertisements were subject to censorship and that insertions in publications could not be bought by advertisers and then filled by material passed on as editorial copy. The result of this increased censorship was a period of stagnation in the advertising industry.[16]

Advertising was allowed a little respite between 1921 and 1928, during the period known as the New Economic Policy (NEP). NEP began primarily as an agricultural measure acting as an incentive for peasants to produce more food for the towns; however, it expanded to allow for commodity exchange between town and country and finally as an encouragement for industrial production.[17] This change of focus (seen by some as being at odds with previous ideology) led to a more prominent role for the market in the state's economic sector.[18] There was a rich private enterprise sector in the Soviet Union, fronted by entrepreneurs who played an important role as wholesalers and in 1922 to 1923 controlled seventy-five percent of the retail trade.[19] In fact, as Tolstikova argued, the NEP allowed for competition between businesses that relied on advertising, and therefore produced ample examples of advertising, which she described as "calming, romantic and in ornamental styles."[20]

General commercial activity continued to use product and service advertising and even though parts of the population became excited about the prospects of consumption, which NEP allowed, others were highly critical, sensing a return to capitalism through the indulgence in consumerist tendencies, including the creation of artificial demands for goods through commercial advertising. In addition, advertising contributed to the finances of the Soviet press, with two-thirds of the Soviet government's daily newspaper *Izvestija's* revenue coming from advertisements.[21] However, not everyone was in favor of the private enterprise Nepmen and their advertisements. Members of the Agitreklama "agitation advertising" association distanced themselves from the entrepreneurial activities of the Nepmen. Agitreklama changed the style of advertising in the Soviet Union by using poetry combined with original forms of montage. Members of the Agitreklama, however, were actively against NEP private enterprise, and saw their role not as sellers of goods, but spreaders of information and educators of the masses.[22]

It should be noted that in the early Soviet advertising period, as Tolstikova[23] and Kolesnik[24] both illustrated, the work of the early Soviet advertising figures—namely, artist Rodchenko and poet Mayakovsky—created a fascinating, artistic, and powerful version of commercial messages that hugely resembles early Soviet propaganda, making their work so popular with clients that in a symbolic manner, established the legitimacy "of advertising as a profession."[25] And not to be overlooked in its aesthetic value, early Soviet advertising did not appear boorish and blandly propagandist—in fact, ads by Rodchenko and Mayakovsky earned them silver medals at the 1925 International Exhibition in Paris.[26]

Stalin's iron rule over the post-World War II economy radically changed the Soviet concept of advertising. Since supply and production of consumer goods was now centrally determined by the planners who set 5-year targets for each industry, the need for advertising, either as an aesthetic expression of visual form or as a promotion of goods was rendered virtually unnecessary. Changes to the economic system, implemented by Stalin, meant that advertising decreased significantly from the late 1920s until the 1960s, and any organization offering *reklama* "advertising" in its services would, in reality, supervise shop window displays.[27] In fact, as Tolstikova pointed out in her analysis of the early Soviet advertising of the NEP period, the concept of developing further advertising as a science as promoted by a number of early Soviet advertising artists, as well as seeking answers for the future development of the trade by learning lessons from the West, was seen "not only as unwise, but ideologically dangerous."[28] It must be noted, however, as Susan Reid contends, in rhetoric, "the turn to consumerism and the promotion of cultured trade began under Stalin."[29] In the second Five-Year plan, abundance was declared as one of the goals of socialism and consumption was presented as a modernizing force that can advance social integration, socialist progress, and personal growth for the proletariat.[30] Thus, advertising during the Stalin era was reduced down to its most basic function of promoting consumption of goods.

Khrushchev's "secret speech" in February 1956 saw an end to the most severe period of Soviet history, heralding a new era of growth and economic prosperity, informed by a completely different attitude towards the matter of consumption. As Reid aptly pointed out, "consumption, and living standards more generally, came to the forefront of party rhetoric and state policy during the 1950s, under the conditions of 'peaceful competition' that marked a new, somewhat more relaxed phase of the Cold War."[31] The advertising industry began to grow in the 1960s and 1970s, seeing the creation of large agencies such as Sojuztorgreklama, Glavokooptorgreklama, and Rostorgreklamai, and publishing of a number of magazines giving advice on advertising, such as *Reklama, Kommerčeskij vestnik, Moskovskaja reklama,* and *Novye tovary.*[32] The advertisements at this time followed the official advertising principles—for example, their aim was to educate people's tastes, provide information to consumers, and improve distribution services. As Markham pointed out, the magazine *Sovetskaya Kultura* (Soviet Culture) proclaimed the following as purposes of Soviet advertising: "1) to educate public taste; 2) to develop demand; 3) to help consumer quickly find what they want to buy, 4) to help them buy it easily, and 5) to tell them the price."[33] Advertising was guided by and clearly grounded in ideology, and was therefore to be truthful, concrete, and effective in selling goods and in conforming to the Soviet plans. Soviet advertisements were used to promote "sufficient" goods; that is, goods for which there was a guaranteed supply (through, for example, overproduction).

Soviet advertising was not used to promote goods that were already in demand, as this was seen as a waste of resources. Thus a new product would be developed and sold to distributors without advance advertising. Retailers would find themselves with excess stock and would then carry out advertising at their own expense. The retailer, not the manufacturer, was therefore in control of advertising. When knitting machines were first introduced into the Soviet Union, for example, they were heavily promoted by retailers, in order to educate the population about their use and benefits. Advertisements for "sufficient" goods would also help to absorb the excess demand for those goods that were "scarce." For example, pacific fish was advertised as the increase in the Soviet fishing fleet meant that there was a large supply of fish in contrast with the poor levels of meat production in the 1960s. Germogenova cites the slogan "Eat hake fish," used when there was plenty of hake in many shops.[34] Advertising was also influenced by social considerations; for example, milk was advertised because of its nutritional value,[35] while at the same time, Ludmilla Gricenko-Wells[36] also demonstrated that there was more emphasis on promoting import/export goods than on the domestic production and distribution of goods, making the argument in support of promoting the "socialist prestige" and "visual dynamic" as a value embedded in the function of advertising even more powerful.

At the end of the spectrum, Soviet visual propaganda also engaged in a powerful attack on all things Western, following the simple logic that the more the Western opulence is demonized, the less desirable it would become, making the socialist choice the only desirable outcome. As Yana Hashamova argued, "with undying energy Russian periodicals pointed out the capitalist unemployment, poverty, and exploitation. And naturally the more official Russian ideology demonized the West, the more ordinary Russians fantasized about it."[37]

WESTERN VERSUS SOVIET ADVERTISING

The rise of advertising in the West has undeniably and intricately been linked to the growth of industrial production and economic development. However, as Stuart Ewen pointed out, the process of industrialization was much more complex than simply producing more goods for consumption.[38] "It also entailed a process of socialization which aimed at stabilizing and inculcating fidelity among those whose labour was being conscripted."[39] In fact, as the authors contended, the need to develop an ideology of consumption was intrinsically linked to issues of social control and the need for goods distribution. From this perspective, the similarities with socialist concepts of advertising were striking. In fact, as Jukka Gronow argued, many of the "tricks" of the advertising business were indeed directly borrowed from economically more advanced countries, where a slew of Soviet delegations were sent with the mission of observing and recording strategies that can then be applied to the Soviet way of life.[40] While this approach might seems somewhat paradoxical and contrary to the Marxist-Leninist doctrine of rejecting the Western models of industrial and economic development, it also signals that "one could with great success, as the specialists believed, copy the most advanced technology from the capitalist countries in the more 'socialized' relations of production of Soviet industry and trade. It would as a matter of fact, fit much better into the new socialist than the old capitalist relations of production, where private property relations slowed down its development and hinder its efficient exploitation."[41]

Despite the attempt of Soviet ideologues to create and rationalize the fine distinctions between Soviet and Western advertising, Gronow argued that particularly in the 1930s period of Soviet advertising, one can see clear parallels with the stages of development of Western advertising, "from adverts for 'wundermedicines' promising a cure to all the ills of humankind, with a maximum of textual product information, to advertising images of products portraying their smiling consumers asking the readers whether they have already tasted the product."[42]

However, while similarities existed, there were also significant differences. For one, Soviet advertisements were to be always dignified, without any signs of vulgarity, countering Western advertising, which often stooped to the lower levels in order to make a sale. In addition, Soviet ideologues were clear about the striking distinction of their ads from those produced in the West—namely, Soviet advertising was to inform the buyer about each product or good, and not make a profit. As Randi Cox pointed out, as reflected in the thoughts of R. G. Driubin, a member of the VSNKh Advertising Commission, "in capitalist countries, the main goal of advertising is to increase trade, enliven sales, and serve as a weapon of competition, while here, the main goal of advertising is to increase the cultural level by arousing desire for those goods and products whose consumption will lead to cultural uplift."[43]

Thus, while Western advertising often leads consumers to buy shoddy and unnecessary goods, Soviet advertising was construed to inform the consumer about the usefulness of the product and its genuine necessity. Interestingly, as Cox points out, while Driubun and his colleagues openly condemned Western advertising as deceptive and manipulative, he did not necessarily reject the idea that advertising can be used to manipulate consumers' consciousness. "Driubin's ideal socialist advertising would still be manipulative, but such paternalistic manipulations would be for the benefit of the uneducated consumer, rather than to increase corporate profits."[44]

It must be noted, however, that both in the case of Western and Soviet advertising, the propaganda aspect of promoting consumption was deemed as equally important. In fact, as Cox argued, "while propaganda art created a Marxist narrative focused on the effects of changing the means of production, advertising was necessarily about consumption, about action in the present, not the future."[45]

Therefore, it might be argued that the function of advertising for the Soviet economy, while similar to the Western need for the development of an ideology of consumption as a response to the need for social control and distribution of goods, also had to stretch a step further.[46] Soviet advertising, as Krisztina Fehervary argued, had an additional goal—to educate consumers about new products and technologies, while at the same time, encourage them to modernize and become more discriminating in their personal tastes and habits.[47] "A desire for transparency and truth in comparison to capitalist deceit and misrepresentation was a major principle behind the ways consumer goods were promoted and displayed, echoing modernist avant-garde ideologies from the 1920s in everything from buildings to letter fonts."[48]

Chapter 2

ADVERTISING IN OTHER SOCIALIST STATES

While the Soviet Union was the "ground zero" for initiating and indoctrinating ideologically correct ways of thinking of the function and role of advertising, the rest of the socialist countries were also developing their own, and often somewhat divergent, way of thinking about the need for advertising and the culture of consumption. Naturally, some of the most prominently different conceptualizations of advertising came from countries that had an alternative approach to their own national economies, such as East Germany and Yugoslavia, among others. And even though the Soviet Union was seen as the premiere authority on the scholarship and artistry of advertising, Soviet offices, as Markham pointed out, sought to learn lessons from the marketing experiences of the Eastern European satellite countries.[49] In addition, as Karen Fox, Irina Skorobogatykh, and Olga Saginova also argued in their study of the Soviet evolution of marketing thought, the Soviet Union already had a number of notable experts on marketing, who were well acquainted with the foreign marketing literature, while at the same time, produced Soviet-style marketing, following the guidance of the Marxist-Leninist ideology.[50] At the same time, these very same marketing experts were what the authors called realists, as they understood the value of studying the examples of marketing and advertising practices in other countries.

Among the members of the Eastern socialist bloc, a particularly interesting example in exploring the nexus between advertising as a commercial practice and the socialist planned economy, which rejects its necessity, is the case of Yugoslavia. As Patterson documented in his extensive analysis of the history of advertising and marketing in Yugoslavia, "within Yugoslavia, the controversy hinged on what was widely recognized as the deeper social significance of the country's burgeoning consumer culture and especially its relationship to, and consequences for, the Yugoslav socio-political system and socialism more generally."[51] In Yugoslavia, which was always seen as the "renegade" socialist state, advertising played a particularly important role as the concept of commercial promotion was transformed from a relic of decadent capitalism into a "necessity of modern, rational, socialist production and distribution."[52] A particularly fascinating diversion from the Soviet model of advertising ensued when Yugoslavia broke away from the grip of the Stalinist ideological and political control in the 1950s, which as Patterson pointed out, marked the beginning of a distinctly Yugoslav brand of a market-oriented socialism, which also brought about the transformation of advertising from pure propaganda with zero commercial appeal into a more sophisticated concept of advertising—one that was informed by and often directly borrowed from models in Western Europe and America. This is a unique feature of the Yugoslav development in defining the cultural and economic role of advertising as the growth of the Western, and particularly so American, influences in the sphere of the business practices of advertising became more and more notable, or as Patterson put it, "Yugoslavia has indeed been infected" with the ideas of advertising as the lifeblood of economic growth, thus causing consumer culture to grow often independently, and completely contrary, to economic growth.[53]

In this context, it must also be noted that even though Yugoslavian advertising specialists borrowed business models and marketing practices from the West, they generally tended to shy away from "acknowledging their role as merchants of fantasy and wish fulfillment," and instead, stuck to ideas of promoting consumption that aligned with the "imperatives of socialist politics: it [advertising] remained cool, rational, and circumspect, marked by its claims to offer straightforward, practical, and above all, reliable information to meet consumer needs."[54]

While Yugoslavia certainly presented a rather unique twist in conceptualizing socialist advertising with a flexible openness to the West and reflected through the ideological innovation of the Yugoslav economic system, East Germany (also known at the time as the German Democratic Republic [GDR]), presents another interesting exception to the general trend in developing socialist concepts of advertising. Just like Yugoslavia's position as the "renegade" child of the socialist bloc, East Germany was seen as its final, and most tested, frontier in its role as the only geographical location in the Eastern bloc, which was so openly exposed to the commercial influences of the West (namely, in its exposure to products from West Germany). As Martin Blum points out in his study of nostalgia and material culture in East Germany, the development of the concept of material culture was informed and to a large extent determined by the development of advertising for consumer goods during socialism.[55] In fact, as Blum argued, beginning in 1965, the culture of consumption in East Germany was radically changed with the East German market becoming almost completely sealed off from the West and directed inwards and eastwards. This was accompanied by a strong push for a dramatic shift in advertising as well, which was expected to follow the guidelines set forth in the socialist advertising principles prescribed by the Soviet ideologues. Ironically, as Blum pointed out, "the understanding of advertising in the socialist economy differed fundamentally from its Western equivalent not only in that ads directed customers to purchase certain items, but also in that ads were geared to lead customers away from certain others so as to redirect consumer attention to less desirable products that were readily available."[56] This paradoxical interpretation of the role of advertising led not only to an increased aesthetic of blandness (as there was virtually no need to create an imagined narrative pointing out the advantages of the advertised good) but also further eroded the public trust in the veracity, or necessity, of the advertising copy, which did nothing to create desire for the product, while at the same time, leading East Germans to "author" their own narratives of everyday uses of products and goods, creating a unique and highly personalized product identity outside the boundaries of officially commissioned advertising.

A similarly poignant look into the intersection of culture, consumption, and socialist aesthetics through the expression of fashion comes from Judd Stitziel.[57] In her examination of the culture of consumption and fashion in East Germany, Stitziel makes several direct observations on the role of advertising in the socialist conceptualization of the East German political hardliners, recognizing the critical role that advertising places in consolidating and synchronizing "the two otherwise antagonistic systems of production and consumption."[58] In this extreme rhetoric, the excessive indulgence in consumer advertising in the West was contrasted with the disciplined and very purpose-driven promotion of "good" consumer-citizenship habits in East Germany. As Stitziel pointed out, "East German functionaries sought to distinguish these activities under socialism, however, by contrasting manipulative, misleading, and profiting-seeking advertising (*Reklame*) and market research in the West, with enlightened, educational, and beneficial advertising (*Werbung*) and 'needs research' (*Bedarsforschung*) in the GDR."[59]

While East Germany and Yugoslavia provide an interesting diversion from "Soviet advertising" as usual, it is still important to note that despite the alternative models that these two countries adopted in addressing the challenges posed by a planned economy with carefully controlled supply and demand chain of production and the need to compete with the West in terms of modernization and lifestyles, advertising continued to present a unique juncture where cultural narratives, economic arguments, and political control were hotly contested. Of interest to this study is the public discourse which surrounded the discussion and conceptual development of advertising in Bulgaria, where the tensions and contradictions of the socialist system of production and the need to foster a socialist consumer mindset engendered a fascinating attempt to maintain a system that was economically and political viable, while at the same, offered a rational response to the demands of growing consumer awareness. This, of course, is not a dilemma unique to the condition of Bulgaria alone; however, Bulgaria is uniquely situated for this analysis as its geographical location in close proximity to Yugoslavia made the alternative models of advertising readily accessible while at the same, among all socialist states, Bulgaria was known to have maintained the closest ideological axis to Moscow, frequently deemed its most loyal satellite state (and casually also known as the U.S.S.R's 16th republic). In fact, early Bulgarian advertising maintained a much closer resemblance to the Soviet model than that of the Yugoslav Republic. A typical Bulgarian ad was usually busy with type, exalting the quality of the product in terms of its utility and modern functionality, rarely accompanied by an enticing visual portraying its actual physical dimension. For example, a shoe ad will often feature a hand-drawn illustration of it, rather than a luxurious photo of it, coupled with verbose description of materials the shoe is made of (typically rubber or vinyl), its high versatility (it's both practical and easy to clean), as well as its durability (won't wear down even after many hours of wear and tear). Similarly, an advertisement promoting a vacation at a seaside resort would be comprised entirely of type, engaging no visual appeals or imaginative devices favoring a functional approach, envisioning ads as nothing more than content carrier for utilitarian purposes.

DEFINING SOCIALIST CONSUMPTION: THE CURIOUS CASE OF BULGARIA

Bulgaria became a communist country after World War II, and had an orthodox command economy in which almost everything was centrally planned by the communist government.[60] Inspired by the vision of the Soviet Revolution, the creation of a "socialist way of life" was the first item of business for the Bulgarian Communist Party upon its accession to power in 1944. Guided by the ideology of the Bolsheviks, who firmly believed that the human condition must be changed in order to achieve the Soviet state of mind, the Bulgarian communists began a massive propaganda effort to promote the Soviet values of urban modernity, while at the same time, swiftly eradicating the remnants of backward bourgeois thinking. This was a particularly challenging task, given that the Bulgarian socialist revolution took place in a predominantly rural society, where peasant behaviors were hard to convert to the communist ideology. Alongside the effort to promote new ascetic values that suppressed consumption and restricted wage policies, the Party also focused on establishing an economic foundation of heavy industries in order to move the country into a modern, industrialized society, rather than an agrarian one. As Kristen Godshee contends, the Bulgarian state was quite successful in its development, although the concentration on heavy industry drew scarce resources away from the production of consumer goods, creating a deficit in what was available for consumption on the domestic market.[61]

The push for a political definition of consumer culture came with the April Plenum of 1956. The so-called "April Line"—the roadmap of Bulgarian socialism—established the official rules of moving rapidly towards achieving progress in every sphere of the socialist development. The Bulgarian Communist Party defined a series of measures it called "the Great Leap Forward," designed to move the country forward, both economically and socially speaking. As Mary Neuburger contended, "the Party's shift in tactics coincides with the subtle shift towards appealing to and satisfying the consumer needs of populations across the bloc, often in conjunction with asserting a 'national path to socialism.'"[62] This movement towards defining socialist consumerism, as Neuburger further contends, was parallel and perhaps served as a direct response to the crisis of legitimacy of the regimes that rocked the Eastern bloc in the 1950s and 1960s. To further strengthen the foundation of the socialist idea in Bulgaria, for example, the Party initiated the construction of the first socialist town of Dimitrovgrad in 1948, which was designed for the optimal socialist living and working conditions, where the "New Man" of the socialist kind will grow organically within the context of the new socialist material culture.

However, as Ulf Brunnbauer pointed out, one of the mistakes that the party ideologists committed was assuming "that the 'socialist way of life' would emerge more or less automatically, once the new material/socialist conditions were established."[63] In fact, just two years after the April Plenum, Todor Zhivkov, the Bulgarian Communist Party leader, admitted these challenges by stating "communist education and re-education is a complicated, difficult and protracted process which is proceeding slower, and is more arduous, than the changes in political and economic life because the consciousness of the people usually lags behind the social development,"[64] thus recognizing the importance of the ideological processes at work, which can cultivate and inform both a political and a cultural understanding of consumption.

In the 1950s and 1960s, the issue of style and form as pertaining to material culture, once widely suspect under Stalin's rules, was now an existential question for the socialist way of life, trying to basically answer one guiding question, "What was the appropriate style for the socialist modernity?"[65]

For Bulgaria, which was at the time experiencing significant economic growth, this meant finding a way to catalyze this success into the cultural sphere as well. There, the challenge was much larger to overcome and more difficult to define as it pertained directly to the make-up of the Bulgarian population, predominantly rural and therefore less prone to accept the ideas of socialist "urban modernity." A strategic move on the part of the Communist Party was the rapid urbanization that encouraged, and often forced, peasants out of their habitats and into the socialist city, where the socialist environment was meant to provide the proper schooling for the socialist way of life. And if in the late 1940s and early 1950s the stress was on curbing consumption and promoting the virtue of self-denying work, led by nothing but class consciousness, in the 1950s and 1960s, the situation in Bulgaria quickly began to take a new turn. As Ulf Brunnbauer pointed out, in the 1960s, Bulgaria also became increasingly aware of Western consumer goods, brought by the influx of Western tourists into the country and the ability of Bulgarians to travel abroad, as well as the presence of Western cultural products—music, movies, etcetera—in the country.[66] As a result, the government found it increasingly difficult to satisfy growing consumer expectations, which it helped to raise by the promise of constantly rising living standards, further widening the gap between the imagined prosperity of the socialist land and the much more visible and tangible markets of Western superiority, evidenced in an endless array of consumer goods.

During the 1970s, the economic growth of Bulgaria continued, albeit in much slower terms, alongside the growing effort of the Communist Party to further push the cultivation of the "New Man" and his aesthetic education. Around this time, a much larger effort was seen in restricting and controlling the population's taste in goods, household objects, and dressing habits, aimed to eradicate the "tastelessness" frequently associated with Western influences and seen as remnants of the bourgeois culture of the Bulgarian capitalist past. A particular target of the efforts to promote socialist harmony and beauty were Western consumer goods, often seen as trashy and kitschy, and therefore incompatible with the socialist manifestation of good taste. These efforts become especially restrictive and stifling as the degree of surveillance and control over the population grew stronger and more aggressive. Combined with the economic decline of the 1980s and a growing sense of discontent and popular cynicism directed towards the socialist system, the Bulgarian socialist future began to look a lot less like a dream and a lot more like a nightmare. As Brunnbauer argued, the Pandora's Box of consumerism turned into one of the most powerful forces de-legitimizing the socialist system.[67]

BETWEEN GOOD TASTE AND GOOD MORALS: HOW SOCIALIST ADVERTISING CAME TO BE

The turning point in determining matters of cultural policy in Bulgaria was initiated by the 8th Congress of the Bulgarian Communist Party in 1963, which as Mila Mineva pointed out, set the tone for the "creation of the new socialist man," thus setting the need to promote and foster a new cultivation of the socialist ethics, as expressed through a cultured approach to the production, consumption, and innovation of goods, all intended for the harmonic and all-encompassing development of the socialist citizen.[68]

Measured in less ideological terms, the proclamations of the 8th Congress simply meant that part of the effort to reform the existing political line of the Communist Party is going to be directed towards the engendering of a consumer culture, recognizing the importance of defining the new socialist consumption as opposed to the bourgeois vice of excess and self-indulgence, while promoting the collective benefit of stimulating production through a disciplined and rational consumption of goods. To achieve this goal, the Communist Party translated the idea of promoting consumption by unveiling a mass number of department stores (State Universal Stores) that offered a varied array of consumer goods, carefully arranged in meticulously engineered visual displays in store windows, serving as one of the first forms of advertising to the consumer. As Mineva pointed out, the visualization of consumer culture took place in these very same store windows, where products were "imagined" rather than demonstrated, serving first and foremost, "an information and educational function—to be modern, aesthetic and useful to the people who observe them."[69]

The concept of promoting consumption, while not directly appearing until 1971 in the Bulgarian press, overtly finds discussion in various forums. For example, a brief report from May 1971 in *Rabotnichesko Delo* displays a photo of the newly opened Sofia Home of Fashion shopping center. In the photo, the socialist advertising window is evident, showing mannequins dressed in "modern" suits, while customers peruse over the fashion items. Of particular interest is the brief report accompanying the photo, which states, "The new store offers a new unique feature, where customers can check the items themselves, instead of having to ask for a shop attendant to show the item from behind the counter."[70] As Mineva argued, the window served as the optimal tool of visualizing the merchandise—however, that wasn't enough. "The window simply exemplifies, but does not effectively transfer the ideological value of the advertised good."[71] Perhaps that is the rationale behind the new fashion store, which offers not just the visual ad, but also the opportunity to physically interact with the item, further heightening the proof of quality—a strategy that while allowing a first-hand experience with the advertised object, still denies the frills of imagined luxury and self-indulgence upon which Western-style advertising was construed.

A much more conceptual discussion of the merits and role of advertising in the Soviet culture took place on the pages of *Kultura*. For example, in an article translated from Russian and published in 1971, Larisa Koznetsova, a Soviet authority on fashion, discusses the ephemeral, yet critically important relationship between fashion, consumer culture, and advertising. While the title of the article "Mini, Midi, Maxi" focuses on the mixed messages in the Western fashion world concerning the proper length of the woman's skirt, Koznetsova makes an argument defending the pragmatic function of Soviet fashion as a undeniable proof "that our prosperity is also leading us towards growing consumption needs." On the issue of advertising, Koznetsova argues:

> Advertising creates a constant state of over excitement which sometimes can lead to a dangerous craziness called "consuming goods." In addition, it doesn't take too much effort to realize that the lines of our ideological struggle in some parts coincide with the lines marking the stitches of our blazers, our coats and the clothes we wear, in the sense that a well-tailored pair of pants can capture the imagination of weaker minds and manipulate it ferociously.[72]

In her attack against Western advertising that stressed self-centered, empty consumption, Koznetsova warns the reader that even in fashion one must exercise control, and once again, reject the "imagistic modes" of representations that Western advertising uses in favor of a rational and well-reasoned choice based on real value and quality versus an imagined one. As Judd Stitziel confirmed, "official propaganda used this emphasis on moderation and thrift to claim that in socialism, good taste provided the basis for a truly democratic society by counteracting the bourgeois and capitalist proclivity for conspicuous consumption."[73]

Parallel to the subtle critique of Western advertising and its emphasis on empty, self-centered buying impulses, were also some telling examples of published letters to the editor. In the June 4, 1971, issue of *Rabotnichesko Delo*, we see the following argument against the hypnotic influence of all things foreign:

> The word "imported" has the following impact—supplying a household with consumer goods they really don't need, dressing a pretentious girl with a blouse that fits her poorly. Foreign goods are coveted irrationally, often without even inquiring into their real origin. Is it blind belief which leads us to worship every piece of garbage just because it is foreign?
>
> The reason for this is not because we feel inferior and incapable of producing quality goods ourselves. It's a matter of evaluation—evaluation of quality and beauty. Often beauty is associated only with prestige and not with aesthetic or the joy of the soul. Judging and evaluation is only possible if you have the proper foundation and the right sense of aesthetics. Coveting the foreign shows poor ideas, immature taste and a lack of any sense of aesthetic culture. The blind worship of foreign goods is an obstacle, particularly for the young person, whose tastes are still forming. Preventing him or her from reaching the depth of aesthetic knowledge without which, he or she will remain tasteless and mediocre.[74]

While the author of this letter offers a clear damnation of what he sees is the blind worship of foreign goods, it also poignantly stresses the indoctrination aspect of this culture critique. In every word of this letter, we see the denial of the Western concept of consumption as competitive and prestige-driven, and therefore, wrong, while offering praise to the rational, educational, and informed by proper aesthetic consumer choice that socialism instills and teaches in the moral fiber of its social standards.

The idea of a cultured consumption went beyond offering a critique for what cultured consumption is not. For example, in an advice column, we found the following recommendations:

> Our socialist development required a higher culture of domesticity. Our home has to look contemporary. We must organize multiple exhibits and expos and answer exciting questions such as how to grow home plants, how to match

colours, how to pick fabrics, etc. Clothes have to be beautiful and comfortable, functional and matching the figure, modern without being too flashy, with excellent tailoring and perfect fabrics.[75]

While this column does not necessarily address the concept of advertising, it stressed the important relationship between the economic benefit of promoting controlled consumption and the ideological benefit of promoting what Susan Reid described as "a normative conception of good taste in furnishing and home decorating, based, like those for dress, on modernist, rationalist, imperatives of simplicity, functionality, and 'no excess.'"[76] In this functional dimension of the socialist ideology, advertising was also seen from its early inception as a purely economic activity, "a compass for the buyer," a rational attempt to solve the issue of oversupply of goods that don't sell over the need to create demand for new goods. Soon enough, however, critics discovered the ideological function of advertising as a powerful educational tool that can effectively discipline taste—"an instrument enabling the construction of the ultimate socialist consumer."[77] The mechanical language used to describe the functions of advertising here is not accidental—the need to "engineer" and "construct" a new type of citizen-consumer has been outlined as a major function of advertising, both as a tool to promote economic growth, but also as a tool to mold the political-ideological and cultural education of people.[78] In this vein, it is not unusual to see discussions on the pages of the Bulgarian newspapers, arguing in support of fostering proper youth education through the aesthetic of advertising. Thus, for example, Georgi Bokov argued in support of the need to further articulate the educational and cultural function of consumption from the pages of *Kultura*:

> Many good articles have been written on the issue of defining the taste of young people, their striving for the beautiful, the practical, the original in advertising, clothing and domestic design. At the same time, we have to continue to criticize the uncommon and uncharacteristic tendencies among our people to choose hollow consumerism, egoism, snobbishness, and the rejection of the socialist sensibilities of aesthetic and morality.[79]

In most basic terms, then, the role envisioned here for advertising, and its cultural producers, was to be defined by its pedagogical functions, not its market implications. As Mila Mineva astutely argued, "during socialism, advertising was legitimated through its ideological function rather than through economic efficiency; it took on the role of educator of the new 'socialist citizen' and was expected to change the structure of traditional consumption—a function, to be sure, bestowed on it as early as the nineteenth century—and to create modern models of consumption."[80] As George Faraday and others have observed, cultural producers easily occupy the intellectual-educator position during socialism.[81]

On the other hand, a parallel discourse to the one articulating the value and worth of the Soviet citizen-consumer who shops out of necessity, with rational precision, while always opting out for the modern and aesthetically pleasing products, was taking place. This discursive approach also served a powerful ideological function—by pointing out the ills of Western advertising that promotes empty consumption for the profit of greedy corporate capitalists, it strived to once again, emphasize the superiority of the Soviet approach that promotes a wholesome, rational, and culturally informed consumption. "There was also continued *ideological* antipathy towards consumerism, which was still regarded as inherently bourgeois and potentially corrosive of the collectivist, activist spirit."[82] For instance, in defense of Soviet advertising, Ivan Slavov wrote for *Kultura*:

> Socialist and bourgeois mass culture are clearly different—the latter is based upon specific social-psychological circumstances that could be found in the consumer psychology of Western societies. The slogan is "enrich (enhance)" yourself which when applied to culture and expression becomes mass culture. And just because there are means for mass communication, it doesn't mean that our culture distributed through these media will also be "mass culture" aka Tom Jones. Ours is spiritually pure, spiritually enriching. Not based upon possession, but based upon emotional and creative needs. We reject consumerism based only on possession—we embrace consumption based on signs of progressive thinking.[83]

It is interesting to see how the concept of "mass" as understood in socialist and Western terms connotes also two very different interpretations of "culture." Mass, in the Western sense, means belonging to an amorphous crowd, crude and unrefined, catering to a sense of possession that serves no purpose but to quench individual needs and desires. Mass, in the Soviet sense, is understood as belonging to the collective, and expressing a common goal that leads to enhancement beyond the individual needs, elevating one beyond the personal and onto the common good. In a sense, mass culture, aka Tom Jones, is understood as one that lacks the appreciation of the aesthetic that the socialist citizen aims for, but is also delineated against a culture that builds itself on consumer psychology while denying the recognition of the ideological elements that the Soviet mode of consumption is supposed to evoke.

While it was important to elaborate how the Soviet culture of consumption and advertising was markedly more superior to that of the West, it was also necessary to convince the Bulgarian readers that Western advertising was indeed a corrupting force that serves no purpose other than the profiteering of greedy capitalists with eyewitness reports directly from the West. As Yana Hashamova contended, "under these circumstances Soviet ideology demonized Western opulence—lustrous cars, elegant suits, and gleaming windows—because it was perceived as signifying the immorality of an unjust society and because almost every Soviet citizen living in a communal apartment, trying for years to save for a car, dreamed of these Western standards."[84] In an excerpt from a commentary on the negative consequences of advertising in the United States, we read:

> Commercialism and advertising have become America's daily nightmare. A number of U.S. scientists, socialists and functionaries have begun to acknowledge this fact. They are starting to contemplate ways in which this negative phenomenon could be curbed, since doing away with it entirely is simply impossible. All of their efforts, however, have failed miserably. The accusations of the decadent influence of the advertising industry are multiplying by the hour. Advertising has a destructive effect on society, however, all articulation of such criticism is in vain because the leadership of the U.S. business continues to ignore the norms of good ethical behaviour. Its main goal is to make profit which immediately prevents it from offering a critical look into the function of advertising.[85]

Clearly, the commentary offers a conflicting account of how the uneasy dynamics between consumerism and advertising is to be understood. On the one hand, it acknowledges the inevitability of the practice of advertising in a market driven economy—an admission that shows a new direction away from the orthodox communist view that consumer driven advertising is unnecessary and could successfully be eliminated in a socialist economy. On the other hand, we also see the admission of the idea that advertising can be used to promote an "ethical" approach to consumerism, which while not entirely well defined, suggests taking a fresh look at the utility of advertising beyond its purely economic function.

An interesting critique of the content of Western advertising was also reprinted from Russian in *Kultura*, focusing on the use of sex appeal in American and other Western advertising. In this critical piece, the famous Soviet sexologist Igor Kon argued that the overindulgence in sexual imagery—what he calls "the commercial eroticism" of advertising—is just another capitalist exploitation of human sexuality for profit:

> The commercial eroticism has taken over advertising and has become a self-sustained industry in its own merit. As a subject of mass consumption and slimy advertising, sex has become an object to be consumed just like fillet-o-fish or aspirin. Visual eroticism serves the function of compensating for the limited and unsatisfactory realities of life.[86]

This poignant analysis of the "sex sells" motto of Western advertising indicates a perceptive and ideologically based outward critique that is meant to discount practices of advertising that only promote excessive and overindulgent consumption, but to point out that this overindulgent consumption can also be morally corrupt. As Judd Stitziel argued, "the attempt to cultivate good taste through the media and fashion shows often involved presentation of images of 'false' or 'tasteless' fashion—especially Western ones—as a foil for 'correct' styles."[87] Thus, Western advertising is not only exploitive and manipulative, the argument goes, but is also morally corrupt and ethically incomprehensible.

A particularly fascinating take on the role of visual propaganda is offered in an issue of *Kultura* under the title "The Problems of Visual Propaganda." In it, Bozhan Todorov offered a relatively harsh critique of the Bulgarian socialist approach to advertising and in general, visual decoration.[88] He argued that the power of advertising is vast and "ruthless" as it informs good taste and "impacts as well as educates with its tricky inevitability of unpretentiousness and seeming unimportance." Todorov contended that understanding the grammar of the visuals—their language, rhetoric, and power—is paramount and should be studied carefully in order to avoid the danger of the overdone decoration, of vanity and emphasis on the superficialities of appearance. Here, once more, we see the argument of measured frugality masked as a token of modernism and progressiveness, simultaneously rejecting fussiness and "visual noise" as very bad taste. Todorov continued:

> We should consider that in some countries people live surrounded by an enormous flow of visuals, among massive visual noise and the competition of the screaming and drastic representations could only be overcome by the active form and the well-delivered propaganda values. In Sofia's window displays in almost every store we see the photo of an attractive lady who does nothing more than holding the consumer item in her hand. Isn't this the most rudimentary form of persuasion? Does this "naked" declaration do anything in terms of its active propaganda function?[89]

Todorov's critique unveils another important challenge that Bulgarian advertising was forced to reckon with—the issue of representing the advertising object not merely as an item of utility and functionality, but also as an "imagined" and, more importantly, "desired" object. As Mila Mineva pointed out, Bulgarian advertising specialists soon realized that presenting the advertised object simply from the point of view of providing basic product information wouldn't suffice.[90] It is through the realization of the techniques of presenting the product as an object of desire, one that can be imagined as a "modern lifestyle," one worth emulating and striving for, that the socialist advertising principles can come full circle. Here, Todorov stated:

> Such a primitive view of advertising can also be witnessed on the pages of our newspapers and magazines, and particularly those intended to represent us abroad. All we see is a photo of the product with a simple layout that does not speak to a high level of visual literacy. This banal solution to our advertising needs often has to compete against advertisements which along with their brutal-commercial character and anti-humanistic traits, also carry a high de-

gree of persuasive effectiveness. Our solution—let's merge the art of advertising with good graphic design to improve the effectiveness of our visual propaganda.[91]

While acknowledging the deficient visual sophistication of Bulgarian advertising, Todorov's critique also signals a growing awareness of the "morally corrupting" but equally tempting Western advertisements that create desire through imagined possibilities. A similar concern is raised in the following brief sidebar: "The well-fed, well-dressed, living in a decently furnished apartment person, is not an ideal we should be aspiring to achieve. We should strive to achieve aesthetic values and high aesthetic standards which are integral to our socialist way of living." [92]

The recognition of the failures of the Soviet style of advertising reached its culminating point in the following article by Konstantin Todorov:

> We need to recognize the need to build and incorporate brand image and trademarks in the minds of the consumers. We need to "show" the products in a manner which is found attractive by our clients. This means that we need to integrate the efforts on the part of the companies and retail industry to develop firms whose sole purpose is to handle the propaganda-advertising functions of the promotional process.
>
> The international codex of advertising which was ratified by the International Congress of Socialist Advertising in the fall of 1988 in Vilnius (Lithuania) established the need for young specialists and advertising professionals whose job will be to professionalize the advertising field in the socialist spirit and also, establish the rules for loyal and fair competition on the advertising field.[93]

And while the concern with moving goods and eliminating surpluses in a planned economy by applying a carefully engineered and well-researched plan as the one suggested above wasn't new—as Patrick Patterson pointed out, "the industry's representation of its own work naturally became laden with 'psychologized,' scientific (or pseudoscientific) characterizations of the power of advertising and marketing"—the open invitation to acknowledge the professional value inherit in the practices of advertising indicates a sharp turn in the discursive tone of the public debate surrounding advertising.[94] It is also critically important to point out that this most open proclamation in defense of advertising comes on the eve of the breakdown of the communist regime in Bulgaria, heralded in a rather paradoxical way by a discussion on the necessity and utility of commercial advertising.

The very effort to conceptualize advertising in the socialist societies constitutes somewhat of a paradox—widely condemned by the early Soviet ideologues as a product of a corrupt and exploitive economic system, advertising was caught in the crossfire of political, ideological, and economic tension.

Initially, the practice of advertising was seen as a commercially motivated waste of resources made redundant by a media system free of the need to raise revenues and more importantly, by planned economic production that did not create competition or the need for product differentiation. However, this rigid way of thinking about the utility of advertising soon began to change as the rise of popular desire and the recognition of the need to promote consumption fundamentally transformed the Soviet policy on production, consumption, and along with it, the practice of advertising. In fact, the official acknowledgment of advertising in the Soviet bloc took place in 1957, at the first conference of Advertising Workers of Socialist Countries held in Prague, whose sole goal was to define the purpose of advertising in a socialist economy. As Susan Reid pointed out, "the role of domestic advertising in a command economy, then, was *not* to generate inauthentic and insatiable consumer demand, as in the capitalist West. On the contrary, it was to promote 'rational consumption' and to predict and manage popular desire."[95]

In its function, then, Soviet advertising advocated a shift from a Western emphasis on "the self" to a collective response to production, sponsored and defined by directives from the state. However, in trying to delineate the goals of Soviet advertising from those of capitalist advertising, Soviet ideologues failed to see the striking parallel between the need to promote consumption and the necessity of maintaining social control, which was also a fundamental tenet of the early origins of Western advertising. A similar need to distance the goals of Western ad men from those of the revolutionary socialist propaganda masters was also popularized in the West. To illustrate this trend, Stuart Ewen quoted William Allen White in his defense of advertising as a form of advanced capitalist production, "I would cut out the advertising and fill the editorial and news pages with material supplied by communist and reds. That would stop buying—distribution of things. It would bring an impasse in civilization, which would immediately begin to decay."[96] Ironically, as Krisztina Fehervary contended, socialist advertising, just like its Western counterpart, brought up a population of *homo consumens,* "without perhaps the same raptures and tensions, but dissatisfied nonetheless with the failures of official state consumer culture to provide excitement and aesthetic pleasure."[97]

Following these prescriptions, Bulgarian advertising meandered in its own labyrinths of ideological doctrines and everyday economic and cultural challenges. This chapter explored the rhetorical discourse in the Bulgaria popular press that defined the thematic treatment and conceptualization of advertising. While clearly guided by the official party line on economic growth and production, the debate surrounding advertising had notably cultural overtones—advertising was construed not only as an economically viable method to stimulate consumption, but was also construed as a means of defining cultural taste, moral standing, and socialist aesthetic. More importantly, the challenge in defining the role of advertising in the Bulgarian socialist society was understood in direct opposition to what advertising stood for in the Western world. While American and Western advertising was deemed distasteful and morally corrupt, the Bulgarian version of advertising was meant to cultivate "good taste" and "socialist consumer habits," which in turn were to guide, properly domesticate, and channel consumers' desires, therefore helping to harmonize production and consumption, supply and demand.

The concept of mass consumption, however, as Ivaylo Ditchev pointed out, served as the basic legitimization of communism itself, the strategic goal of which was to satisfy the growing needs of the workers.[98] From this angle, he argued, there was no difference between the strategic goals of capitalism and socialism, except the socialists' moral condemnation of this very same exact consumption and their desperate attempt to separate the "progressive" consumption of the East from the reactionary consumption of the West. "The paradox is that communism simultaneously creates the norm and the practice of mass consumption—the desire, and the sanction of it. Without desire, there is no growth, without growth, there is no capitalism, without sanction, there is no totalitarian political power."[99]

And while Ditchev's argument points out the remarkable similarities between the socialist and capitalist conceptualization of consumption, it is the cultural and ideological meaning invested in advertising that made the socialist and Western display of consumption quite different. As Anne Cronin contended, "advertising has an ideological function of naturalizing and disseminating capitalist principles of social organization: it is politically implicated in transmitting certain capitalist ideals about the legitimacy of social structures based on private ownership and exchange."[100] In its socialist version, advertising as an ideological and cultural form was only meant to promote good taste and the socialist way of life, and thus was entirely stripped of its visually provocative elements that can create desire for material possessions or personal gains. As Krisztina Fehervary[101] concluded, "it was within this particular configuration of authoritarian politics and material worlds that iconic Western goods took on the significance they did, and their properties acquired the power to project fantastic understandings of the 'system' that produced them."

At the same time, the articulation of what really constitutes good taste and socialist aesthetic, and particularly so in the realm of advertising, remains remarkably thin. This could partially be explained by the fact that as Svetlana Kolesnik pointed out, "during the long years of a state monopolistic socialism, the aesthetic component of mass consumer products received little or no attention."[102] As a result, advertised goods held no visual appeal, or as Mila Mineva pointed out, in advertising, the element of desirability was conspicuously absent. This trend is further exemplified by the historical narrative surrounding the evolution of advertising, yet the process of recognizing the necessity to supply not only ideological rhetoric, but an element of "real want" in the process of creating advertising remained largely ignored.[103]

The problem, as Patterson pointed out, was further exacerbated by the governments' efforts to celebrate the socialist achievement and promote a culture of consumption, in advertising, and in other media, which he argued, quickly became a socialist "culture industry" with real similarities to the much demonized "media machines" of the West.[104] "Socialist consumers, it turned out, were quickly trained to expect more: a constantly-expanding array of goods, services, and experiences, all to be supplied in constantly-increasing quantity and quality."[105]

At the end, it becomes clear from these samplings from the rhetorical discourse in defense of advertising that the concept of socialist advertising in Bulgaria, and perhaps, similarly so in the rest of the Balkan socialist states, was caught in an uneasy, and sometimes tumultuous relationship with culture, the economy, and politics—defined by an ever growing awareness of the need to recognize the role of consumption not as an act of sheer necessity and state control, but based on individual choice and competitive visual presentation, that can make us not only imagine the "modern lifestyle of socialism" but envision it and live it through the tempting and inviting world of commercial advertising. In doing so, that temptation built a new way to think about and envision both women and men, as it projected not only the much coveted view of the way men and women led imagined, but nonetheless visually exciting lives in the West, but also because it provided a pedagogical site of cultural production of new gender norms and expectations.

NOTES

1. Markham, James, "Is Advertising Important in the Soviet Economy? *Journal of Marketing*, 28 (1964): 31–37; Swayne, Linda, "Soviet Advertising: Communism Imitates Capitalism to Survive. In *The role of advertising*, eds., Charles. H. Sandage and Vernon Fryburger (Homewood, IL: R. D. Irwin, 1960), 93–104; Goldman, Marshall, "Product Differentiation and Advertising: Some Lessons from Soviet Experience," *The Journal of Political Economy*, 68 (1960): 346–57; Hanson, Phillip, *Advertising and Socialism: The Nature and Extent of Consumer Advertising in the Soviet Union, Hungary and Yugoslavia* (White Plains, NY: International Arts and Sciences Press, 1974).

2. Siebert, Fred, Peterson, Theodore, and Schramm, Wilbur, *Four Theories of the Press* (Urbana: University of Illinois Press, 1963).

3. Kolesnik, Svetlana, "Advertising and Cultural Politics," *Journal of Communication* 41, 2 (1991): 46–54; Gricenko-Wells, Ludmilla, "Western Concepts, Russian Perspectives: Meanings of Advertising in the Former Soviet Union," *Journal of Advertising* 23, 1 (1994): 83–95; Patterson, Patrick, "Truth Half Told: Finding the Perfect Pitch for Advertising and Marketing in Socialist Yugoslavia, 1950–1991," *Enterprise and Society* 4 (2003): 179–225; Reid, Susan, and Crowley, David, *Style and Socialism: Modernity and Material Culture in Post-War Eastern Europe* (New York: Berg, 2000); Tolstikova, Natasha, "Early Soviet Advertising: We Have to Extract All the Stinking Bourgeois Elements," *Journalism History* 33, 1 (2007): 42–50.

4. Patterson, "Truth Half Told"; Svab, Alenka, "Consuming Western Image of Well-Being: Shopping Tourism in Socialist Slovenia," *Cultural Studies* 16, 1 (2002): 63–79; Reid, Susan, "Cold War in the Kitchen: Gender and the De-Stalinization of Consumer Taste in the Soviet Union under Khrushchev," *Slavic Review*, 61, 2 (2002): 211–52.
5. Patterson, "Truth Half Told," 180.
6. Tolstikova, Natasha, "Early Soviet Advertising."
7. Babbie, Earl, *The Practice of Social Research* (Belmont, CA: Wadsworth Publishing Company, 2010), 325.
8. Nord, David, "The nature of historical research," in *Research Methods in Mass Communication*, eds. Guido Stempel and B. H. Westley (Upper Saddle River, NJ: Prentice-Hall, 1989), 289.
9. Ibid.
10. Bryan, Carter, "Communist Advertising: Its Status and Functions," *Journalism Quarterly* (1962): 500–506.
11. Markham, "Is Advertising Important in the Soviet Economy?," 31.
12. Ibid.
13. Tolstikova, "Early Soviet Advertising," 42.
14. Hanson, *Advertising and Socialism*.
15. Tolstikova, "Early Soviet Advertising."
16. Vorošilov, Vladimir, *Marketingovye Kommunikacii v ž urnalistike* [Marketing communications and journalism] (Saint Petersburg: Izdatel´stvo Mixajlova, 2000).
17. Kochen, Lionel, and Keep, John, *The Making of Modern Russia* (London: Penguin, 1990).
18. Nove, Alec, *An Economic History of the USSR, 1917–1991* (London: Penguin, 1992).
19. Kochen and Keep, *The Making of Modern Russia*.
20. Tolstikova, "Early Soviet Advertising," 45.
21. Hanson, *Advertising and Socialism*.
22. Ljaxov, V. N., *Sovetskij Reklamnyj Plakat 1917–1932* [The Soviet advertising poster 1917–1932] (Moscow: Sovetskij Xudožnik, 1972).
23. Tolstikova, "Early Soviet Advertising."
24. Kolesnik, "Advertising and Cultural Politics."
25. Kolesnik, "Advertising and Cultural Politics," 50.
26. Ibid.
27. Hanson, *Advertising and Socialism*, 21.
28. Tolstikova, "Early Soviet Advertising," 48.
29. Reid, "Cold War in the Kitchen," 221.
30. Ibid.
31. Ibid., 212.
32. Vorošilov, *Marketingovye Kommunikacii v ž urnalistike*
33. Markham, "Is Advertising Important in the Soviet Economy?," 36.
34. Germogenova, L. J., "*Èffektivnaja Reklama v Rossii. Praktika i Rrekomendacii*" [The effectiveness of advertising in Russia: Practices and recommendations] (Moscow: RusPartner Ltd., 1994), 13.
35. Hanson, *Advertising and Socialism*.
36. Gricenko-Wells, "Western Concepts, Russian Perspectives."
37. Hashamova, Yana, "Post-Soviet Russian Film and the Trauma of Globalization," *Consumption Markets & Culture* 1 (2004), 55.
38. Ewen, Stuart, *Captains of Consciousness: Advertising and the Social Roots of the Consumer Culture* (New York: McGraw-Hill, 1976).
39. Ibid., 6.
40. Gronow, Jukka, *Caviar with Champagne: Common Luxury and the Ideals of the Good Life in Stalin's Russia* (Oxford: Berg, 2003).
41. Ibid., 79.
42. Ibid., 82.

43. As quoted in Cox, Randi. "NEP Without Nepmen! Soviet Advertising and the Transition to Socialism," in *Everyday Life in Early Soviet Russia: Taking the Revolution Inside*, ed. Christina Kiaer and Eric Naiman (Bloomington: Indiana University Press, 2006), 132.

44. Cox, "NEP Without Nepmen!," 131.

45. Ibid., 136.

46. Ewen, *Captains of Consciousness*.

47. Fehervary, Krisztina, "Goods and States: The Political Logic of State-Socialist Material Culture," *Comparative Studies in Society and History*, 51 (2006): 426–59.

48. Ibid., 437.

49. Markham, "Is Advertising Important in the Soviet Economy?"

50. Fox, Karen, Irina Skorobogatykh, and Saginova, Olga, "The Soviet Evolution of Marketing Thought, 1961–1991: From Marx to Marketing," *Marketing Theory*, 5 (2005): 283–307.

51. Patterson, "Truth Half Told," 181.

52. Ibid., 182.

53. Ibid., 190.

54. Ibid., 192–94.

55. Blum, Martin, "Remaking the East German Past: Ostalgie, Identity, and Material Culture. *Journal of Popular Culture*, 34, 3 (2000): 229–53.

56. Ibid., 238.

57. Stitziel, Judd, *Fashioning Socialism: Clothing, Politics, and Consumer Culture in East Germany* (Oxford: Berg, 2005).

58. Ibid., 17.

59. Ibid., 17.

60. Lampe, John, *The Bulgarian Economy in the Twentieth Century* (London: Croom Helm, 1986).

61. Ghodsee, Kristen, "Potions, Lotions and Lipstick: The Gendered Consumption of Cosmetics and Perfumery in Socialist and Post-Socialist Urban Bulgaria," *Women's Studies International Forum*, 30, 1 (2007): 26–39.

62. Neuburger, Mary, "Pants, Veils, and Matters of Dress: Unraveling the Fabric of Women's Lives in Communist Bulgaria," in *Style and Socialism: Modernity and Material Culture in Post-War Eastern Europe*, eds. David Rowley and Susan Reid (Oxford: Berg Publishing, 2000), 181.

63. Brunnbauer, Ulf, "Making Bulgarians Socialist: The Fatherland Front in Communist Bulgaria," *East European Politics and Societies* 22, 1 (2008): 48.

64. As quoted in Brunnbauer, "Making Bulgarians Socialist," 49.

65. Reid and Crowley, *Style and Socialism,* 3.

66. Brunnbauer, "Making Bulgarians Socialist."

67. Ibid.

68. Mineva, Mila, "Stories and Images of Socialist Consumption" [in Bulgarian], *Sociologicheski Problemi* 1–2 (2003): 143–65.

69. Ibid., 151.

70. The photo with the caption ran in *Rabotnichesko Delo*, 1971, 4.

71. Mineva, "Stories and Images of Socialist Consumption," 153.

72. Koznetsova, Larisa, "Mini, Midi, Maxi" [in Bulgarian], *Kultura* 8 (1971): 3.

73. Stitziel, *Fashioning Socialism*. 55.

74. Letter to the editor, *Rabotnichesko Delo*, 1971, 4.

75. Advice column, *Rabotnichesko Delo*, 1971, 2.

76. Reid, "Cold War in the Kitchen," 242.

77. As quoted in Mineva, "Stories and Images of Socialist Consumption," 156.

78. Ibid.

79. Bokov, Georgi, "The Great Responsibility of Bulgarian Journalism" [in Bulgarian], *Kultura* 10 (1976): 8.

80. Mineva, Mila, "Made in Bulgaria: The National as Advertising Repertoire," *Eurozine*, originally published in *Critique & Humanism* 25 (2008) [in Bulgarian], 8.

81. Faraday, George, *Revolt of the Filmmakers: The Struggle for Artistic Autonomy and the Fall of the Soviet Film Industry* (University Park: Pennsylvania State University Press, 2000).

82. Reid, "Cold War in the Kitchen," 242.
83. Slavov, Ivan, "Against the Consumerist Psychology" [in Bulgarian], *Kultura* 48 (1971): 3.
84. Hashamova, Yana, "Post-Soviet Russian Film," 55.
85. Commentary ran in *Kultura* 1976, 8.
86. Kon, Igor, "The Appeal of Commercial Eroticism" [in Bulgarian], *Kultura* 51 (1971): 3.
87. Stitziel, *Fashioning Socialism*. 56.
88. Todorov, Bozhan, "The Problems of Visual Propaganda" [in Bulgarian], *Kultura* 18 (1971): 3.
89. Ibid.
90. Mineva, "Stories and Images of Socialist Consumption."
91. Todorov, "The Problems of Visual Propaganda," 3.
92. Appeared in *Kultura*, 1976, 3.
93. Todorov, Konstantin, "The Need for Advertising" [in Bulgarian], *Kultura* 4 (1989): 1.
94. Patterson, "Truth Half Told," 212.
95. Reid, "Cold War in the Kitchen," 218.
96. Ewen, *Captains of Consciousness*, 42.
97. Fehervary, "Goods and States," 441.
98. Ditchev, Ivaylo, "Die Konsumentenschmiede: Versuch über das kommunistische Begehren," in *Zurück aus der Zukunft. Osteuropäische Kulturen in Zeitalter des Poskommunismus*, ed. B. Groys (Frankfurt: Suhrkamp, 2007) [an abbreviated version of this article was published in *Kultura*, February 22, 2007, in Bulgarian].
99. Ibid., 4.
100. Cronin, Anne, "Regimes of Mediation: Advertising Practitioners as Cultural Intermediaries?" *Consumption Markets & Culture* 4 (2004): 362.
101. Fehervary, "Goods and States," 455–56.
102. Kolesnik, Svetlana, "Advertising and Cultural Politics," 44.
103. Mineva, "Stories and Images of Socialist Consumption."
104. Patterson, "Truth Half Told."
105. Ibid., 23.

Chapter Three

Liberating Women

The Role of Media in Defining Femininity in the Post-Socialist Transition

The late 1970s and 1980s are often described as a time of quiet turbulence in Eastern Europe. In an unassuming, yet persistent way, the proliferation of any unorthodox ideas, whether political, cultural, or economic, signaled the beginning of a move towards "openness." At the same time, these new ideas were also paving the way for transforming the conversation about sex and the gender concepts it defined—as clinically controlled and sanitized as they might have been—into an actual discourse. This shift was certainly indicative that new subversive cultural forces were working underground in the labyrinth of socialist gender ideologies, contextualized in markedly different historic circumstances. As Ann Oakley stated, "what is defined as 'sexual' in content or implication varies infinitely from one culture to another within the same culture in different historical periods."[1]

Moreover, what was presented by the official propaganda organs of the state as a "maturing" version of socialism also meant that the growing awareness of the socialist citizens both of their oppressive political environment and the competitive advantage of the Western world could no longer be kept behind the "Iron Curtain." At the core of this tension, many scholars have pointed out, laid the issue of consumption, which meandered between the discourse on the economy of shortages and the discourse on the unofficial so-called, "black" market.[2] Contrary to the popular belief in the West that consumption in the socialist East did not exist, as Adele Barker demonstrated, it was in the last decade of the communist rule that Eastern Europe began to experience consumption to which the pervasive second economy of the black market stood as an undisputable testimony.[3] As a result of this burgeoning exchange of goods and services taking place under the radar of the watchful eye of the state, the social fiber of the society was slowly but surely unraveling into what Denise Roman called "a prestige-based consumption society, and not a monied one."[4]

What this shift indicated in purely economic terms was an opportunity to direct the effort of finding one's place in the economic structure away from the role of producer and into the role of consumer. And while this was true for both men and women, it was a particularly transformative process for women, whose role in the economic superstructure of the state was multidimensional. What is more, partaking in these new, non-commissioned channels of consumption indicated to women that in some way, they are engaging in a subversive act, an attempt to define their new, independent sense of self, outside the boundaries of what is dictated by the state, while simultaneously embracing commodification as a performed ritual of femininity. As Katherine Verdery has also argued, in societies where there was little to consume, consumption itself became a political act, a way to demonstrate resistance to the regime's control over the intimate details of everyday life.[5] Kristen Ghodsee also confirmed, "in a society where the state actively tried to homogenize the sexes, women could resist the state by continuing to emphasize their femininity."[6]

This idea of asserting one's femininity through an act of consumption purely directed towards one's self was not only what was lacking in the early socialist style of advertising, but was also what helped construe an image of the well-kept woman both as a valorized commodity and a desirable ideal. As Beth Holmgren explained, "In the absence of capitalist market their [women's] extreme preoccupation with 'looking feminine' (read bourgeoisie feminine) and obtaining hard-to-get makeup and stylish clothes *also* signified a personalized triumph over state-imposed norms and consumer priorities."[7]

If consumer awareness of the allures of commodities was greatly influential in determining the degree to which women and men, but particularly women, were willing to rethink and renegotiate the gender norms and sexual behaviors guiding their socialist existence, then the complexity of this transformative process must be acknowledged. As Biljana Kasic warns, there is a certain degree of ambiguity involved in analyzing commercialization alongside sexuality.[8] Yet, one of the most readily available and noticeable places where a shift in both the public's and the state's attitude toward gender norms was sexual expression, a fact that cannot be overlooked simply as the less pleasant byproduct of the progressive demise of the authoritative regimes in the East.

Here, it must also be noted that regional differences between the countries of the Eastern bloc to a great degree guided, if not entirely determined the speed of breaking the silence around erotic pleasures. For example, as both Kasic[9] and Žikić[10] contend, in former Yugoslavia, erotic content was not marginalized but, on the contrary, had a large circulation and was rather popular. Besides profitability, there could be several more reasons why the socialist establishment was relatively tolerant towards the emergence of pornography in the Yugoslav media. In socialist Yugoslavia, the cultural establishment did not hold a unique stance against "erotica" in the media.[11] While some blamed it for being "insulting of public morals" others thought that it helped "break the old taboos about human sexuality" and that photos of the naked female body and similar content contributed to the equality of the sexes.[12] A similar degree of openness and acceptance towards sexual content that would have been considered a taboo during previous decades was also chronicled by Ana Magó-Maghiar.[13] Magó-Maghiar's analysis of the presentations of sexuality in Hungarian culture calls for an attempt to historicize and contextualize the Hungarian's media incorporation of political erotica, paying particular attention to the cultural policies of the Hungarian Communist establishment in the early 1980s. Under the guise of a more relaxed approach to the planned economy and as a move away from enforcing control toward exhibiting more tolerance for diverse cultural production, the state inadvertently allowed for a more explicit take on issues of sexuality.

While it appears that communist states like Hungary and former Yugoslavia embraced the topic of sex in a more relaxed and less stringent fashion, other states like Bulgaria were more reluctant, if not entirely opposed to "opening Pandora's box" on sexual discourse. The most rigorous resistance to this idea came from the Soviets. In the Soviet Union, even though newspapers and magazines were among the first to tackle the subject of sex, they did so in a rather tactile fashion, utilizing "the tools of the trade developed over decades of Soviet press making: bogus statistics pontificating 'scientific expert'; and heavily ideologized interpretations."[14]

In the case of Bulgaria, the pages of the popular magazines changed, albeit not drastically. While the media remained tight-lipped on the subject of sex, an attempt at signaling a change of course took place when several of the women's magazines, including *Zhenata Dnes*, changed the size of their pages and the typography of their nameplates. Beginning in 1979, *Zhenata Dnes*, for example, fronted a smaller, but much glossier and slicker looking format. Inside the magazine, the layout and design of the page was greatly revamped, away from the dull, mechanical appearance of boring typefaces and hand-draw illustrations into larger-sized photo formats with visually striking typographic presence and image hierarchy, drawing more attention to the content, without drowning the readers with the bland, uniform design of the past.

The change was also felt in terms of the thematic selection of the feature articles and analyses. A major ideological shift occured, focusing on men and their role in the social fiber of the communist society and the family as a whole, indicating that the traditionally reserved area of discussion focusing on gender was also being redirected towards a more inclusive conversation about social roles and responsibilities. This shift was evident in the fact that many more articles were authored by male journalists in addition to the previous scientific advice, especially on the issue of women's health and reproductive functions. Male reporters were now writing about women's and men's issues alike. Headlines, such as "Fathers: An attempt at an honest portrait," "The contemporary men: Does he know himself?" "In the labyrinth of emancipation," and "In search of the father," all signaled that the conversation on gender was at least redirecting its course, if not switching direction altogether. *Zhenata Dnes* even ran its first cover featuring a family portrait, rather than a photo or a painting of a woman, which had been the conventional approach of the magazine up to the 1970s.

A similar trend was also noted by Massino in Romania's sister publication to *Zhenata Dnes*, *Femeia*.[15] Massino's analysis of the magazine's content revealed that towards the late 1960s, men began to make frequent appearances on the pages of the magazine, in roles far from the traditionally imagined realm of masculine behavior. "Just as the modern socialist woman was able to balance work, home and family—and looking good while doing—so too, the magazine reasoned the modern socialist husband could change diapers, vacuum and cook (as well as bring home bacon)."[16]

However, the visual changes and the progressive sounding headlines were not necessarily accompanied by a similar shift in ideological tone. As Krasimira Daskalova argued, "virtually no difference can be detected in style and substance between the sociological writings published during as opposed to after communism."[17] Daskalova's observations over the state of sociological commentary in the context of the Bulgarian popular media were informed by her analysis of the way in which women were discussed in the output of sociological research. She pointed out that women were always viewed and spoken of in impersonal terms, from a presumed vantage point of objectivity, indicating what she described as "a communist era tradition of sociological writing on women, the purpose of which was to justify the state's pro-natalist policies by stressing the included welfare provisions—lauded as care for the woman and family."[18] While this continued to be the case on the pages of women's magazines, it must also be noted that at least on the surface, the so-called "maternity discourse"[19] or mother-centered welfare ideologically dressed as a "policy for women" was shifting to include discussion of men's contribution to this policy, albeit unconvincingly informed and disappointingly uninspired in its call for action.

EVOLVING GENDER ROLES: ENTER THE MALE

To shift the attention away from the already fairly conventional discussion on the "woman question," magazine editors experimented with introducing new rubrics one would least expect to see on the pages of publications presumed to cater towards the interest of housewives and female workers. In 1979, *Zhenata Dnes* introduced a series of young men's confessions, under the title "The thoughts of a young man," running in every monthly issue. In this series of articles, as the editors' note indicated, the idea was to present a forum for young men to express their views of gender relations, without being censored or monitored by anyone in an official role, whether it be a sociologist, an editor, or an expert of any kind. One glimpse in the mind of the contemporary man comes from Todor Gergishanov, who argues against the popular socialist ideology that women are indeed equal with men at the workplace, and must be held to the same standards of productivity as men. Gergishanov admits that men have taken advantage of this so-called "emancipation" in order not to enhance the positioning of women in the workplace, but to cover up for their own lack of performance, using women's job productivity as a measuring yardstick for their own labor output.

A similar mix of ideas on what the achievements of women under socialism have amounted to is expressed by another article in the same series, authored by Georgi Apostolov. In it, Apostolov attempts to present what he understands the contemporary male psyche to be about. Meandering between both biological and sociological rationale, Apostolov's writing style is deliberately ambiguous, often praising the stoicism of Bulgarian women who have survived so much hardship in the process of climbing up the socialist gender emancipation ladder. While he acknowledges that men have always been favored in the social hierarchy because of their physical ability to usurp and sustain power, he also admits that in the current social arrangement, "women have made a very successful entry in a number of typical men's roles, and undoubtedly have proven some of their qualities, which have been largely underestimated. There is no doubt that in the social sphere, she [the woman] is not inferior to man."[20]

This tactic was also noted by Mira Marody and Anna Giza-Poleszczuk in their study of the representational discourse of Polish women in popular magazines, pointing out that the theme that women are more clever and mature than men was common.[21] Simultaneous with this frank admission of women's worth, however, there was also the qualifying statement that women are often naturally more vulnerable and submissive to social traditions, and often unable to reconcile their own desires to compete alongside men for social recognition when deep inside, they are unable to overcome their own sense of insecurity about their standing in the world. This, according to Apostolov, creates a "minefield in the relationship between the sexes. That creates somewhat of a paradox—she, the tender one, the loving one, the one bubbling with hidden and obvious desires, wants to attract the stronger sex, while at the same time, she wants to be treated like a delicate creature, to be courted and to be adored."[22] This "paradox," as the author seems to imply, is a result of internalizing a "misplaced" desire to emancipate—seeking opportunity outside of what has been a comfortable zone of social and economic confidence for women (the domestic sphere) has left women feeling out of touch with what is "natural" and fitting for their proper function in society (the public sphere). Placing the responsibility of "negotiating" gender relations entirely on the shoulders of women, the author concludes: "All of this makes me think that it is the woman who determines how she is to be treated by the man. That is why she must remain first and foremost, a woman, to continue to want to carry in herself that which makes her different from the man, and which makes the man want to respect and recognize her."[23]

It becomes clear from this honest account of the young man's thoughts about relationships between the sexes that although communist ideology claimed to be inspired by an equality between the sexes and aspiring to create new forms of gender relations, in essence, it artfully twisted the idea of gender emancipation to serve on the one hand, as a great motivational tool to get women involved in the workforce and personally rewarded for their effort to continue to grow the economy, while at the same time, continuing to actively subscribe to and heavily endorse the ideal of a patriarchal society, where the mother figure—and now—the delicate wife are the only two desirable alternatives for the domestic persona fitted for the socialist woman. Not only are these ideological prescriptions cleverly disguised as honest and genuine first person accounts, coming from "the random guy on the street," but they also squarely put the responsibility of redefining the gender order on women, creating yet again the illusion of choice and symbolic power, while extracting all of its practical applications in the realities of everyday life.

This discursive approach, while manipulative and self-serving, was also quite telling of the contradictory goals of the socialist regimes and their paradoxical incompatibilities. As Susan Gal and Gail Kligman contended, "they wanted workers as well as mothers, token leaders as well as quiescent typists," pointing to the inherent contradictions that lurk beneath the seemingly iron-clad logic of the progressive socialist gender emancipation.[24] This idea clearly remained unchanged even in the 1970s and 1980s as the socialist regimes in the Balkans collectively marched towards a less than certain economic future.

Perhaps the most fascinating demonstration of this ideological tension is the final column in the series, authored by a young attorney by the name of Nikolay Bankov. Bankov's account, he reveals in the opening paragraphs, is based both on his personal observations, but also on his experiences as a divorce lawyer who has had a first hand opportunity to observe what can go wrong in the relationship between the sexes. Using his recollections from handling divorce cases, Bankov argues that gender emancipation somehow has also entered not only the sphere of labor opportunities for women, but also has threatened the male identity and the role of the husband in the traditional family structure. Not only that, he argued, women have also pushed the envelope of what he calls "wrongly conceived sense of gender entitlement," often mistreating their husbands and humiliating them in public during the divorce process. In short, Bankov shares his concern about what he sees as a very alarming, borderline dangerous, reversal of gender roles, for which he blames women and their ill-construed sense of empowerment. "The weaker sex has gotten so over its head, that the so called 'women's tenderness' is only to be lamented by less than manly husbands. That is why it is very difficult today to espouse a position of male master and to try to educate young women about what is right and wrong in today's gender relations."[25]

What appears first as a humorous spin on the weaker/stronger sex dichotomy quickly turns into a diatribe against women's transgressing what Bankov calls "the natural biological boundaries that should never been trespassed."[26] Bankov is also fairly outraged by what he calls the feminization of many of the typical manly professions and the dangerous consequences of women's mass exodus from the family sphere into the labor force. He calls for a reflection on the past, when women were mostly seen in their functions of wives and mothers, and yet, as he states, "always equal and respected." "In the past, the man was a man, and the woman was a woman. No one ever overdramatized mothering children or doing housework!," Bankov argues, essentially blaming socialist women for being oversensitive and spoiled by the socialist emancipation.[27]

Even more so, Bankov voices his dissatisfaction with the fact that many of the young Bulgarian women are too rebellious and too aggressive to submit to a man's command. "I don't believe there is a place in the world where women speak so much about freedom in the marriage while at the same time, enjoy so many privileges," he continued. And to further ridicule what he certainly sees as the undesirable consequences of advocating equality between the sexes, he says, "even babushkas are over-emancipated and after 30–40 years of marriage are rushing to get divorced."[28]

Bankov's misogynist rant is actually not only directed towards women who are too entitled and therefore, more liberated than they need to be, but is also a critical pronouncement over the institutional utility of divorce itself. What socialist demagogues have boasted as a right granted to all women who find themselves in marriages that don't work, demonstrating the progressiveness of the socialist gender ideology against the backwards logic of the bourgeoisie mentality that stigmatized divorce as a morally corrupt practice, here is presented as just another way for women to act too entitled, and therefore, outside the norms of acceptable behavior. Describing elderly women who seek divorce, as "babushkas turned into liberated Amazons" is a great illustration of the prevailing attitude towards the social relevance of divorce itself. There are hardly any positive traits associated with divorce, and when divorce is spoken of, it almost exclusively is discussed within the context of direct and indirect consequences for the woman, and not the man. In fact, as Mira Marody and Anna Giza-Poleszczuk argued, divorced women were either portrayed as unhappy or as wicked and crafty, making divorce appear as an undesirable social practice, relegating the former wife into a trouble maker treated with disdain as a potential rival and "the other."[29]

Bankov's article concludes in a tone of appeasement, which nonetheless fails to mask his paternalistic and patriarchal conventional thinking. "Let's confess to the woman than she can do some manly jobs, but let's also ask her to do more of her womanly chores. Because if she is indeed able to replace the man, no man can replace her."[30] This statement also demonstrates at the level of ideology what Karen Remmler described as the paradox of the "patriarchal-paternalistic" state, or the "father state" that appears to provide for women's needs while at the same time, continues, "perpetuating gender specific values in the social realm."[31]

As the 1980s rolled around, the material conditions of the socialist economy were beginning to show clear signs of decline, indicating that the socialist project is not entirely delivering on its promise. In the Eastern bloc, from the German Democratic Republic, to the communist corner of the Balkans, the socialist states were struggling with a number of economic and social challenges, including declining standards of living, reduced industrial output, and a growing sense of discontent among the working proletariat. As the economic challenges grew even bigger and the deficits in meeting the consumer demands widened, women found themselves literally in the center of these difficult times. Katrin Sieg described these new conditions best when she argued, "the conditions between the promise of equality and the praxis of women's socioeconomic disadvantagement sharpened."[32]

In an attempt to respond to these changing perceptions about the reality of being a woman in a less than perfect socialist utopia, the discourse about gender began to transform itself in what Sieg described as "socialist feminist discourse." Sieg examined the emergence of socialist feminist literature in the GDR, explaining its essence as "the articulation of a radical critique of the patriarchy with the goal of a fundamental social change."[33] However, while this critique called for reconsideration of the calcified social structures of gender equality, they also continued to espouse the same egalitarian rhetoric, with an unusual twist. The gender strategy focused the conversation about women squarely on women's struggles and their ongoing battle to integrate themselves in the labor force while remaining good wives, mothers, and caregivers, shifting the public discussion towards men and their participation in the socialist project.

To further quench criticisms that women's positioning in the work force has been marginalized by the traditional division of labor that assigned them more service oriented jobs and less leadership oriented occupations, magazines began publishing articles that drew the public's attention to professions that have been "feminized" in the process of labor division in the socialist economy. A slew of titles such as "Profession: Male Nurse," "Searching for Dad," or "A Man in the Kindergarten," began to appear in the pages of the publications. These types of articles certainly present a reversal of course for the typical conversation that took place on the pages of women's magazines, frequently dictated and informed by rather predictable, stifling prescriptions of socialist gender norms and behavior. Inspired to some degree by the climate of social discontent that also signaled to the communist elites that a change of course is necessary if power is to be sustained, magazine editors turned their attention to what they view as a radical change in their general approach to the subject of gender relations.

And yet, the effort to change the gender discourse never materialized beyond scratching the surface. In fact, they further calcified the prevailing view of uncontested patriarchy as the norm. A particularly fitting illustration is presented in the article "A Man in the Kindergarten." The article, intended as a profile of Comrade Ivelin Mitkov, who chose the unusual profession of caregiver to young children, is just another artful manipulation presenting gender roles, carefully crafted to appear ideologically progressive, while at the same time pushing the traditional imperative of patriarchy, while professing its wide ranging benefits for the socialist women and their children. The article tells Mitkov's story, stressing his "manly" approach to the task of engaging and educating young children—for example, instead of engaging in conventional play, Mitkov brings in a construction set that he uses as a mini-model for the city plan of Tolbuhin (a small Bulgarian town named after a famous Soviet general) only to demonstrate that the kindergarten abounds with technically inclined children, whose special skills can thus be identified from an early age and channeled for the benefit of the economy. In fact, the author argues Mitkov's presence in the daycare facility has become such a hit that parents are now pleading to be included on a waiting list so their children can, too, be part of such a progressive pedagogical approach. The article goes beyond a Soviet-driven praise of engagement pedagogy that anticipates the active participation of young children who learn how to socialize through work. When asked what it is that Mitkov gives the children that is different from his female colleagues, at first, he hesitates to answer with certainty but states nonetheless:

> What I can tell when I observe my female colleagues is what I can't do like them. They show a different emotion in their interaction with the children. They act motherly, and I talk to the young children just like I talk to you. It is also possible that I am more organized, more action oriented. Especially with boys, a man's role model is very important and they miss that a lot. You noticed how the boys swarmed around when the photographer [also a male] came in, didn't you? In general, raising children in a females-only environment is like raising children in family without a father.[34]

Mitkov's expertise as a pedagogue goes unquestioned and is further solidified by stressing his educational qualifications—a degree in early childhood education—legitimizing his dismissal of women, and in this case, women who act "motherly," as effective educators. Describing his female colleagues as emotional, hence, potentially irrational, disorganized, therefore, chaotic, as well as lacking in action, hence, uninspiringly passive, Mitkov practically strips women of their credentials to do one thing well—be mothers and caregivers to their children. What is more, in his account of the importance of the "male presence" in the life of a young child, Mitkov also implicitly condemns the single mother as practically unable to offer the "right" context for learning, as the single-parent family environment is not only deficient, but also potentially ineffectual when it comes to raising a well-rounded young individual. This diversion from the conventional focus on women's lot in society serves as an illustration of the subversive ways in which male power was expressed—often in seemingly minor and innocuous forms of subjugation that reiterate the conventional gender disposition allying women with low-level domestic work and subordinating their social and domestic functions to those of men.

While the focus of the discourse surrounding gender conventions featured mostly men entering spheres of domestic and family obligations previously reserved exclusively for women, the progressiveness of the socialist ideal was not abandoned yet. On the contrary, the rhetoric around the proper political, social, and economic role of women was now venturing into a new area of illustrative emancipation. So far, the idea of the socialist female citizen who achieves a new social status and a new consciousness was defined almost entirely through the importance of work, whether contributing to the economy or catering to domestic duties.

In the 1980s a new role for women also found its place on the ideological agenda of the communist elites; women have conquered so many areas of economic and social contribution and they are ready to take on a new challenge—the military force. In the true spirit of the socialist Amazon warrior,[35] we now begin to see women whose professional aspirations include joining their male counterparts as professional military personnel. In an article titled "An Experiment: Girls in the Line of Duty," a male reporter offers a two-page portrait of the new generation of young Bulgarian women whose aspirations stretch beyond the factory assembly line and the kitchen duties. Mirroring the entry of men into "women's only" line of work, women are now doing the same, with a slight twist. As the author points out, "the only point of contention is the uniform, which appears too strict."[36] The author spends most of the length of his feature describing the entrance exams and physical tests young women have to pass in order to be admitted to the ranks of cadets in the military academy and the unique and highly patriotic task these young women take upon themselves. But the story also serves to differentiate the function of females in combat compared to their male counterparts. While it appears that the goal of the text is to showcase women's desire for self-realization as the only motive behind what the author describes as the "militarization" of the Bulgarian woman, he is also quick to point out that in "peaceful" times, the place of women in the military ranks is far from adding more numbers to the country's defense capacity. Rather, Peshev states, the reason is the individual drive of each woman to be recognized as able in every sphere, offering an ideologically neutral gender pronouncement on the motivation behind women's desire to take on a new challenge.

Ironically, while the story profiling the male teacher in the kindergarten was intended to show that a different—read here male—expertise has the potential to positively transform the educational experience of young children, the article focusing on women in the military does not treat their presence in the battlefield as a contribution to the military might, but rather, as a novelty act. Describing the whole initiative as an "experiment" also indicates the lack of confidence in women's ability to measure up to the task of defending the nation. The images accompanying the story are also telling in their own merit—the photos feature women in civilian clothes waiting at the gates of the military academy, who, once admitted, transform themselves into uniform-clad, cut from the same mold soldiers, under the command of a male superior officer. The text argues against seeing females joining the army as an attempt to feminize the military, yet the conclusive paragraphs indicate otherwise. Focusing on the issue of uniforms, the author states that the military authorities should not ignore the calls for revising the uniform of the army as a whimsical female request. "The young ladies have an inborn appreciation for beauty. Do we need to underestimate their desire to be fashionable and sophisticated simply by discrediting their demands as fleeting female caprices?"[37] By zeroing the discussion on looks—clearly an external manifestation of women's motivations and ambitions—the article undermines the fundamental ideological argument of emancipation by perpetuating the myth that sheer presence and numbers can account for a genuine attempt at integrating women in every aspect of public life, including the military. In addition, this article also appears to support a hypothesis Nadia Kaneva and I posited, essentially arguing that during communism, women were portrayed in visual media in larger numbers but not necessarily in progressive or ground-breaking social positions, interactions, and occupations, leading us to conclude that the strategy behind this was "for the 'glorification' of women or, conversely, [as] a form of 'segregation' which makes women's symbolic elevation more palatable because they are not directly compared to men by appearing in the same photograph."[38] As Karen Remmler also noted, part of this seemingly progressive approach in presenting women was indeed a strategic move on the part of the communist establishment to continue to control the way in which women appeared in the public consciousness. "Thus, women were 'represented' in the most literal sense of the word. The state presented them, that is, took care of their needs for them, while the social semiotic system represented them in terms of traditional universalistic images of femininity."[39]

BEAUTY, THE BEAST, AND SOCIALISM'S DEMISE

The changing spirits of the 1980s were beginning to show not only in the topics that occupied the pages of women's magazines, but also in the manner in which women were visually represented. The images of women began to soften down and appear more feminine, displaying varying degrees of physicality, although not suggestive by any standard. In these images, the woman appears less confident, more consumed with the problems of the day, to some extent defying the long-lasting image of the previous decade of the self-assured, fighter spirit communist mother/functionary. When women were discussed, it appears that the focus on these discussions was reconfigured— the woman's function in the social context of socialism is now to be understood in the exclusive role of mother, perhaps to a great extent as a direct response to the steadily declining birth rates across the entire socialist camp.

Within this general sense of changing ideas about femininity, the visual shift was particularly striking. Not only were women seen more frequently in roles other than professional vocations, but they were also more noticeably "feminine." Irene Dolling's analysis of women's portrayals in East German magazines as referenced in the work of Karen Remmler offers a compelling explanation of this trend.[40] Dolling's analysis of the visual representations of East German women showed that the higher the professional standing a woman enjoyed, the more "feminized" her visual representation was. In one way, these women have already demonstrated that their competency can be and indeed is non-distinguishable when it comes to visual portrayals. But the more powerful a woman's professional positioning becomes, Dolling argued, the more feminine they were portrayed by the magazines in an attempt to minimize the threat they posed to the status quo. Femininity, then, becomes political currency that now can be manipulated to change the way women are presented and perceived as social agency. As Remmler argued, "they were at once recognizable as women, that is, sexual objects, according to Dolling, fulfilling the expectation of both male and female viewers that equality at the workplace did not relieve women from the stereotype of being feminine and thus capable of reproducing and/or being sexually available."[41]

In fact, at this stage, for the first time we see discussions of beauty as the sole subject of concern, beyond matters of cosmetics and exercise intended to improve the female body's stamina and aesthetics of appearances. An illustration of this trend in Bulgarian magazines is the first article on Miss University, a beauty pageant for female college students held at Sofia University, featured in a 1990 double spread in *Zhenata Dnes*. The article, accompanied by a medley of photographs of girls parading on the catwalks, applying make-up, or just anxiously waiting to get their turn in the spotlight, was certainly a novelty not seen in mainstream socialist media in Bulgaria and Romania prior to the 1980s. This, however, was not the case in countries like Hungary, for example, as demonstrated by Ana Magó-Maghiar in her analysis of the representations of sexuality in Hungarian popular culture.[42] Magó-Maghiar creates a compelling argument that demonstrates how Hungarian media had a much more liberated attitude towards sexuality and the nude body and effectively used erotica to wage a political battle with the repressive ideologies of the paternalistic state. However, she also pointed out that this ideological battle was very much rigged in the interest of the "brotherhood of men," dismissing almost entirely the possibility of engaging women in a transformative action against the gender status quo of socialism:

> On the one hand it [discourse on sexuality] mocks young, beautiful women for using their sexual powers for material gains, while it forgets about the (s)exploitation inherent in profit-making or the social stigma that surrounds these activities. On the other hand it derides older women as asexual losers stressing the incompatibility of the two sides of the whore/Madonna or sex-discourse/sanitized image of sexuality dichotomy. Female "success" is naturally amoral, but older and ugly women are stupid not to understand that no "decent" man could want them.[43]

A similar trend can also be noticed in the desire of Bulgarian magazines to follow perhaps in the footsteps of their more "progressive" sister publications from the Central European region, by featuring more and more articles focusing on the young and the beautiful rather than the middle age female "seasoned" worker, who was often juxtaposed—both visually, but also symbolically—with the less experienced, naïve young woman, who is hesitantly finding her way through her journey to becoming the modern socialist woman. As a sign of this shift, for instance, the fashion advice section that sanctioned the proper dress code for "hefty, overweight" women, now addressed them as "those women who are not fashion models." And if that ideal prior to the 1980s rarely, if ever, included being attractive, the theme of visual beauty as a descriptor and a desirable characteristic of the woman became a common theme in the magazine's transforming discourse. This diversion into the realm of physical appearance was also a sign that as Rasa Balockaite has argued, Eastern Europe began to "rediscover and popularize the myth of femininity which was discarded, subdued and erased during the Soviet period."[44] That myth, to borrow from Naomi Woolf's famous work, now also included a "beauty myth" which was equally imbued with ideological intentions and manipulative goals.

This sudden desire to recalibrate the cultural parameters of acceptable standards of appearance was nothing more than a move towards softening the control over the cultural flow in the socialist states, in many ways a direct response to the growing discontent with the stifling directives of what it meant to lead one's life "the socialist way." A number of other economic and cultural factors, such as an increased exchange of contacts and experiences with Western content and cultural products, as well opening of the borders for greater access to the outside world also contributed to the official desire to accept and endorse beauty, and the need to care for oneself as an expression of self-interest and not because one needs to effectively and efficiently contribute to the growth of the economy. This, in turn, led the Soviet states to formally acknowledge the importance of physical beauty and its importance for the well-being of the Soviet woman.

Elizabeth Waters offered one of the very first cultural analyses of the popularity of beauty contests in the former Soviet Union in an attempt to explain the willing and eager acceptance of the Soviet public of the concept of beauty "parades."[45] Prior to the 1980s, this concept not only appears foreign and undesirable, but very possibly could have been sanctioned as an unacceptable indiscretion to the socialist norms of gender behavior. Waters acknowledged that the popularity of beauty pageants and their almost seamless integration in Soviet culture had a lot to do with the uneasy relationship the Soviet Union maintained with the West. By openly rejecting its indulgence, the Soviet Union was secretly longing to invent its own, better "socialist" version of it. As demonstrated in an earlier chapter, this clearly was also the case with advertising. Now, it appears the same spirit of co-opting Western trends in the socialist way of life impregnated the concept of beauty and its status as a marker of success for women, previously absent in the desexualized public and private roles women were allowed to occupy.

In the 1980s and early 1990s, it became more and more obvious that those discrepancies were unbridgeable, unless the Soviets began to make real strides towards embracing a new cultural politics that recognized and to some extent, incorporated, the importance of image and the importance of beauty as a sight for public pleasure. As Waters wrote, "young Soviet women wore bikinis on the beach and raised hemlines in city streets; Soviet advertising and cinema began to incorporate in their repertoire 'tasteful' female nudity. Wide sections of the Soviet public, in other words, were growing accustomed to the female body on public display, to the female as a recognized source of visual pleasure."[46]

Tatyana Mamonova offers yet another interesting look at the sexual identity and objectification of the Soviet and Eastern European woman.[47] The eroticization of the female body by men is recognized as the patriarchy's international norm, she argued, and the opening of the former communist society for this kind of expression of male dominance allowed sexism to move on to a more blatant, visual form. Beauty contests, Mamonova asserted, were the ultimate testimony to this change. She provided an excellent example to support her argument—the budget for the final contest at Miss Russia before the collapse of the regime was around 1.5 million rubles. The organizers naturally were counting on a substantial return. "They planned to use the winners of the show for commercial purposes, which means good money, including hard currency."[48] Men essentially transformed the female body into immovable—or movable—property and have objectified it in the most obtrusive and materialistic manner.

That growing familiarity and acceptance of the female body as a site for visual pleasure signaled to the public at large a thaw in the rigor of the ideological canon of socialism and its uneasy relationship with the subject of sexual agency. Similarly, the desire to appear beautiful in public, be appreciated for it, and even more so, potentially earn material rewards for it, became a particular point of attraction for young women across the region. To be pretty now also meant to be open to ideas and influences from the West, interpreted to be a tangible achievement of a better standard of living. As Waters again aptly asserted, "the consumer goods and modes of leisure of the 'capitalist countries' were the objects of far more interest than their parliamentary systems,"[49] arguing, that beauty pageants, as virtually devoid of political meaning at the expense of being understood as manifestation of personal freedom—in this case the freedom to flaunt one's physical attributes and be applauded and rewarded for it—indicated their seamless integration in the cultural complexity of the late socialist period. "The beauty contest could thus be seen as doubly justified, both as a political and cultural prerequisite."[50]

An unintended consequence of the loosening of control over the physical appearance of women emerged disguised as consumerism under a new codename—fashion modeling. The increasing growth of alternative economic transactions that began to form a new middle class of socialist consumers in the early 1980s also meant that women and men would begin to notice and covet products that they were previously either denied, or were always described as deficit. Among those products, one that becomes immediately associated with the idea of the visual display of beauty was the output of the fashion industry. As noted earlier, socialist fashion and socialist advertising were essentially the cultural forces in charge of making socialist goods desirable and wanted by the working class. Therefore, fashion was at the forefront of not only spelling out the canon of proper dress according to the socialist ideologues, but also as the place where women could now readily find fashion ideas they can admire and long after in the privacy of their homes. Now, they can also see clothes and fashion trends they can actively seek and acquire without being sanctioned for acting outside the canon of proper socialist consumption.

Fashion magazines were also the venue where some of the very first pleas for rethinking socialist femininity and the images it promulgated took place. Djurdja Bartlett illustrated this trend with the launch of the first "proper" fashion magazine, *Zhurnal Mod*, in 1988.[51] Located on Moscow's fashion street and equipped with the latest technology for fashion photography and high-end production, *Zhurnal Mod* demonstrated a new direction in the socialist ideology of what Bartlett called "glamour under control." Despite remaining under the ever-watchful eye of the socialist party, the new fashion journals were allowed a degree of creative freedom in nurturing an atmosphere of controlled consumer practices, which the socialist regimes saw as the least dangerous way to calm growing economic tensions down, while at the same time, introduce social distinction in a supposedly classless socialist order.[52] As Bartlett recalls, the journal's editor, Lydia Orlova, pleaded in the inaugural issue that women have been forced to prove themselves as workers and sportswomen for decades, and it was time to show that they were "simply women."[53]

The idea of "controlled glamour" or as I would like to call it, "sanctioned beauty" was certainly not new to the countries of the Central European region. As noted earlier, countries like East Germany, Czechoslovakia, and Hungary had a different approach to meeting growing consumer demand among their socialist populace. This, in turn, also influenced and determined their approach to women's fashion and the liberty with which they interpreted the gender ideologies prescribed by the socialist regime. For example, as a result of the Hungarian economic reforms of 1968, Hungarian fashion houses began to produce limited quantities of high quality clothes that adapted Western modes but still adhered to the socialism conceptualization of good taste. The Czech and Polish state fashion houses followed suit and also opened their elite shops, catering to the desires and consumer needs of a growing middle class of socialist female consumers. Women, in turn, began to realize the duplicity of the regime in denying them access to fashion trends and styles, which became more and more available through the growing exchange of travel and consumer goods from the West. As Bartlett argued, "Foreign travel, Western fashion magazines and Western films and music not only provide experiences that enriched the cultural capital of the middle classes, but also encouraged them to explore new sartorial choices."[54]

Perhaps the launch of the East German's chain of over four hundred socialist luxury shops, under the name of *Exquisit*, best manifested the regime's attempt to quench growing interest and demand in fashion goods, while maintaining control over the coffers of the fashion industry. As a result, consumption grew to a new level, but remained exclusively reserved for the privileged groups of "connected" men and women, whose access to those exclusive deals was granted based upon their affinity and close ties to the Communist Party. Denise Roman described this layer of the communist privilege as "a certain positioning within the nomenklatura or as a cultural personality, and particularly through involvement in the widespread system of personal relations, traffic and influence, and *baksheesh.*"[55] The fact that the masses continued to be denied access to widely available "quality" goods contributed further to the escalation of distrust between the communist establishment and the "ordinary" citizens of the working class.

If the production of socialist luxury goods failed to meet the demands for volume and quality that the growing class of socialist consumers expected, the media and fashion industry continued their attempt to capitalize on the consumer curiosity for all things Western, albeit within the confines of the socialist ideological dogma on gender and femininity. As demonstrated by Waters in her analysis of the popularity of beauty pageants, the currency of physical appearance was soon noticed by none other than the Western fashion industry and its own media outlets. "Aware of the potential of the large Soviet market for clothes of stylish Western cut and of the USSR's untapped supply of potential models, the German firm *Burda Moden*, partnered in a join venture to produce fashion magazine in Russia, became a promoter of beauty contests."[56] In fact, *Soviet Burda*, which launched in March 1987 with a circulation of 240,000 copies, was the first joint media venture between the Soviet Union and the West, and was fully supported by none other than the patron of perestroika, Mikhail Gorbachev.[57] It seems that *Soviet Burda* encompassed at the time what the socialist regime was hoping for—an influential fashion magazine from the West, which, instead of following every trend in the latest fashion, promotes practical clothes for "normal" women.

However, the sense of normalcy *Soviet Burda* promoted soon began to exhaust its appeal, as women across Eastern Europe were growing more and more aware not only of their economic and social exploitation that defined their pitiable self-image projected in socialist media outlets, but also of the wide ranging choices available to their Western counterparts. It appeared that normal was not what women craved, normal was what women dreaded and did everything in their power to avoid. Not only that, but now added to the list of desirable features of the ideal woman was also the need to be "beautiful" or "presentable," which was stressed over and over again both as a personal characteristic and as an attribute of success. Beauty, therefore, can be entrepreneurial as well, an idea that seamlessly appeared to integrate itself with the socialist conventions of womanhood—now women could be "loving, caring *and* beautiful."[58]

THE RISE OF PORN CULTURE: FROM BEAUTY TO EROTICA

In Bulgaria, the wave of awakening to what it meant to be a woman featured prominently on the pages of women's magazines. The entire tone of the reports that focused on women's conditions in late socialism began to sound a lot more critical and self-reflective, capturing the growing social tension of the late 1980s and the early 1990s. Curiously, the regular pieces in *Zhenata Dnes* that featured women's professional achievements as equal to those of men were replaced by feature articles showcasing social problems anchored in the family and the youth. The word "socialism" seemed to have mysteriously disappeared from the pages of the magazine, replaced by discussions of women's struggles with alcoholism, domestic abuse, and the need for sexual education. For example, articles with titles such as "The Bulgarian Woman on Monday," "A Report, Written With a Baby in One Arm," and "How Long Are We Going to Talk About the Second Sex?" all indicated a shift away from the subdued tone of feminine critique into a bolder version of self-reflectivity.

However, even within the new atmosphere of a more emboldened writing style and a harsher social critique, the thematic approach of the articles veered very timidly away from the dominant socialist gender paradigm. As an illustration of the editors' attempt to remain relevant in a time of growing interest in content from the West, free of the ideological magnifying glass and socialist demagoguery, *Zhenata Dnes* ran its first commentary on pornography. Ironically, the trend of smuggling and distributing hard and soft pornography was already a common occurrence on the emerging black market of the Balkan states. In Yugoslavia, for example, porn was seen as a common rebellious tactic against the political establishment. In Bulgaria, such "taboo" content was also available, but was not necessarily invested with the same ideological intent as it has been in the Central European countries.[59] Therefore, the 1980 piece that ran in the magazine, titled "In the Footsteps of Pornography," albeit an edited reprint of an article that originally ran in the French magazine *Antoinette*, was a novelty in the Bulgarian cultural climate. The article, authored by a journalist by the name of Monica Malfatto, reads like a classic feminist attack of pornography as exploitative of women's bodies, while exhibiting in many ways support for the official political line on pornography pushed by the Communist party. Malfatto summed it up:

> Pornography, just like alcohol and opiates, helps its consumers to escape reality. For this condition, they [porn consumers] do not seek responsibility from themselves, not from the social order. In the new society, pornography serves the goal of distracting people from social ills, to keep them passive and to throw them into further degree of alienation from one another.[60]

This obvious critique of pornography is particularly telling as it encompasses the tensions of the changing cultural climate of socialism. The socialist political establishment began to entertain the idea of more openness in its treatment of topics pertaining to the body—sex, erotica, and to some extent, even soft forms of porn—only as an attempt to mitigate, if not entirely suppress, the growing discontent with the dismal economic output and stifling lack of political freedom. Such an unorthodox departure from the previously puritanical, strangely scientific, and comically inept communist approach to sexuality was necessitated by the growing influx of provocative materials from the West. To some extent, this budding sense of openness to sexuality was coming from the "brotherly" nations in Central Europe, as well as from the nascent industry of home-grown publications that borrowed conceptual treatment of nudity, pornography, and erotica from iconic Western media sources, such as *Playboy*, *Penthouse*, etcetera.

This trend has been widely documented in the works of both Helena Goscilo[61] and Eliot Borenstein,[62] who in turn offer compelling accounts of how sexuality was transformed by the collapse of communism in the early 1990s. In her examination of the politics of porn in post-Soviet Russia, Goscilo demonstrated that prior to 1990, finding this type of media content would have been next to impossible, but "by mid-1992 pornography was thriving as a mainstay of the novelties introduced, along with kiwis and deodorants into Russia's capital."[63] Similarly, Borenstein argued that the novelty of porn in the former Soviet Union was what he called "doubly ubiquitous: not only was the first post-Soviet decade marked by a proliferation of pornographic texts and images on newsstands, televisions, and even shopping bags, but pornography seemed all the more pervasive in that it featured prominently in the standard litany of woes afflicting post-socialist society."[64]

In this sense, it was not unusual to see discussion of AIDS and other sexually transmitted diseases in the same exact vicinity as the nude bodies of soft-erotica models. A clear example of this trend is Russia's first men's magazine, *Andrei*, which began circulating in 1991 and proclaimed its goal was a political fight against sexual oppression. As Borenstein documents, the magazine's publisher, Aleksei Veitlser stated that, "Our magazine began as a political action. It was the sexual revolution."[65] This liberal magazine was "arguing for an eroticism based on liberation, beauty, and morality, of which the intelligentsia could be proud."[66] However, the magazine's basic "economic task was to sell sexual images of Russian women to Russian men," clearly signifying an economic, market-driven argument behind the boon of erotic magazines as well as other media at the dawn of the transition.[67] In fact, *Andrei* claimed that unlike its Western competition (*Playboy*), it was more respectful of Russian women; it put them "on a pedestal of admiration; unlike invader magazines, of which there are more and more in the kiosks. The invaders' task is simple: to prove that everything Western is better, more expensive, stronger—and also to turn our women into cheap export that is ready for anything."[68] The Russian post-communist, glasnost-inspired interest in sex, therefore, was both liberating and protecting women—liberating them from the oppressiveness of the communist sexless past all the while protecting them from being exploited by the vulgar sexuality on display, modeled widely in the Western world.

This loosening of the discursive control over the conversation about women's bodies and sexuality on the eve of the disintegration of the Soviet bloc is particularly telling as it clearly exhibits the communist establishment's desperate attempt to appear open to the idea of cultural transformation. However, it also manifested the strong hold and parochial approach that the cultural activists of the socialist ideology (the aparachiks) continued to demonstrate in their treatment of gender relations and definitions of femininity. On the one hand, their attitude towards topics of sex and the female body has obviously changed, allowing for a more provocative visualization of these trends in the public space. On the other hand, we continue to see an active exercise of ideological control over who defines what is desirable and acceptable in the new cultural conditions of the transition. What appears as an invitation to more openness to the West revealed the tendency to deliberately handpick and present only a limited view of appropriate roles and behaviors for women intended to evoke a new sensuality and femininity, yet calculatingly continuing to subscribe to the age-old patriarchal gender constructions.

TURBO FOLK AND TURBO SEXUALITY

A particularly potent mix of women's bodies on display and pornography in the same exact cultural junction was evident in the growing popularity of the musical genre of turbo folk that originated in the former Yugoslavia and quickly gained immense popularity in the Balkan region. The music itself, a rather strange mix of folkloric rhythms native to the region and some trite musical chords from the 1980s and early 1990s popular disco, became widely accepted and sought after as means of entertainment. This genre was also popular because it was easy to memorize and even easier to replicate and hum. Songs usually dealt with matters of love, money, and earthly possessions, focusing on the material, rather than the emotional aspects of everyday life.[69] Tea Nikolic described turbo folk as "a musical genre that represents a mixture of commercial electronic dance-sound and kitsch folk music with an oriental tone."[70]

The really fascinating fact about the turbo-folk genre is that its most attractive performers are female, displaying a new level of heightened sexuality unparalleled even within the relatively more liberal cultural and social politics of the former Yugoslav republic. In fact, as Nikolic also pointed out, the first woman to even undress and behave seductively on Serbian television was one of the most prominent stars of the turbo-folk movement, Fahreta Janic, who is best known by her musical alias Lepa Brena. Not only did Lepa Brena set a new standard of behavior through her highly sensual performances and explicit lyrics. She also opened the gate for a number of aspiring young performers who perfected the genres of the turbo folk, while popularizing a very particular physical appearance for the female performer: extremely sexual, and in more recent times, artificially enhanced by plastic surgery and other cosmetic procedures, the turbo-folk performer encompassed everything that the communist woman wasn't—desirable, provocative, a femme fatale, who seductively crossed over a new breed of exotic sexuality infused with the rhythm of the Balkan region while readily mimicking a model of attractiveness directly borrowed from Western ideals. Excessively large breasts, small waist, blonde hair, pouty lips, and glamorous make-up all secured the instant success of the turbo-folk genre. Coupled with the magnetic power of the market, where this specific look sells top dollars, the formula of turbo folk became an instant success. As Nikolic quotes one of the sex symbols of the industry Jelana Karleusa: "All of us in this business are in fact whores. Not in the literal sense of that word, but something similar to that. The real skill is to sell yourself well."[71]

The turbo-folk phenomenon certainly set the stage for a new visual aesthetic both in terms of mediated performance and in terms of visualizing women's bodies in spaces previously occupied by a very deliberate absence of women's physicality and sexuality. The idea of the naked body was certainly not new to the media climate of former Yugoslavia. As Biljana Žikić showed, magazines such as the popular Serbian publication *Start* already used those strategies to promote what the editors considered a new, more liberal attitude towards sex.[72] This strategy naturally boosted circulation and produced financial benefits uncommon in the socialist press. Žikić recounts a specific issue of the magazine from 1979 meant to commemorate the magazine's tenth anniversary. To celebrate the occasion, the editors of *Start* put a beautiful woman on the cover, which the male editor, writing about the editorial decision, wanted to make sure stood for a collective image of all women—"she is to be anonymous . . . neither blonde nor dark-haired, her whole body should be shown and she should look the buyer in the eye provocatively, not vulgarly."[73]

Žikić explained that the inclusion of nude women in the magazine, which also boasted the very first nude centerfold in the history of Yugoslav journalism, was not sexist or exploitive of women, but was seen as liberating and "modern" because it borrowed much admired models of media content from the West. In line with the ironclad logic of market profitability and the currency of the nude body, *Start's* male editor is quoted by Žikić, stating that "nowadays few people see anything provocative in them [nude female bodies], not to mention anything lascivious: they naturally belong to *Start*, as grapes grow on the vine."[74]

The trend of greater acceptance towards content that was previously banned both because it was unbecoming of the socialist citizen, but also because it was considered immoral and offensive to the sanctity of the human body, also translated into wider availability of soft erotica, such as suggestive, nude images of women from the covers or centerfolds of Western magazines. Virtually overnight, this trend also translated into wide availability of pornographic content on television. In both Serbia and Bulgaria, the booming industry of ever-proliferating media outlets, including a mushrooming of private, unregulated TV channels that found themselves competing for audience attention, and, incapable of filling the slots of their programming blocks with original content, turned to the instant appeal of pornographic content as their weapon to fight for recognition and viewership. As Nikolic argued, "it was exactly media—which was in every other way closed—that 'opened the sexual views' of viewers."[75]

Interestingly, in the case of Serbia, pornography was also a political tool used by nationalists, who were willing to deregulate the national air to allow for morally questionable content to be broadcast in hopes of increasing birth rates among the populations. Somehow, their argument went, pornographic movies will promote a desire for sex, and eventually lead towards continuing the national gene pool.[76] The wide availability of pornographic content, which beamed into families' living rooms at the odd hours of the night served a two-fold function—on the one hand, it inadvertently led toward a transformation of sexual norms by removing socialist taboos associated with sexuality and the female body, while on the other hand, it also became a political tool of exploiting female sexuality for goals very similar to those of the communist gender order. Thus, the wide availability of such content blurred the boundaries between what is considered obscene and what is considered pornographic, reminding us of Marilyn French's argument: "Obscenity is a moral idea; pornography is a political practice. Obscenity is abstract; pornography is concrete."[77] Ironically, pornography also serves as a normalizing social practice and its appeal and popularity were considered indicators of a healthy national interest in sex, free of dangerous deviations and abnormalities. As Nikolic quotes a Serbian sociologist's evaluation of the impact of this transformative cultural trend:

> Compared to the life of our ancestors, the sex life of our contemporaries is characterized, above all, by its greater liberty. Innocence and shyness, are, as old fashion virtues, replaced by the greater sexual freedom, which through the vulgarization of sexology and other sciences in the media, is often imposed as obligatory in order to avoid any suspicion of abnormality.[78]

A similarly fascinating account of how pornography and sexual content permeated the vacuum left behind by the socialist's ideology of the body also comes from East Germany, a socialist bloc member that has been widely influenced by its powerful Western counterpart. In East Germany, the impact of the disintegration of the Soviet ideology appeared to have resonated most vigorously because of its immediate vicinity and instantaneous access to the previously denied goods and services of the Western world. The gender identities of East German women and the cultural transformation they endured are particularly telling as they show the ambiguity of bodily agency more so than in other countries of the former Eastern bloc. In fact, as Beret Norman notes in his discussion of what he calls the "sex wave" or the erotic invasion of the West into the culture of the GDR, the material goods, namely, bananas, oranges, and Western cigarette brands, were the most representative materials by which citizens of the GDR could experience a break away from the tangible limitations of living in the East.[79] However, Norman also points out that one specific area of material production—namely, erotic and pornographic films—immediately filled a space previously non-existent in the culture of the socialist republic. To illustrate this, Norman cites a 1989 report in *Der Spiegel*, Germany's premiere magazine, proclaiming, "As far as pornography is concerned, the GDR is 'No man's land.' In the stodgy stench of socialism as it really existed porn was seen as a decadent outgrowth of capitalism."[80]

The West/East dichotomy in thinking about female bodies, sex, and ultimately, pornography, was clearly an ideologically convenient, yet overly simplified way to explain and understand the fine cultural differences defining the profound ways in which women's lived identities were altered in the post-socialist transition. In the resulting euphoria of gaining access to previously forbidden products of a culture longed after for many decades, women in East Germany became exposed to new economic realities, which arguably did very little to change the already determined way in which they perceived their bodies both as instruments of social engineering and as cultural artifacts.

As Karen Remmler remarked, the fundamentally different economic systems of the East and the West (in the case of her observations, the GDR and the FRG) determined to a great extent the different semiotic constructions of the female body.[81] Remmler also noted that the capitalist economic system that in part normalizes the commodification of the female body was certainly different from the socialist, non-private, and advertising-free economy of the East, which while not entirely free of objectifying the female body, did not engage to the same extent in using the female body as a commodity as the Western media did. And yet, "the actual representation of the female body was not bound by the political borders," Remmler argued, pointing to the fact that while economic conditions might have informed differently the gender identities of women in the East and the West, the exposure to similar media content—and in the case of this book, the seductive content of Western advertising—might have wielded similar influences in the material experiences of living everyday gender.

In Bulgaria, the change in the ideological climate not only became apparent in the thematic shift of magazines such as *Zhenata Dnes*, but was also formally acknowledged by the editorial team in an open letter to its readers. On December 18, 1989, just a few weeks after Bulgaria's own revolution to bring down the communist regime, editors of the magazine revealed the reasons behind the significant lag in circulation. While acknowledging the financial difficulties triggered by the economic collapse, the main goal of the editorial was to acknowledge the historic changes sweeping through the social and political foundation of the country. In their attempt to refocus the political discourse on matters related to gender policy, the editors boldly claimed that the Bulgarian woman is the one who has endured the hardest consequences of the many decades of totalitarian oppression. And yet, despite the seemingly rebellious tone of the piece, it still remained transfixed on the economic hardships of women, rather than on the warped gender ideology that, for so many years, the magazine itself unquestionably propagated. Ironically, women's righteous indignation expressed in this piece also encapsulated and demonstrated the virtual impossibility to criticize gender politics in the post-socialist climate. Criticizing the gender regime was not simply a matter of pointing fingers and laying blame on an oppressive political structure that demanded women's participation in the labor forces while pushing them into an unbearable cycle of public and private production duties. More importantly, it also meant calling for a complete overhaul of the patriarchal system of beliefs that for many years have laid dormant under the surface of the progressive gender policies of the socialist emancipation.

As a result of the economic hardships the magazine itself faced, the publication of *Zhenata Dnes* ceased for a short while and renewed its regular publishing cycle in the early 1990s. At the time, the magazine appeared completely revamped—in a significantly smaller, standardized page size, it featured a colorful cover displaying a model, with a modern hairdo and fashionable make-up, alongside a number of inviting teaser headlines—a format directly imported from Western publications, which became the standard of the publication industry. The same trend was also adopted by other fashion magazines of the socialist time, such as *Bozhur* and *Lada*, which westernized their pages, in order to make themselves more competitive and appealing to an increasingly picky female readership. Because of the opening of the press towards a liberal market of competition, Bulgaria, just like the rest of the Balkan region witnessed a mushrooming of magazines that catered to the growing consumer interests of women.

These magazines, as Krasimira Daskalova noted, began to appear around 1984, but really picked up in popularity and circulation around 1989, following the commercialization of the press and what Daskalova described as "the real explosion" of the magazine business.[82] Magazine titles such as *Vsichko za Vseki* (Everything for Everybody), *Traditsii* (Traditions), and *Hubava Zhena* (Pretty Woman) were among the new circulating titles, alongside the revival of the old traditional magazines. In addition to the more mainstream publications, the market also imploded with magazine titles that thrived upon objectifying women's sexuality and turning a quick profit in a market eager for this type of tantalizing exposure. Among those, titles such as *Az i Ti* (You and I), *Adam i Eva* (Adam and Eve), *Eros*, etcetera, targeted mostly a male audience with the goal of entertaining and sexually provoking their readers, while at the same time, importing, and often cleverly domesticating, Western ideas of sexuality. A particularly ironic observation is offered by Krasimira Daskalova who noted that the son of the only female minister of culture Elka Kostantinova, was also the publisher of one of Bulgaria's home grown pornographic magazines, while his mother was still in office.[83] And while the debate about the widely accessible and freely distributed pornography that could be found literally on every street corner—negligently nestled on magazine stands next to serious news publications, or better yet, sold at kiosks adjacent to second-hand textbooks in chemistry or mathematics—continued to rage on, the implosion of the porn genre proved to be certainly both a money generating business and a cultural force that dictated and implicitly began to encode a new way of thinking about and looking at women. Roumiana Deltcheva described the following in her account of the developments in mass culture and media during the post-totalitarian transition:

> The "pornographic network" gained enormous dimensions—starting from the sales of Emmanuelle at every street corner to the Playboy photographs (pirated) which periodically appeared in leading daily and weekly newspapers. In this context, the multitude of contests for "Miss Erotic Dancing," "Miss Monokini," "Miss Naked Body/Miss Eve," or the ever present advertisements for a "truly erotic striptease" in the restaurants of the bigger towns should not cause any surprise or shock.[84]

If beauty contest and pornographic videos propagated degrading and reductionist images of womanhood, they also pioneered a rather magnetic way to transform the desire to exercise agency through looking good into the desire to exercise the right to be politically relevant. That also meant that the body could now be used as an empowering vehicle towards legitimizing political participation, a tool for propagating and visualizing the very essence of the female public presence. The idea of nude protests, for example, began as an offshoot of student protests against the communist establishment, creating a rather potent mix of political and sexual power. That mix was powerfully intoxicating because of its potential to transform and invigorate the stale and oppressive political status quo. As Nadia Kaneva and I noted elsewhere, *Demokratzia*, the main opposition newspaper in Bulgaria after 1989, sponsored a topless beauty contest and—upon publishing the photo of the winner—argued that a new sense of liberation was being expressed through the symbolic act of stripping the clothes and the artificial morals of the communist past.[85]

While the boom in media ventures spans over a wide range of outlets, starting from newspapers, into radio stations and TV stations, it was magazines that continued to be the major vehicle of advertising experiments, at the same time serving as the primary purveyors of standards of femininity and new ideas about womanhood. Indeed, in the vacuum of the ideologically imposed concept of gender equality and public and private functions of men and women, magazines began to fill the void with new, rejuvenated versions of femininity, which were presented not only as visually stimulating because of their bodily displays and sexualized context, but also because they offered a fresh new way to think, and more importantly, imagine what it meant to be a woman.

These trends were particularly well exemplified in the budding advertising business and its quick rise as a regular content provider in all media. Ads for Italian pantyhose, German sawing machines, Bulgarian and foreign perfumes and cosmetics, typewriters, and condoms appeared sporadically on the pages of the magazines. Most of the time, this arbitrary mix simply demonstrated a lack of understanding on the part of the magazine production team how advertising is supposed to work in the first place. Product placement appeared frequently alongside long articles featuring women's issues and in an almost comical, and certainly not particularly inviting way. The advertisements themselves were inundated by endless copy extolling the quality of the new product, describing it as "unparalleled," "top of the line," of "unquestionable quality," literally blurring the distinction between editorial content, product advertisements, and scientific report. This unimaginative approach to writing copy and visualizing content showed how novice and amateurish the Bulgarian advertising business was, but it also signaled a transition from the previously familiar world of scientific lingo that made product information both impersonal yet invested with undisputable facts about quality and value.

As a result, the typical ad of the early 1990s was heavy on copy and light on visuals, similar to the early advertising of the twentieth century in the United States. Appearing a lot more like a news column and a lot less like an ad for a product that women would desire, the ads would include a logo showing the name of the brand, and engage kickers such as "Innovation on the Bulgarian market," with a catchy promo headline, cleverly masking the real "selling" strategy behind it. Ironically, instead of "visualizing" the actual product, the ad would spend a lot of time "describing" its packaging.

To illustrate this point, consider a 1995 ad for a cosmetic line named "Dori Lux," featuring a variety of products, from lipsticks, and facial creams to nail polish and face powder. The ad reads, "The high quality of the cosmetic products are in total harmony with its elegant and sophisticated packaging." They meet the high European standards and reach the client in immaculate condition, because in the first private factory for color cosmetics "Dori Lux," as the ad reads, "the products are sealed in tiny vacuumed packages." It is obvious from this lackluster copy that the strength of the product lies not in its visualization or appealing presentation, but in the copy that guarantees meeting the new standards of consumer expectations—that of the West, in this case represented by Europe, and that of sophisticated packages that won't fall apart or won't spoil the good, as they have done in the past. In fact, the issue of poor packaging was a major complaint raised by Kristen Ghodsee's informants who shared their experiences consuming cosmetics during socialism and in the post-socialist transition.[86] A similar emphasis on failing quality of packages was also acknowledged in Mila Mineva's work, whose overview of the visual construction of the socialist consumption delineated poor packaging as one of the major reasons for unimpressive sales of Bulgarian perfumes among the socialist consumers.[87] Mineva argues that a consumer good is not longer just an object, but becomes the focus of the consumer's gaze, who infuses it with expectations of quality and value that must emanate from its visual presentation. This certainly was not the case in the early days of post-socialist advertising, as the majority of ads featured lengthy copy, stressing function and utility, rather than visual appeal and desirability.

Another example of the same approach featured a Western product—the Gillette lady's razor—finally made available on the Bulgarian market. Although the ad itself only showed a black and white photo of the razor, it masterfully blended the pseudo-scientific appearance of a factual report with copy written to appeal to the vanity of the female readership. "The dream—silky, soft, beautiful legs which look fantastic. Is that even possible? Yes, if you are using the infallible method for hair removal invented by Gillette, which made this dream a reality for millions of American women."

POST-SOCIALIST BEAUTY AS A COMMODITY

Another interesting trend in the advertising of the early post-socialist era is the abundance of ads that clearly target women's interests and consumer needs, while boasting improvement in their quality of life. I call these types of selling strategies the "domesticating" of advertising as they tend to not only culturally situate the products as visualized and desired within the imaginative boundaries of domestic life, but also because they implicitly tend to associate the value imbued in these products with the utilitarian functionality of womanhood, particularly in the new conditions of the post-socialist economy. In the early and mid 1990s, the majority of print ads appear to be promoting household products, such as sewing machines, refrigerators, cleaning supplies, etcetera, which presented an alternative way to think about household chores. In the new context of the private economy, domestic chores do not need to be a drag, these advertisements seemed to imply, because the products advertised are meant to make the process of caring for one's responsibility in the sphere of the home less arduous, but more importantly, a lot more enjoyable. An Indesit washing machine will save you time and effort, a good refrigerator will also cut your time in the kitchen in half because now you can cook and store food for a longer period of time, and a sewing machine by Husqvarna will make all of your fashion dreams come true.

A simple visual scan over the advertising content of the 1990s magazines reveals that not only were the majority of goods either advertised to women (as consumers) or advertised via women (as models), but that in both cases, the implicit goal was to cultivate a new aesthetic for the post-socialist femininity. The woman visualized in these ads is attractive, often provocatively looking back at the consumer, projecting a new sense of confidence and attention to appearance. In doing so, she is wearing Italian pantyhose, high-heel shoes, immaculate make-up, and lots of flashy jewelry, displaying utmost attention to virtually everything that distinguishes her as a woman. Interestingly, even when the product has very little or nothing at all to do with being feminine, the gaze of the spectator is still envisioning the female body, and the woman herself, as infusing the object advertised with feminine, and therefore, sexually desirable gestures. As Krasimira Daskalova pointed out, the new magazine culture also instituted a new ideal of femininity—the "feminine" woman was now "the most common and widespread image of women in Bulgarian society at large."[88]

Additionally, she argued, women's magazines also began pushing a certain set of skills that signaled a desire to reconstitute the image of the woman as one that is both polished and cared for, but also defined the woman's roles and duties through consumer objects of desire while reconditioning her sense of femininity in the realm of the domicile. Daskalova also remarked that the new female readership magazines made possible by the variety of product advertisements, now offered new recipes and "do-it-yourself" fashion tips, associating those with tangible objects for consumption that make the once coveted item finally "imaginable." While these ads appear "to serve preexisting interests and needs, they actually contribute to the formation, and encourage the cultivation, of an array of traditional domestic skills. By advertising activities and objects in which 'every woman' should interest herself, writings of this sort posit standards and ideals of womanhood."[89]

The paradoxical outcome of this new phenomenon of creating desire through advertising also meant that the much longed after ideal of the West is nothing more than a post-socialist adaptation of Betty Friedan's "feminine mystique," a continuation of the patriarchal tradition of the woman as a self-negating creature, who now also has a new goal—doing so, while looking beautiful and flawless, using the "magical" consumer products that her Western "sisters" have long enjoyed.

While advertising was enjoying a growing success as a novel cultural artifact, it was also quickly recognized by the private entrepreneurs venturing in media production as a source of immense revenues. That model of private ownership was the engine behind the production of new and original content and worked as a charm for the budding business of media in the post-socialist environment. As a result of the general collapse of the state, the infrastructure of the socialist media monolith was left drained of resources, but intact and up for grabs, creating a "no man's land" for the newly emerging capital holders. As Kristen Ghodsee also noted, the magazines of the post-socialist Bulgarian media environment were abundant in advertising, in which a very deliberate image of the woman was being constructed. "The ads are typical as they feature very young, thin, flawless woman smiling, confident and often, scantily clad, often promoting a cosmetic product."[90]

Even when the product did not have anything to do with the physical appearance of women, it nonetheless evoked an association with the woman—and specifically, her body—as a symbolic "stamp" of quality, as far as both the product and the actual ad for it were concerned. A good illustration of this trend is an ad for the Bulgarian brand of typewriter Isotimpex. The ad, which ran in *Bhozur* magazine, features a young woman, dressed in a mini skirt, looking playfully over her shoulder, while holding effortlessly the typewriter in her right arm. She appears very attractive and her body posture is somewhat inviting, with her legs forming a v-shape framing the typewriter, nonchalantly dangling by her side. A similar ad also showcases the newest in computer software and hardware, where another attractive young woman is featured jumping playfully over an oversized computer keyboard, wearing nothing but a revealing one piece bathing suit.

While one might argue the use of a seductive young female model was simply an unimaginative approach on the part of a naïve, yet eager to explore new sales strategies advertising business, it must also be noted that associating the typewriter or the computer accessories with the female body is not entirely accidental. For instance, the secretarial profession during the socialist period was entirely feminized, allowing for an interpretation that visualizes a connection between a typewriter and a female model. However, the fact that the model is very attractive and appears to treat the typewriter and the keyboard almost as weapons of seduction tells us a lot more about the new labor conditions of the market economy. As Ghodsee noted in her work, "women are aware of the new beauty standard and accept them as a way to get ahead in a competitive labor market."[91] Similarly, a typewriter in the hands of a beautiful woman could be seen both as a tool of earning her wage and as a tool of advancing one's professional stance, especially through the sexual innuendo of the model's entire physical presentation.

The editorial content that appeared on the pages of women's magazines sustained a major makeover. In the mid and late 1990s, the pages of the new publications as well as the old, hard-liner ideological bastion of gender norms, such as *Zhenata Dnes,* switched their attention to women's most valued attributes in the conditions of the market—their bodies and their beauty. Articles detoured from their previously ideologically constraining tone, moralizing about the duties and responsibilities of women to others—family members, social groups, party delegates—into the indulgent sphere of self-care, where the sole benefactor of the woman's desire to improve is the woman herself. Most of the reports, therefore, focused on beauty advice, accompanied by a number of "sponsored" products, information about the latest trends in dieting and exercising, and even venturing into the world of plastic surgery and other medical procedures intended to improve women's physical attractiveness. As Daskalova also noted, "one message conveyed is that beauty is a woman's most valuable asset, and every woman should try to make herself sexually attractive to men."[92]

Advertising was further aided by the myriad of articles literally teaching women the "abc's" of owning one's sexual agency and using it to advance one's goals, especially in the professional environment, where the pressure to succeed along with the limited array of job opportunities forced women to resort to unconventional strategies in order to reach a new measure of success. As a result, an abundance of articles, most of which were direct reprints of articles published in the Western press, skillfully taught women how to "flirt in the office," how to "sell their beauty," or "how to use sex appeal to advance one's career." It was not at all unusual to see articles with sexually playful titles, such as "The Art of Seduction: Sex As a Play," "Sex School and the Art of Flirting," "The Erotic Zones of the Body," and "18 Moments of Orgasm," often illustrated with provocative images that meant to stimulate both the imagination and pique the interest of a growingly selective, yet equally enchanted magazine audience.

Even more telling in this direction are articles that were written by Bulgarian authors who offered the "local" response to the growing "feminizing" of the discourse on womanhood in the post-socialist conditions. Articles continued to rely on the authority of the scientific expert, however, this time around the advice offered had nothing to do with being efficient in meeting the socialist woman's duties at home and at the factory, and everything to do with meeting the expectation to look good. Consequently, Djurdja Bartlett pointed out, "An immaculate, individualized look became the ideal for millions of women in socialist countries, who made great sacrifices trying to achieve it."[93] As an illustration, consider an article in *Bhozur* magazine, titled, "Venus's weapon" with the unusual subtitle, "Do you have a hobby?" The article, written by Dr. Zlatka Papazova—a dermatologist and a cosmetologist—offers step-by-step directions on how to improve the appearance of one's breasts. In a strangely misfit scientific tone, the article lists specific exercises, stretches, and mechanical moves a woman can practice in order to make her smaller breast grow larger, advising on "how to care for one's breasts so they can turn into a real weapon of beauty."[94]

Similarly, an article on sex appeal and career building, written by a male author by the name of Vasil Simeonov, advises women on how to use the Western culture of office affairs to advance one's professional positioning. The article, accompanied by a cut-out photo collage featuring a fully clothed man, wearing a Wall Street-banker type raincoat and a partially clad young woman, sitting by what appears to be an office window, wearing nothing but a bra, is an almost comical handbook on how to channel a woman's sexual power to achieve professional advancement in her career. At first glance, the article tackles a subject that while many knew existed during communism, and perhaps in a much more abusive and exploitive way, was never really a subject of public conversations. In this sense, the fact that the author has ventured to discuss a topic considered taboo can been seen as a sign of a new, more enlightened approach towards the topic of sex, free of the shame and embarrassment previously associated with it. However, the ideas provided by the text do very little to condemn the culture of abuse of power at the workplace, while blatantly legitimizing and normalizing the use of women's sexuality and specifically, sexual affairs with one's superiors, in order to gain career advancement. Simeonov writes:

> The women of the former communist countries discovered a long time ago mechanisms for building stable careers in the old conditions—party activism, professionalism, mixed with ideological overtones, submission. Sex, it seems, was not a dominating factor in a society, where party functionaries determined everything. . . . Now we have to think differently and it should not be a surprise that office sex appeal will overtake the "party-style" appeal as much more elegant and sophisticated.[95]

What the author seems to imply is that the woman of today has always been artfully exploiting and crafting ways to get ahead in her social and professional development. The desire to get ahead no matter what is not foreign to the socialist woman, who has learned a long time ago how to use her assets to gain the outcomes she desires. Now, it seems, sex is legitimately added to the list of secret weapons a woman can use, and rightfully so, both because she is tired of the party-imposed rules of the game, but also because having an office affair is seen as a token of forwarding-thinking, displaying a Westernized and liberated sense of self-worth, and empowering her to dictate her own rules. Essentially, this new approach to envisioning one's power through the agency of sex is aided by the media, or as Helena Goscilo pointed out, "all media, with varying degree of sophistry and sophistication, convey the message that sexual desire and desirability (of a visible, marketable sort) are critical to a full life, to popularity, happiness, etc.," and in this case, also career success.[96]

It is also interesting to point out that the encouragement that women receive in pursuing their professional goals through whatever means necessary, including sex, ironically, and yet, not surprisingly, comes from a male author, whose patronizing tone simultaneously serves as a sign of social progressiveness and a gender backlash. This irony is further exemplified in the case of a rubric *Bhozur* magazine featured, titled, "Who Are We, Women?" Naturally, the expectation for who will respond to this question is women themselves; however, in this case, the question and answer session hosted by the editorial team of the magazine was hosted by four men, members of what will be considered the intellectual and cultural elite of the transition—an art critic, a journalist and a photographer, a film director, and an actor. The selection of the "esteemed" panel is not accidental—the journalist behind the idea, Paloma Ilieva, explained her motivation for posing the questions she did to the commentators she selected as an attempt to find answers outside of the confused circle of identity crisis in which women seem to be stuck. The questions that were posited barely even touched the surface of the fundamental shift in political and economic realties bound to affect gender relations. On the contrary, the questions asked were almost lighthearted, rather than soul-searching, "What do you find attractive about a woman?" or "Would you formulate your idea of the woman—the real one, the dreamed one, the desired one?" One of the responses to this question artfully illustrates how changing ways in which men think about women might be seen as a break away from the regimented Puritanism of the socialist time. At the same time, they merely act as a substitution for the same old patriarchal rituals of repression. Here is Georgi Papakochev's response:

> What generally can you say is the symbol of the woman? This is complex alchemy of everything big and beautiful, which man has received from the women surrounding him. It encompasses the idea of the mother, the loving wife, the ever-giving woman. Or as Ilia Beshkov [a famous Bulgarian artist] once said, if I recall correctly: "The woman seeks out the man so she can realize herself as a woman through his being a man."[97]

The seemingly endearing and poetic portrait that Papakochev paints of the Bulgarian woman reflects the parochial ideology of sexual complementarity, which seems to fit perfectly in the mixed modes of patriarchy and post-socialism. The woman is described as a mother, a wife, and a giving soul, one whose very identity is only possible and imaginable through the existence of a man. This also confirmed Daskalova's view that "cultural stereotypes about weak and vulnerable women perpetuate socialized forms of domination. Thus, deeply ingrained, patriarchal attitudes, habits, opinions and judgments are difficult to change, especially if women remain insensitive to, and therefore, complicitous in, their own domination."[98]

Even when the magazines appear to break out of the socialist patterns of thinking that have become so embedded in women's discourses, they continue to frame issues within the traditional and familiar cultural norms of femininity, constraining women's roles to serving their domestic duties, and now, also tending to their appearance. Consider an article from *Zhenata Dnes* titled "The Luxury of Being Single." While trying to promote the idea of a woman's personal choice to remain unmarried and consequently, not to bear children, as a sign of the new progressive mindset, the article also condones the stereotypes of femininity by claiming that single women must treat their independence as a luxury, not as a widely accepted and socially desirable trend. Even more telling is the advice that the article offers women for the "good kind" of solitude, equating the single woman with a lonely, and therefore, potentially unhappy woman. The very first advice is "say yes to daily care for your physical appearance!" A similar stress on the importance of appearance and attractiveness is also echoed several years later under the title "It's a Question of Choice." In it, the author almost immediately acknowledges the predominance of looking good as the advantage point of the independent woman—she is single by choice, she is empowered by her sense of independence, but "the young, modern and ambitious woman is always elegant, with immaculate appearance." Here, the choice to remain unmarried is not treated as a luxury, but is seen as one of the most important achievements of "modern times."

The notion of evoking modernity as a sign of progressive gender ideology is certainly not new, as it is reminiscent in many ways of the early socialist ideologues' desire to paint a new—and consequently modern—picture of society that conceptualized and envisioned women's role as fully engaged in the workforce and in public life. In the conditions of post-socialism, however, to be modern has taken a whole new meaning, which ironically promotes a return to domesticity and patriarchy, disguised as a progressive gender paradigm. As Aniko Imre argues, "While the single woman has emerged in the region in the past two decades, she is hardly a celebrated model of female independence. . . . She tends to be seen as an overworked victim of global capitalism, who has no time to build meaningful relationships with men, which would lead to a fulfilling life as a mother."[99] This phenomenon is also discussed within the Western context of women's social positioning by Naomi Wolf who has argued that the beauty myth is a powerfully, universally applicable grand narrative designed to keep women in positions of subordination. "As soon as a woman's primary social value could no longer be defined as the attainment of virtuous domesticity, the beauty myth redefined it as the attainment of virtuous beauty."[100] This is certainly true in the case of Balkan women whose new social and political realities were suddenly inundated not only with a wide range of discursive renditions of the new post-socialist femininities, but also with an onslaught of media that offered most seductive and hard to resist messages about how to live the "good life," all the while looking beautiful and ignoring the economic realities of the failed socialist experiment.

NOTES

1. Oakley, Ann, "Sexuality," in *Feminism and Sexuality: A Reader*, eds. Stevi Jackson and Sue Scott (New York: Columbia University Press, 1996), 35.
2. Reid, Susan, and Crowley, David, *Style and Socialism: Modernity and Material Culture in Post-War Eastern Europe* (New York: Berg, 2000); Roman, Denise, *Fragmented Identities: Popular Culture, Sex, and Everyday Life in Post-Communist Romania* (Lanham: Lexington Books, 2003); Kaneva, Nadia, and Ibroscheva, Elza, "Media and the Birth of the Post-Communist Consumer," in *Media Transformations in the Post-Communist World*, eds. Peter Gross and Karol Jakubowicz (Lanham: Lexington Books, 2012), 67–85; Verdery, Katherine, *What Was Socialism, And What Comes Next?* (Princeton: Princeton University Press, 1996).
3. Barker, Adele Marie, "Rereading Russia," in *Consuming Russia: Popular culture, sex, and society*, ed. Adele M. Barker (Durham: Duke University Press, 1999), 1–9.
4. Roman, Denise, *Fragmented Identities: Popular Culture, Sex, and Everyday Life in Post-Communist Romania* (Lanham: Lexington Books, 2003), 50.
5. Verdery, Katherine, *What Was Socialism, and What Comes Next?* (Princeton: Princeton University Press, 1996).
6. Ghodsee, Kristen, "Potions, Lotions and Lipstick: The Gendered Consumption of Cosmetics and Perfumery in Socialist and Post-Socialist Urban Bulgaria," *Women's Studies International Forum*, 30, 1 (2007): 27.
7. Holmgren, Beth, "Bug Inspectors and Beauty Queens: The Problem of Translating Feminism in Russian," in *Post-communism and the Body Politic*, ed. Ellen Berry (New York: New York University Press, 1995), 22.
8. Kasic, Biljana "The Spatiality of Identities and Sexualities: Is 'Transition' a Challenging Point at All?," in *Sexuality and Gender in Post-Communist Eastern Europe and Russia*, eds. Alesandar Stulhofer and Theo Sanfort (New York: The Haworth Press, 2005), 95–102.
9. Kasic, "The Spatiality of Identities and Sexualities."
10. Žikić, Biljana, "Dissidents Liked Pretty Girls: Nudity, Pornography and Quality Press in Socialism," *Medij. Istraz*, 16, 1 (2009): 53–71.
11. Ibid.
12. Quoted in Senjković, R. *Izgubljeno u Prijenosu: Pop Iskustvo soc Culture* (Zagreb: Institut za etnologiju i folkloristiku, 2008), 69.
13. Magó-Maghiar, Ana, "Representations of Sexuality in Hungarian Popular Culture of the 1980s," *Medij. Istraz*, 16, 1 (2009): 73–95.
14. Gessen, Masha, "Sex in Media and the Birth of the Sex Media in Russia," in *Post-Communism and the Body Politics*, ed. Ellen Berry (New York: New York University Press, 1995), 203.
15. Massino, Jill, "From Black Caviar to Blackouts: Gender, Consumption, and Lifestyle in Ceausescu's Romania," in *Communism Unwrapped: Consumption in Cold War Eastern Europe*, eds. Paulina Bren and Mary Neuburger (Oxford: Oxford University Press, 2012).
16. Massino, "From Black Caviar to Blackouts," 234.

Chapter 3

17. Daskalova, Krasimira, "Women's Problems, Women's Discourses in Post-Communist Bulgaria," in *Reproducing Gender: Politics, Publics and Everyday Life After Socialism*, eds. Susan Gal and Gail Kligman (Princeton: Princeton University Press, 2000), 352.
18. Ibid., 352.
19. Magó-Maghiar, "Representations of Sexuality in Hungarian Popular Culture," quoting Adamik, M., *"Az államszocializmus és a 'nőkérdés.'" "A legnayobb ígéret—a legnagyobb megaláztatás"* ["State socialism and the 'Woman Problem'"(PhD dissertation, 2000).
20. Apostolov, Georgi, "The Thoughts of a Young Man," *Zhenata Dnes*, 7 (1979): 12.
21. Marody, Mira, and Giza-Poleszczuk, Anna, "Changing Images of Identity in Poland: From the Self-Sacrificing to the Self-Investing Woman?," in *Reproducing Gender: Politics, Publics and Everyday Life After Socialism*, eds. Susan Gal and Gail Kligman (Princeton: Princeton University Press, 2000), 151–76.
22. Apostolov, "The Thoughts of a Young Man," 12.
23. Ibid.
24. Gall, Susan, and Kligman, Gail (eds.), *Reproducing Gender: Politics, Publics and Everyday Life After Socialism* (Princeton: Princeton University Press, 2000).
25. Bankov, Nikolay, "The Thoughts of a Young Man," *Zhenata Dnes*, 9 (1979): 20.
26. Ibid.
27. Ibid.
28. Ibid.
29. Marody & Giza-Poleszczuk, "Changing Images of Identity in Poland," 157.
30. Bankov, "The Thoughts of a Young Man," 20.
31. Remmler, Karen, "Deciphering the Body of Memory: Writing by Former East German Women Writers," in *Post-Communism and the Body Politic*, ed. Ellen Berry (New York: New York University Press, 1995), 136.
32. Sieg, Katrin, "Sex, Subjectivity, and Socialism: Feminist Discourse in East Germany," in *Post-Communism and the Body Politic*, ed. Ellen Berry (New York: New York University Press, 1995), 107.
33. Ibid., 108.
34. Hristova, Julia, "A Man in the Kindergarten, *Zhenata Dnes*, 2 (1989): 18–19.
35. Kotzeva, Tatyana, "Reimagining Bulgarian women: The Marxist legacy and Women's self-identity," in *Gender and Identity in Central and Eastern Europe*, ed. Chris Corrin (London: Frank Cass Publishers, 1999), 83–99.
36. Peshev, Georgi, "An Experiment: Girls in the Line of Duty," *Zhenata Dnes*, 2 (1989): 30–31.
37. Ibid.
38. Kaneva, Nadia, and Ibroscheva, Elza, "Hidden in Public View: A Critical Analysis of Visual Representations of Women in the Communist Bulgarian Press," *Feminist Media Studies*, iFirst (online). doi:10.1080/14680777.2011.604341, 8.
39. Remmler, "Deciphering the Body of Memory," 137.
40. Ibid.
41. Ibid., 137.
42. Magó-Maghiar, "Representations of Sexuality in Hungarian Popular Culture."
43. Ibid, 92.
44. Balockaite, Rasa, "Go West . . ." Myths of femininity and feminist utopias in East and West. *Eurozine* (2009), accessed June 11, 2012, from http://www.eurozine.com/articles/2009-08-14-balockaite-en.html.
45. Waters, Elizabeth, "Soviet Beauty Contests," in *Sex and Russian Society*, eds. Igor Kon and James Riordian (London: Pluto Press, 1993), 116–35.
46. Ibid., 117.
47. Mamonova, Tatyana, *Russian Women's Studies: Essays on Sexism in Soviet Culture* (Oxford: Pergamon Press, 1994).
48. Ibid., 161.
49. Waters, "Soviet Beauty Contests," 118.
50. Ibid.

51. Bartlett, Djurdja, *FashionEast: The Spectre that Haunted Socialism* (Cambridge, MA: MIT Press, 2010).
52. Ibid.
53. As quoted in Bartlett, 236.
54. Ibid., 242.
55. Roman, *Fragmented Identities*, 50 (emphasis in the original text).
56. Waters, "Soviet Beauty Contests," 119.
57. Bartlett, *FashionEast*.
58. Waters, "Soviet Beauty Contests," 124.
59. Magó-Maghiar, "Representations of Sexuality in Hungarian Popular Culture."
60. Malfatto, Monica, "In the Footsteps of Pornography," *Zhenata Dnes*, 8 (1980): 33.
61. Goscilo, Helena, *Dehexing Sex: Russian Womanhood During and after Glasnost* (Ann Arbor: University of Michigan, 1996).
62. Borenstein, Eliot, *Overkill: Sex and Violence in Contemporary Russian Popular Culture* (Ithaca and London: Cornell University Press. 2008).
63. Goscilo, *Dehexing Sex*, 135.
64. Borenstein, *Overkill*, 53.
65. Ibid., 239.
66. Ibid.
67. Ibid., 244.
68. Ibid., 242–43.
69. Ibroscheva, Elza, "The New Eastern European Woman: A Gold-digger or an Independent Spirit?" *Global Media Journal*, 5, 9, accessed July 11, 2011, http://lass.purduecal.edu/cca/gmj/fa06/gmj_fa06_ibroscheva.htm.
70. Nikolic, Tea, "Serbian Sexual Response: Gender and Sexuality in Serbia During the 1990s," in *Sexuality and Gender in Post-Communist Eastern Europe and Russia*, eds. Alesandar Stulhofer and Theo Sanfort (New York: The Haworth Press, 2005), 132.
71. Quoted in Nikolic, "Serbian Sexual Response," 133–34.
72. Žikić, "Dissidents Liked Pretty Girls."
73. Quoted in Žikić, "Dissidents Liked Pretty Girls," 58.
74. Ibid.
75. Nikolic, "Serbian Sexual Response," 135.
76. Ibid.
77. French, Marilyn, *The War Against Women* (New York: Ballantine Books, 1993), 167.
78. Quoted in Nikolic, "Serbian Sexual Response," 138.
79. Norman, Beret, "'Test the West': East German Performance Art Takes on Western Advertising," *The Journal of Popular Culture*, 34 (2000): 255–67.
80. Ibid., 262.
81. Remmler, "Deciphering the Body of Memory."
82. Daskalova, "Women's Problems, Women's Discourses."
83. Ibid.
84. Deltcheva, Roumiana, "New Tendencies in Post-Totalitarian Bulgaria: Mass Culture and the Media," *Europe-Asia Studies*, 48, 2 (1996): 307.
85. Kaneva and Ibroscheva, "Hidden in Public View."
86. Ghodsee, "Potions, Lotions and Lipstick."
87. Mineva, Mila, "Stories and Images of Socialist Consumption" [in Bulgarian], *Sociologicheski Problemi*, 1–2 (2003): 143–65.
88. Daskalova, "Women's Politics, Women's Discourses," 348.
89. Ibid., 349.
90. Ghodsee, "Potions, Lotions and Lipstick," 34.
91. Ibid., 38.
92. Daskalova, "Women's Problems, Women's Discourses," 349.
93. Bartlett, *FashionEast*, 243.
94. Papazova, Zlatka, "Venus's Weapon," *Bhozur* 3 (1991): 38.
95. Simeonov, Vasil, "Affair at the Office," *Bhozur* 7 (1995): 37.
96. Goscilo, *Dehexing Sex*, 140.

97. Ilieva, Paloma, "Who Are We, Women?" *Bhozur* 7 (1995): 38 (Papakochev was interviewed by Ilieva).
98. Daskalova, "Women's Problems, Women's Discourses," 362.
99. Imre, Aniko, "Sex and the Postsocialist City," *FlowTV* (2009), accessed June 9, 2012, http://flowtv.org/2009/07/sex-and-the-postsocialist-city.
100. Wolf, Naomi, *The Beauty Myth* (New York: Morrow, 1991).

Chapter Four

Of Vodka, Watermelons, and Other Sexy Fruit

Advertising and the Objectification of Women in Bulgaria

During the long-standing conflict between the West and the East, the propaganda effort to present each camp as ideologically superior and in fact, exceeding in every aspect of social and cultural life, was well documented and evidence of it abounded on both sides of the Atlantic. Western nations boasted about the quality of individual life and the advantages of innovation and luxury, while the Eastern bloc paraded social consciousness and communal welfare. Disguised in this larger ideological conflict, however, were also subtle commentaries on how gender identities were constructed and presented to the world at large, both as expressions of cultural norms, but also as a political tool for defining and controlling power relations.

In this ideological contest, the socialist states saw an opportunity in proclaiming gender emancipation unparalleled in the West. During the years of the Cold War, the one thing that the East was often seen excelling at and quite frequently, envied for, was the status of women in the socialist world. Women from the former Soviet bloc enjoyed rights and privileges that Western women could only dare to imagine. While American women struggled to introduce and implement the Equal Rights Amendment, for example, Soviet women experienced equal rights firsthand. Laws that provided three years of maternity leave and widely available state-sponsored childcare were just a few of the "protectionist" laws established by the socialist states in their attempt to resolve what they termed the "woman question" in a truly Marxist fashion.[1] Naturally, to support these ideas the powerful propaganda machine of the socialist state disseminated images of women in hard hats, women pilots, and women doctors in white lab coats, which widely supported the illusion that women in the socialist countries had indeed been liberated and had found the perfect balance between handling a career and raising a family. Thus, in sync with the Communist Party line, socialist women "felt" free to reject individualism and self-serving motives, and instead, "chose" to devote their energy to the common good, exercising their remarkable ability to serve their families while also attending to their public duties.

Today, the post-socialist woman is much more than a token of visual propaganda. In this chapter, I focus the primary discussion on one specific example of a contemporary advertising campaign for the Bulgarian Vodka Flirt. I selected alcoholic beverages based on their popularity as a consumer product but also because according to a recent study, the average frequency of drunkenness rose by 40 percent among all Eastern European countries, with an increase in girls leading the way. Additionally, researchers have stipulated that the dramatic changes that have taken place in the Eastern European nations are related to the socioeconomic conditions, as well as the development of new advertising norms and exposure to the global marketing of alcoholic beverages.[2] I also chose Vodka Flirt because it serves as an exemplary case of how women's imagery has been transformed in the advertising space of the post-communist transition. I selected this specific brand because according to the only study to date that includes data from Eastern Europe, Vodka Flirt was the top most recognized brand of vodka in Bulgaria (vodka also ranked as the most popular type of alcohol), but more importantly, because Vodka Flirt also ranked as the most frequently mentioned alcoholic beverage, the most appealing alcoholic beverage, and the beverage that has the most appealing marketing practices, including most popular TV ads, outdoor billboards, and print ads. In fact, it is perhaps safe to say that Flirt not only enjoys a fairly notable brand positioning in the Bulgarian alcohol advertising market, but it has also practically permeated popular culture with its popular ad campaigns, becoming a common topic of conversation and even a popular tagline in the urban vernacular of Bulgarian youth.

MEDIA IMAGES OF SOCIALIST WOMEN

The power of images was not lost on the ideologues of the communist regimes. In fact, the Soviet propaganda machine from an early stage used the potential of political ideas and their visual renditions to mobilize and organize the masses into collective action. As Nadezhda Azhgikhina argued, the Soviet culture, generously subsidized by the state, became a sort of a "dream factory," while the press, and the media in general, were a "bazaar of dreams," "tirelessly drumming new myths and images in public consciousness, creating another reality, which many Soviet people perceived as 'more real than reality itself.'"[3]

These included ideological constructions of womanhood that were further solidified in the public consciousness by the constant barrage of images of mythical heroines next to real women—tractor-drivers, pilots, mechanics, and political functionaries, thus building a very strong, and fairly stereotypical, public perception of what a woman should look like. Similarly, Barbara Einhorn, in perhaps the most widely read and cited book on the issue of Eastern European women, writing about the expectations of Western feminist scholars for the future development of women in Eastern Europe, put it succinctly: "The image of the female tractor driver is out, as is Superwoman wearing a hard-hat on a building site," describing the defining stage in reconstructing and defining female imagery in the mass media in the countries of Eastern Europe.[4]

Throughout communism, images of women were extremely didactic and had a most important ideological function to perform. In fact, a quick look into the popular female images and stereotypes in the press throughout the history of the socialist regimes allows us to outline the specific features and paradoxes of that era and to understand the essence of the socialist ideologies of gender. Part of the ideological motivation of the press to maintain the image of the socialist woman as an epitome of successful emancipation represented the idea that women have mastered control over the "parasite" needs of leisure and aesthetics, the decadent trend of self-indulgence through fashion and beauty and instead, have focused narrowly (and appropriately so) on functional, productive-driven activities.[5] As Tatyana Kotzeva explained "the visual space of the socialist society was inhabited by the new Amazons—they were labeled 'doers,' 'fighters,' 'functionaries,' 'labourer,' 'activists,' and so on."[6] More importantly, the socialist gender ideology while proclaiming the triumph of woman in taming the revolutionary energy, showed that "women's appropriation of a progressive masculine discourse was not to their benefit but rather functioned to curb a 'transgressive femininity,'"[7] leading, in turn, to engendering a manufactured and controlled idea of femininity that had nothing to do with women's self-expression and everything to do with the party line on gender equality.

Thus, the typical socialist woman was devoid of any playfulness or coquetry, let alone sexuality. As Azhgikhina explained, "of all feminine manifestations, only motherly love in moderate quantities was tolerated; women actively mastered men's skills, acquired education and took part in public life," all the while dressed in conservative suits, lacking any fashion sense and appearing utterly asexual.[8] Doina Pasca-Harsanyi described,

> They [women] could not dress fashionably, wear makeup, or look attractive in any way. Anyone who looks at pictures of the most prominent female nomen-

klatura, forced to imitate the generic asexual communist "comrade" will understand the lack of appeal to young women.[9]

This stifling ideological control over the public image of the socialist woman soon proved to be difficult to maintain as public discontent with the repressive communist system grew and eventually brought about its demise. In the years immediately following the collapse of communism, a dramatic shift took place, transforming not only the entire political process for women, but also their visual representations. The image of the fashion model and the beauty queen came to reign supreme in the mass media, immediately and successfully replacing the communist woman. This change came almost naturally as a backlash against the socialist aesthetics and the artificial stereotypes of womanhood maintained by the socialist ideology. Consciousness fostered by the totalitarian regime and expressed in the mythical heroine of the past was rejected and replaced with a full display of beauty, sexuality, and hyper-femininity. This trend was readily embraced by the mushrooming of independent media outlets, heralded by the commercial appeal of advertising, which flagrantly used female images of liberated, rebellious, and bursting with sexual energy young women, often celebrated as a visual symbol of the rejection of the communist past and its stifling mores.

REVISITING BEAUTY, BODY, AND SEXUALITY IN THE POST-SOCIALIST TRANSITION

It is interesting to trace the growing importance of beauty and style as markers of success for Eastern European women and the complex way in which these markers became connected to the market economy and its commercial engine, advertising. Kristen Ghodsee, for example, shed light on how Bulgarian women employed in the tourism industry became winners in the transition to market economy because they used accrued cultural capital through their strategic contacts with foreign tourists and industry resources.[10] As she explained, cultural capital includes world experiences, education, and other skills related to one's social advancement, but it also means "the acquisition of good taste. . . . This kind of cultural capital is also referred to as symbolic capital, because an individual's public 'performance' of these discerning tastes symbolizes personal 'success' to others in her social milieu."[11]

The concept of good taste and how it relates to one's standing in the social environment appears to be of critical importance to Bulgarian women as it not only determined the way in which others deem one's social status but because it also determined the way in which women themselves establish their own self-worth. And even more so, the matter of taste and sense of worldliness also translated into an appreciation for and personal involvement with beauty and striving for constant improvement of one's physical appearance. Here, the work of Mette Svendsen examining the relationship of beauty and aerobics in post-communist Romania is particularly illuminating.[12] In her ethnographic study of how Romanian women construct their identity through the investment in body care and the consumption of Western practices such as that of aerobic exercise, Svendsen explored the presentational status of the body in the post-communist transition. In doing so, the author argues that for Romanian women, and by extension, for other Eastern European women, "beauty operates as a moral imperative, as a defining feature of femininity, as a dream and a necessity. Taken together, these functions make beautify (or body care) an essential field of activity for women."[13] Moreover, as she discovered in interviewing her subjects, for Romanian women being in shape and being recognized as beautiful not just by means of one's genetic predisposition for beauty, but also, by one's deliberate and purposive cultivation of a beautiful body, is a sign of independence and control that situates female agency in an empowered position, transforming the body into what Svendsen calls "body capital."[14]

It is interesting to explore where women in the post-communist transition first got introduced to sources of "body capital." In the case of Romanian women, as Svendsen pointed out, the practice of aerobics, which had clearly American roots, also led women to consider the American woman as the paradigm of beauty and social standing that women in Eastern Europe should aspire to achieve. This was also true of Bulgarian women who worked in the tourism industry during communism, according to Ghodsee.[15] However, for those women who had little or no opportunity to be in contact with Westerners, I would also argue, Western advertising as well as local advertising that directly borrowed and frequently mimicked images and marketing strategies from Western commercial campaigns, served the same purpose, where images of women stood for tokens of progress, beauty, and liberation, experiences women in Bulgaria, and women across Eastern Europe recognized as vastly missing from their socialist realities.

In the post-socialist transition, the sense of femininity became defined by Western media imports, packed with deliberate images of idealized women, often in a sexually suggestive manner. Two social and cultural by-products of the transition—the proliferation of the "pop-folk" music genre and the deliberate images of womanhood it promoted as well as the rise of the new class of violent elites, known as the mafia—have direct connection to the changing standards of femininity in Bulgaria. In fact, as Ghodsee argued, the two are intrinsically connected as the women who rose to fame as performers of pop folk music were often financially supported and romantically involved with powerful members of the mafia.[16] While both of these phenomena are clearly rife with problematic social consequences, from defining artificial standards of beauty and questionable behavior set forth as models for the young women who watch the sexually provocative music videos, to the hypercommercialism promoted by the conspicuous display of wealth, the more disturbing outcome of this music genre's popularity is the association of women's good looks with the potential to find a rich lover, who in return would guarantee a virtually endless influx of money.

In a similar vein, Vesa Kurkela[17] and Timothy Rice[18] note the importance of the pop folk music genre as both widely celebrated by the Bulgarian masses and simultaneously loathed by the Bulgarian elites. As Kurkela observed in his study of the *chalga* genre and its political and nationalistic overtones, in the cultural climate of the transition that has created an atmosphere favorable to the hyper-reality of *chalga* and pop-folk, politically correct eroticism was frequently and purposefully replaced by sexist soft porn.[19] Kurkela also contended that this trend was particularly noticeable on the covers of music cassettes of various *chalga* groups—in fact, by the *chalga* music producers' own admission, when the *chalga* group's visual appearance was not provocative enough, it would deliberately be switched with a photo of a seductively dressed or totally nude female. In tracing this phenomena back to the cultural history of the region and its complex relationship with the West, Kurkela concluded "after the sultans and fairytale figures with 'Eastern' treasures have been transformed into mafia businessmen and Western luxury goods, the target of irony is no longer the East but the Western life and the dreams connected to it."[20]

A similar phenomenon was also recognized by Jasmina Lukic in her examination of the images of women in Serbian popular media.[21] Lukic argued that in the post-communist media, there were two dominating images of women—those of women connected to powerful politicians and those of women in the entertainment business. The second one was particularly popular as it promoted a very deliberate image of femininity. "Typically, a young girl in very sexy, revealing clothes would sing about her wish of love for 'him' and for 'his mother,' to serve him or wait for him, to forgive him (what required forgiving was not often specified). Thus, somewhat ironically, open sexuality was harnessed to national values and patriarchal traditions that were otherwise quite repressive of sexuality."[22]

The trend towards the revitalization of the ideal of traditional female beauty, the sexualization of the female body and the relegation of women to the sphere of domesticity appeared to be a most natural occurrence during the post-socialist transition. In her study of the role of style and fashion in post-communist Bulgaria, Elitza Ranova noted that instead of embracing feminist thought, many Eastern European women returned to traditional ideas of femininity by stressing innate differences between the sexes and the cultivation of attractive personal appearance.[23] "In this context, care for the self and a 're-sexualization' of the socialist asexual female body is combined with aspiration to the standards of conventional gender roles."[24] Ranova also confirmed that Bulgarian women's tendency to associate their prospects for success and social recognition with their physical appearance, money, and wealth has been intrinsically link to the emphasis on good looks and sexualized bodies in the Bulgarian popular culture.

In her analysis of the changes in gender discourses in the Bulgaria post-communist transition, Krasimira Daskalova noted a similar trend, closely related to the rapid proliferation of women-oriented magazines.[25] While she acknowledged that most of these publications focused narrowly on tips on style and fashion and preoccupied the attention of their female readers with advertisements for products that improve one's body image, including medical procedures such as plastic surgery, she also pointed out that "one message conveyed is that beauty is a woman's most valuable asset, and every woman should try to make herself sexually attractive to men."[26] Simultaneously, Daskalova herself recognized that the complexity of the cultural climate of the transition cannot be reduced to a simple count of the number of beauty magazines in wide circulation and the messages they convey, but she also noted that since consumerism (as an ideology rather than an actual practice) is only now openly advertised in Bulgarian society, it is hard to ignore the curious convergence of growing consumer awareness, a heighted interest in beauty as a paramount goal and the advertising that engenders these ideas.

And although it is tempting to think of the eroticization of the post-socialist female body as a direct consequence of the resurgence of patriarchy and the masculinization of the democratic transition, it must be noted that the process of sexualizing the female body in the post-socialist transition is not entirely a forced-upon act of masculine domination. To support this claim, Denise Roman described the complex and often contradictory myriad influences that women in Eastern Europe become exposed to—rise in traditional Orthodoxy, the return to pre-communist village values, and more importantly, "a provocative *feminine mystique* of Western origins stressing beauty as a paramount goal."[27] These conflicting factors of influence, Roman argues, have led Eastern European women to a rather unexpected turn—the women of post-communism have adopted a new understanding of being feminine that includes rejecting modernization and all the turmoil that it brings, and with it, rejecting the ideas of Western feminism. "If, for feminists following the Western model, emancipation means autonomy and taking a public job, for the average woman emancipation means dependency and the right to be a housewife, thus return to the private sphere."[28] In a similar "backlash" reaction, Eastern European women sought an outlet for a collective "rebellion" against the restrictive range of expressions of femininity sanctioned during communism and the poor aesthetic of their appearance in reverting to a much more provocative dress and sexualized appearance compared to that of communism.

FLIRTING WITH GENDER DISASTER

With the advent of the market economy and the consumer consciousness that it inevitably promotes, the rise of advertising expenditure and the exposure to advertising messages have become commonplace in the post-socialist countries. During the transition, advertising debuted in its purely commercial, revenue-driven form on the Bulgarian market, introduced mainly by international companies looking for profit opportunities in newly emerging markets.[29] This, in turn, led to fundamental changes in the local advertising landscape. Today in Bulgaria advertising expenditure has risen from $4.3 million in 1996 to $325 million in 2007, and even with the economic downturn that has affected the growth of media profitability all over the world, the annual advertising revenue in the media sector alone for 2012 is reported at $256 million, with the potential to grow as the media markets rebound from the crisis.[30] In fact, as David Berry noted, the rise of lifestyle magazines, and perhaps all advertising supported media, is creating a new form of consumption and identity, with "images portraying the 'new woman' and depicting new social freedoms associated with rising patterns of consumption."[31] As a result, the visual space of Bulgarian media, and specifically, Bulgarian advertising, quickly became overpopulated with sexualized depictions of womanhood. Women's bodies became commodified and transformed into valuable currency, used to sell virtually any product. This trend has been particularly magnified and exploited in the advertising campaigns for alcohol, which have brought a number of ethical and legal issues to the forefront of public debate.

Among those campaigns, Vodka Flirt has claimed a top position as an alcohol brand known for its sexually provocative ads, according to a recent survey.[32] The first campaign for the brand started in 2004 when Vodka Flirt launched its pioneering sexually suggestive print campaign, carrying the tagline "It's Open Season." The campaign consisted of a series of photographs of the bare back torsos of female and male models, displaying prominent tattoos of wild animals engaged in a hunting pursuit. The models' bodies, only partially revealed, are photographed locked in a sexually suggestive embrace, with deliberate camera angles (mostly close-ups) and compositional elements of the shots (featuring partial nudity while obscuring the face or the entire body of the female and male models). Clearly, while the portrayals of nudity and gender in these ads appeared in a subtler, less blatant way, it nonetheless featured prominently the metaphor of sexual pursuit—one tattooed animal hunting the other—reinforcing fairly stereotypical, male dominated ideas of gender relations. An illustrative example of this trend is one of the campaign ads in which we see the tattoo of the male model represented by a tiger, engaging in an aggressive pursuit of the vulnerable gazelle tattooed on the female model's arm. This image clearly mimics the power-driven visualization of the hunting pursuit—just like the tiger conquers and subdues the gazelle into submission, so does the male in his pursuit for sexual pleasure.

Once Vodka Flirt broke into the market, it started to engage in a series of much more aggressive campaigns in an attempt to build a distinct brand, simultaneously competing with a ballooning number of vodka brands as well as other alcohol varieties, many of which already used hypersexualized portrayals and sexually risqué behavior to advertise their product. In 2005, Vodka Flirt introduced the "Angels" campaign under the slogan *Are you ready for tonight?*, which focused on the idea of what might be construed as male and female "sexual" angels, inspiring the young men and women featured in the ads to take on new sexual adventures. The campaign had both print and TV components and was considered a success in positioning the brand even further on the alcoholic beverage market in Bulgaria. The common theme in both the print and the video ads centered on the idea that the main task of the "sex" angel is to help men and women connect, leading to a sexual escapade, whether in the back seat of a car, or in a bathroom stall, all the while keeping count of how many successful "hookups" the angels have been able to instigate. A particularly glaring example of the hypersexualized portrayal of women is found in one particular TV spot, in which a young woman is seen dancing by herself, being watched closely by a young man at the bar. As the young man decides to make his move, suddenly the "sex" angel, who is also male, appears, leading the young woman into the man's arms, where the angel physically prompts her to intensify her sexual moves by lifting her skirt up her legs, pulling the strap of her revealing top, virtually leading her into the sexual foreplay. Throughout the scene, the young woman appears in somewhat of a stupor, as though she is not herself, almost as if she does not know what she is doing. The sexual game continues as the angel rushes both the young woman and the man into a cab, where they engage in an even more intense stage of their sexual adventure. Eventually, we see them arrive at their final destination, ready for the final stage of the sexual conquest. At this point, we see the angel being thrown out of the apartment, clearly hinting that while this might be a wild night, it certainly does not involve the presence of the third party during the sexual culmination.

Flirt's follow-up campaigns in 2006 under the slogans *Games for the advanced* and *Savor the memories* featured a series of sexually provocative scenarios in which a few young men, and predominantly women, pursue a variety of sexual escapades while searching for new exciting ways to attract potential partners of the opposite sex. Almost all of the "creative" scenarios of the Flirt ads focused on women, and while men are not entirely absent in the theme of sexual adventures, women—directly or indirectly—are the focus of hypersexualized portrayals. For example, in one of the TV ads for the *Are you ready for tonight?* campaign, two young women clad in nothing but sexy lingerie, are taking turns riding an electric bull, practicing their tantalizing moves under the tagline, "Are you ready for tonight?" At the end of the commercial, one of the girls is shown passing the other, looking disheveled from the physical effort, yet showing visible signs of contempt towards her "competition." Set to the rhythm of extremely seductive dance music, the girls are shown in a series of fragmented extreme close-up, engaging in a most provocative foreplay, riding the bull while moving their bodies in a most seductive fashion to the rhythm of the music. It is difficult to overlook the striking similarity between this ad and for example, an erotic video clip, such as seen on the Playboy TV channel. In fact it is not a surprise that Vodka Flirt also hosts regular parties in partnership with *Playboy* (the magazine has its own very popular Bulgarian edition as well as a nude beauty pageant that airs on Bulgarian television)—for which hundreds of young girls audition for a chance to partake in the festivities, frequently mimicking, if not entirely copying, the scenes of the Vodka Flirt ads. Sexually charged, ready for the night and willing to go the distance, the Bulgarian women from the Flirt campaigns have no difficulty incorporating these very same behaviors into real life.

Yet another ad from the same campaign focused on a young woman who seductively engages in a striptease. Throughout the TV commercial, we see her practicing every calculated move perfectly cued in to yet another sexually seductive tune, from dropping her purse on the floor, to unlacing and kicking off her high heels, to sexily unbuttoning her bra, until the accompanying music comes to a screeching halt. So does her routine, as she messes up her steps and has to start rehearsing from the very beginning, getting ready for the night in knowing every step of the sexual ritual. Going through the tedious process of getting dressed all over again, she is eager to resume her practice, the ultimate goal of which is perfection in the game of sexual tantalization.

Another series of TV ads featured under the campaign slogan *Games for the advanced* took the theme of sexual adventure a step further. In a series of thirty-second TV spots, produced and entirely conceptualized by a Bulgarian advertising team, young men and women are featured in different party settings. In one of the ads, a beautiful young woman ordering a drink is seen, attracting the interest of two men, also sitting at the bar. While she is trying to figure out what to do or perhaps which one of the two to pick as her potential partner, her eyes suddenly lead the viewer behind the bar counter, where an attractive young man, the bartender, is washing a glass. Yet this is no ordinary wash—with his long cleaning brush, covered heavily in foam, the bartender starts to glide the brush in suggestive gestures. Cued to the rhythm of the equally sexually provocative tune, featuring the pleasure moans and heavy breathing of a female vocal, the sexual "game" heats up, as the young woman becomes not only interested, but physically engaged in expressing her growing sense of ecstasy. This visually tantalizing sexual game culminates in the closing scene, during which the bartender removes his shirt to reveal his chiseled body and, of course, also, to dry the glass.

Perhaps the culmination of Flirt's sexual theme was the vodka's 2007 campaign that featured an actual porn star, Hungarian born Brigitta Bulgari. In the TV spot, we see the same tested scenario, featuring a nightclub scene and the adventures one can encounter if consuming the right brand of alcohol. In the beginning of the ad, we see Bulgari and what appears to be her roommate, parting for the night, with the roommate sneaking out and secretly wearing Bulgari's belt, with a heart-shaped buckle, the logo of the vodka brand. From this moment on, the ad unveils in two separate stories—one features the intense sexual foreplay with the experienced porn star who seduces and dominates her man, while the other shows her rather inexperienced, clumsy, but somehow sexually inspired roommate, who sees herself venturing in sexual adventures, prompted by nothing less than the "magical" belt she is wearing. The entire video features a tantalizing series of fragments of intense sexual scenes in which both women are seen leading the sexual game, hinting yet again that in sex there lies power, regardless of how exploitive or manipulate it may be.

OF WATERMELONS AND OTHER PASSION (SEXY) FRUITS

The sexual innuendos in advertising spread infectiously as a winning promotional strategy not only for Vodka Flirt, but also for a variety of brands that were seeking a guaranteed attention hook. Vodka Flirt, judging by its successful sales figures and brand recognition among younger audiences, seemed to have managed to carve a niche. An even more interesting trend was now comfortably nestled on advertising billboards, familiar staples of the visual landscape of post-communism. Kristen Ghodsee noted this trend through the comment of a Bulgarian pensioner who said of advertising billboards: "There is not a blank space left in the country. Everything is an advertisement: the trams, the street signs, the apartment blocs, even private cars!"[33]

Just like every space turned into an opportunity to advertise, advertisements themselves became much more than momentous opportunities to sell a product. They became the physical space in which for the first time Bulgarians, Romanians, and their socialist brothers and sisters can visualize and imagine the elements of desire. Advertising, it was quickly realized by the players on the emerging media market, was not only a means to generate revenues and guarantee financial success; it could also be used as instrument of control, where political and cultural dogma can quickly and easily be transformed by exploiting consumers' passions and desires. In a truly capitalist fashion, advertising crossed over into other media, where products became displayed and evaluated, but also, implicitly infused with gendered codes of behavior. For example, a billboard ad for a brand of sausage automatically, and in the cheapest way, meant that it would feature a beautiful young female model shown consuming the sausage in a highly provocative and sexualized manner. The irony, of course, is that the sausage advertised—known in Bulgarian as *kremvirsh*, a common, relatively inexpensive sausage with a characteristic flavor of spices often emblematic of the long queues and depravity triggered by the collapse of communism—is now symbolically invested with sexual desire when for most men and women who witnessed the transition, the *kremvirsh* was anything but an object of sexual desire. As Borenstein also noted in his study of the use of sex in Russian popular culture, "ads routinely featured half-naked, sexually available beauties to promote the most unlikely of products."[34]

On many occasions, female models featured in Bulgarian ads appeared to have been literally copied from advertisements produced in other parts of the globe, featuring very distinct race or ethnic appearance. For example, a billboard ad for the Italian coffee brand Gimoka, conspicuously named "White Label," featured what appeared to be a woman of color, whose buttock is bare and exposed, with one of her breasts peeking out through the fallen strap of her lingerie. She playfully looks over her shoulder into the direction of the viewer, propped against the oversized image of the coffee beans bag. The logo of the coffee company is tattooed on the right cheek of her buttocks as a heart shape that reads, "I Heart Gimoka." This ad is particularly illustrative not only because it sexualizes and commodifies women's bodies, but also because it racializes an exotic "other," a look and appearance uncommon in the Balkans, and recently only becoming widely popular in the collective imagination because of the inundation of images of ethnic and racially diverse women who are often the subject of the porn gaze. The tendency to build the image of the woman of color as one that is different, exotic, distant, yet available, is a demonstrative strategy of building what Patricia Hill Collins calls the "matrix of domination," which through the discourse of advertising—in this case, explicitly racist not only in its degrading visualization of the black female body, but also in its use of the colonizing term "white label"—becomes as natural and commonsensical as thinking about the pure taste you can enjoy while visualizing an ad that features a bottle of mineral water.[35] The language of sex in this case is also the language of racism, for as Alice Walker has also remarked, "where white women are depicted in pornography as 'objects,' Black women are depicted as animals. Where white women are at least depicted as human bodies if not beings, Black women are depicted as shit."[36]

Here, the commodification of the female body by the advertisement for a "White Label" coffee also serves as a reaffirmation of the precarious conditions of the women's post-socialist gender construction project. It demonstrates what Denise Roman terms the "plural subordination," which defines women's subjectivities as sanctioned by the heterosexist and ethno-racist views more often than not intertwined in the moral compass of the patriarchal norms.[37] And while that plural subordination is certainly creating an unflattering and dangerously exploitive view of women who are seen outside the normative ethno-racial makeup of the fairly heterogeneous societies of the Balkans, it also leads towards the establishment of the view that advertising, and by osmosis, media discourse, is a naturally fitted venue where women's diverse sense of sexuality can be displayed, often in an (pseudo) empowering fashion. This view is resonated by Jacqui True's study of the effects of globalization on the Czech post-socialist transition when she remarked that market consumption has been "promoted by the marketing of gender identities in global culture industries and consumer advertising," introducing the post-socialist subject for the first time not only to the culture of consumption and advertising as its vernacular, but also to new, exotic identities and sexualities, whose presentations in the global flow of media content are bound to serve as solid, yet extremely limited, cultural points of reference.[38]

The commodification of women's bodies, it can be argued, was indeed considered to be the equivalent of achieving a Western look and feel for the advertising campaign, especially when it was masterfully done. While Bulgarians slowly but surely were learning how to make better advertising, they were also learning how to be more sophisticated consumers, and therefore, both the market and the audience demanded a different, yet equally inviting style of presenting ideas, brands, and products. This is where the advertising "Mad Men" of the post-socialist transition discovered that products become desirable not only because they are associated with the female body, but also because of the way in which this association is presented. In other words, the beautiful, and often naked, body of the woman is an important, yet insufficient condition to sell the product—it also required mastering the power of suggestion that Bulgarian and other Balkan advertisers themselves were just beginning to learn. So it was not surprising that American and other Western advertising agencies quickly discovered the unrealized potential of the newly emerging markets of Eastern Europe, whose consumers were not only eager to embrace a new lifestyle that promotes consumption as the exercise of the highest degree of personal freedom, but also were ready to spend every penny they earned to legitimize this spirit of liberated consumerism. As Helen Kelly-Holmes pointed out, "advertising and market discourses teach individuals not just about individual products but also about how to live and participate in the consumer society—thus ensuring its survival."[39]

Because of this obvious commonality between the propaganda of the capitalist society, namely, advertising, and the propaganda of the totalitarian society, the two phenomena, Kelly-Holmes argues, function as natural processes of socialization. More importantly, because advertising also served in post-socialism both as a tool to promote a specific worldview but also as a process that naturalizes Western capitalism, its methods and strategies of selling were virtually unquestioned. In the case of Bulgarian advertising, the growing sophistication of the advertising field itself signaled the spread of the idea of promoting products using not just women's bodies per se, but a very deliberate, more recognized, and further improved version of the post-socialist body.

That idea was perfectly embodied by the rising stars of the *chalga* music genre, as previously noted. These young vixens carved a cultural niche for beauty standards and norms of behavior intrinsic to the Balkan region and yet displayed a strange blend infused with Western aesthetics and an unbridled desire to consume. The trend of combining the sex appeal of the *chalga* stars—fronting unnaturally big and artificially enhanced breasts and a face modeled after Barbie—with specific products, especially brands of liquor, quickly became a guaranteed success formula for the advertising business. The profit was instantaneous and mutually beneficial—not only were the manufacturers of the products gaining brand recognition and generating revenues, but also *chalga* stars themselves essentially became popular culture icons, as their thirty-second commercials became an expression of a collective sexual dream come true.

A great illustrative example comes from the Bulgarian alcohol producer Peshtera, whose commercials for a specific kind of alcohol called mastika were the hit of the summer season in 2006, 2007, and 2008. One of the most popular ad campaigns featured two of Bulgarian's budding pop folk stars—Emilia and Galena—dressed in skimpy bathing suits, designed to make their breasts and private areas look like watermelons. Emilia and Galena are seen either serving drinks at a bar, or just walking along the beach, in very minimal bathing attire. As one of the women is seen frolicking on the beach, three young men whose gazes follow her around seem exceedingly excited and visually aroused by the sight of her attractive physique. They decide to cool off their sexual steam by ordering shots of mastika. At the bar, one of the young men is met by the inviting bartender, wearing a similar watermelon-themed bra. The two exchange flirtatious glances and a sexual pun that is not left unnoticed—"It is watermelon season," says the narrator, and "they are ripe and sweet." The ad is an undisputable testimony to the ultimate marriage of clever marketing and product placement, virtually enabled, delivered, and sealed in the consumers' psyche by the presence and visual provocation of the sexualized body of the chalga singer. Not only are the pop folk divas commodified and reduced to the essence of seasonal fruit, but they are also for all intents and purposes consumable and perishable—once the season is over, and the beauty of these young women's physicality expires, so will their relevance and sexual appeal.

This marriage of convenience between the advertising industry and the pop folk genre has also produced a new breed of song writing and video production intended to further capitalize on the potential of the entrainment stars to secure brand recognition for the advertised product. It is not uncommon to see popular music videos and songs that were practically produced to only offer lengthier commercials for the alcohol brand, which references the name of the brand in the lyrical content, while sexy women are seen dancing around, virtually serving as fillers in the now formulaic pop folk music videos. For example, the "Passion in Crystals" campaign, which was also part of Peshtera's attempt to popularize their brand among media audiences, included the release of a hit single with the same title in which the female singer, Galena, was the topless beauty featured in one of the campaign ads. The ultimate manifestation of the commodification of the *chalga* stars and the sex appeal they exude is found on the cover pages of young girls' writing notepads and other school supplies, graced with retouched photos of the new Bulgarian sex idols.

A particularly interesting look at the importance of these cultural artifices is the perspective offered by the advertisers who "dream up" these very deliberate images of women's sexualities. Gancho Ganchev, director and scriptwriter for the Watermelon campaign was asked to do exactly that when thirteen women from varied walks of life filed a gender discrimination lawsuit against Peshtera and named Ganchev as one of the defendants. Ganchev was quick to justify his actions as nothing more than clever advertising, which relies on harmless puns—albeit sexual in nature, never vulgar or demeaning. Here is what he said in one of his interviews:

> My clients believe *chalga* will attract people who drink mastika. They rely on the sex appeal for years now. They came to me with an idea, wanted two folk stars and action on the beach, and I had to make an interesting story. They have their right to do so. I don't refuse. I make the commercials, but never leave the script to the *chalga* singers. They are only part of it. To deliver the message I actually rely on the actors (the male characters). Do I respect those women? Everyone has the right to have their own opinion.[40]

While trying to paint himself like a true professional, whose one and only responsibility is to deliver a final product his clients approve and find desirable, Ganchev also reveals his seemingly misogynist attitude towards women. Not only is he stating that the main action and therefore, the only believable value in the ad is delivered by his male actors, making the women in the commercial appear to be nothing more than decoration, but he also ambiguously refused to answer the question whether he actually respects the *chalga* stars of this commercial. Another statement was issued by the marketing manager of Peshtera, who echoed a similarly dismissive rationale:

> Thirteen women are not a representative sample of the Bulgarian ladies; we show the beauty of the Bulgarian woman. We don't aim to offend her; to the contrary, we wish to glorify what she has and what we are proud of. I don't think there is anything to be ashamed of. To me it is incomprehensible how showing the beauty of a Bulgarian woman can be deemed offensive.[41]

In an almost word by word recreation of Russia's first sex-magazine editor's justification for using women's bodies to sell magazines, it seems advertisers here are adopting the same patronizing, yet complimentary tone, seemingly embracing the woman as an equal but predominantly as a prized possession. Here, we see the male establishment now also in control of the business of advertising, applying a time-honored technique of favoring the culture of "fraternal patriarchate" that rules by benevolent domination and not direct and forceful oppression. Therefore, when women's nude and sexualized bodies are on display, reduced to fruit and offering nothing more than instant gratification, we must recognize that while sexual desire might be expressed by the audience at large, the decision of how this desire is to be presented to the consumer is guided by a sense of macho-liberation mentality, which is particularly dangerous armed with and motivated by the infallible logic of the commercial market.

Discussing the use of sexual imagery in popular media is definitely not a new line of critical inquiry and has indeed occupied the interests of cultural critics, who also see the role of media, and in this case, advertising, as an important domain for the negotiation of gender and feminism.[42] What is fascinating in the case of Bulgaria, and the Balkan region at large, is just how fast, how smooth, and how natural the transition into "porno-chic" has been. It is important to note that the paradox of this heightened sexuality on display stems not only from the collapse of the controlled cultural and moral norms that characterized the communist regime, but also from the fact that Bulgarian women, and perhaps most women in the region, found in this very unbridled expression of sexuality a new form of rebellion against the established, artificial aesthetic norms and stagnant gender roles prescribed by the communist ideology. As Margaret Gallagher argued, "in the Eastern countries the conventional female feminine image represent a genuine aspiration for a woman tired of the tractor driver image of woman as a worker."[43] And while this rebellious spirit of what some called "the new sexual revolution" might have been a refreshing way to face the challenges of the disintegration of the communist ideology, the new sexual mores of the post-socialist transition were quickly commercialized and the sexual liberation of women was "highjacked" in the interest of selling bodies and pushing brands.

NOTES

1. LaFont, Suzanne, *Women in Transition: Voices from Lithuania* (Albany: State University of New York Press, 1998).
2. Kuntsche, Emmanuel, Kuntsche, Sandra, Knibbe, Ronald, Simons-Morton, Bruce, Farhat, Tilda, Hublet, Anne, Bendtsen, Pernille, Godeau, Emmanuelle, and Demetrovics, Zsolt, "Cultural and Gender Convergence in Adolescent Drunkenness: Evidence from 23 European and North American Countries," *Archives of Pediatrics and Adolescent Medicine*, 165, 2 (2011): 152–58. According to this study, which looked at eighty thousand fifteen-year-olds in twenty-three countries, social control of leisure time and lack of alcohol marketing behind the Iron Curtain had seemed to keep adolescent drunkenness down. But in the 1990s, after the fall of the Berlin Wall, increasingly aggressive marketing of alcohol likely helped contribute to an increase in adolescent alcohol use during that decade.
3. Azhgikhina, Nadezhda, "Women as Presented by the Russian Media," A Report for the *United Nations Department of Economic and Social Affairs (DESA)*, accessed July 13, 2008, http://un.org/documents/ecosoc/cn6/1996/media/rmediaen.htm.
4. Einhorn, Barbara, "Imagining Women: Literature and the Media," in *Cinderella goes to Market: Citizenship, Gender and Women's Movements in East Central Europe*, ed. Barbara Einhorn (London: Verso Publishers, 1993), 1.
5. Kotzeva, Tatyana, "Reimagining Bulgarian Women: The Marxist Legacy and Women's Self-Identity," in *Gender and Identity in Central and Eastern Europe*, ed. Chris Corrin (London: Frank Cass Publishers, 1999), 83–99.
6. Ibid., 95.
7. Ibid.
8. Azhgikhina, "Women as Presented by the Russian Media," 5.
9. Pasca-Harsanyi, Doina, "Women in Romania," in *Gender Politics and Post-Communism: Reflections from Eastern Europe and the Former Soviet Union*, eds. Nanette Funk and Magda Mueller (New York: Routledge, 1996), 44.
10. Ghodsee, Kristen, *The Red Riviera: Gender, Tourism and Post-Socialism on the Black Sea* (Durham: Duke University Press, 2005).
11. Ibid., 13.
12. Svendsen, Mette, "The Post-Communist Body: Beauty and Aerobics in Romania," *Anthropology of East Europe Review*, 14, 1 (1996): 8–15.
13. Ibid., 10.
14. Ibid., 14.
15. Ghodsee, *The Red Riviera*.
16. Ghodsee, Kristen, "Potions, Lotions and Lipstick: The Gendered Consumption of Cosmetics and Perfumery in Socialist and Post-Socialist Urban Bulgaria," *Women's Studies International Forum*, 30, 1 (2007): 26–39.
17. Kurkela, Vesa, "Bulgarian *Chalga* on Video: Oriental Stereotypes, Mafia Exoticism, and Politics," in *Balkan Popular Culture and the Ottoman Ecumene*, ed. Donna A. Buchanan (Lanham, MD: Scarecrow Press, 2007): 143–75.
18. Rice, Timothy, "Bulgaria or Chalgaria: The Attenuation of Bulgarian Nationalism in Mass-Mediated Popular Music," *Yearbook of Traditional Music*, 34 (2002): 25–46.
19. Kurkela, "Bulgarian *Chalga* on Video."
20. Ibid., 172.
21. Lukic, Jasmina, "Media Representation of Men and Women in Times of War and Crisis: The Case of Serbia," in *Reproducing Gender: Politics, Publics and Everyday Life After Socialism*, eds. Susan Gal and Gail Kligman (Princeton: Princeton University Press, 2000), 393–424.
22. Ibid., 399.
23. Ranova, Elitza, "Of Gloss, Glitter and Lipstick: Fashion, Femininity and Wealth in Post-Socialist Urban Bulgaria," *Anthropology of East Europe Review*, 24, 2 (2006): 25–34.
24. Ibid., 28.
25. Daskalova, Krasimira, "Women's Problems, Women's Discourses in Post-Communist Bulgaria," in *Reproducing Gender: Politics, Publics and Everyday Life After Socialism*, eds. Susan Gal and Gail Kligman (Princeton: Princeton University Press, 2000).

26. Ibid., 349.

27. Roman, Denise, "Gendering Eastern Europe: Pre-Feminism, Prejudice, and East-West Dialogues in Post-Communist Romania," *Women's Studies International Forum*, 24, 1 (2001): 56 (emphasis by the author).

28. Ibid., 56.

29. Ibroscheva, Elza, "Caught Between East and West? Portrayals of Women and Gender in Bulgarian Television Advertisements," *Sex Roles: Journal of Research*, 57, 5–6 (2007): 409–18.

30. *World Trends in Advertising*, 2007. Published by the World Advertising Research Center (WARC); IREX *Media Sustainability Index*, 2012, accessed July 11, 2012, http://www.irex.org/project/media-sustainability-index-msi-europe-eurasia.

31. Berry, David, "Is Popular Culture Subversive in Romania? An Assessment of Teenage Girls' and Women's Magazines," *Slovo*, 16, 2 (2004): 137.

32. The study, known as ELSA, was a project initiative of STAP (the National Foundation for Alcohol Prevention in the Netherlands), supported by the European Council and released in 2007. It collected data from twenty-four European countries, including Bulgaria, in order to assess and report on the enforcement of national laws and self-regulation of the advertising and marketing of alcoholic beverages in EU member states. This study was also the first of its kind for Bulgaria since its accession to the European Union.

33. Ghodsee, Kristen, "Potions, Lotions and Lipstick," 33.

34. Borenstein, Eliot, *Overkill: Sex and Violence in Contemporary Russian Popular Culture* (Ithaca and London: Cornell University Press, 2008), 88.

35. Collins, Patricia Hill, *Black Feminist Thought* (London: Routledge, 2000).

36. Walker, Alice, "Coming Apart," in *Take Back the Night: Feminist Papers on Pornography*, ed. Laura Lederer (New York: William Morrow and Company, 1980), 103.

37. Roman, Denise, *Fragmented Identities: Popular Culture, Sex, and Everyday Life in Post-Communist Romania* (Lanham, MD: Lexington Books, 2003), 109.

38. True, Jacqui, *Gender Globalization and Post-Socialism: The Czech Republic After Communism* (New York: Columbia University Press, 2003), 103.

39. Kelly-Holmes, Helen, "The Discourse of Western Marketing Professionals in Central and Eastern Europe: Their Role in the Creation of a Context for Marketing and Advertising Messages," *Discourse and Society*, 9, 3 (1998): 342.

40. Guineva, Maria, "Sex, Chalga and Alcohol: Sexual Harassment or Bulgaria's Best Selling Mix," Novinite.com, August 26, 2009, accessed February 8, 2008, http://www.novinite.com/view_news.php?id=107166.

41. Ibid.

42. Winship, Janice, "Women Outdoors: Advertising, Controversy and Disputing Feminism in the 1990s," *International Journal of Cultural Studies*, 3, 1 (2000): 27–55.

43. Gallagher, Margaret, "Velvet Revolution, Social Upheaval, and Women in European Media," in *Women Empowering Communication: A Resource Book on Women and the Globalization of Media*, eds. Margaret Gallagher and Lilia Quindoza-Santiago (London: World Association for Christian Communication, 1993), 117.

Chapter Five

Sex and Politics

Consuming Women's Bodies

The velvet revolution that swept through the Eastern bloc and brought the demise of communism held a remarkably bright promise for all Soviet citizens—authoritative regimes were demolished and the potential of democracy revived the enthusiasm of women and men alike to lay the foundation of a new, just social system of equities. However, that bright promise has not delivered. Instead, patterns of marginalization and increasing social and cultural pressures have become obvious across Eastern Europe: diminished access to the labor market, increasing vulnerability to crime, including human trafficking and forced prostitution, loss of family-oriented social benefits, resurgence of traditional values, but more importantly, a weak parliamentary representation accompanied by a boom of oversexualized portrayals of women in advertising and the media.

Perhaps the most evident manifestation of the hardships of the post-socialist transition for women can be found in their deficient participation in the political discourse. This is particularly evident in the case of Bulgaria, where women's equality was identified with full employment, social benefits, and quota representation in the Communist Party.[1] However, these figures stood for "tokenism of the worst kind," resulting a communist model of pseudo-emancipation.[2] The fall of the Berlin Wall in 1989 and the ensuing democratization did not translate in big qualitative gains either. In the current political climate of transition, Bulgarian women, while still present in power, are often reduced to political posts of less significant scale as the post-socialist parliamentary elections exemplify.[3]

In addition to weak political representation, Bulgarian women face another formidable, yet subtler, obstacle in their struggle to assert a leading position in society—a growing gender bias in the media. Studies of the politics, gender, and media dynamics worldwide reveal that media coverage of female politicians is more negative, tends to focus more on appearance than issues, and in general reinforces deeply rooted social stereotypes.[4] In Eastern Europe, and Bulgaria in particular, these trends have been further amplified by a media system in transition, which meanders between sensationalism and complete rejection of state control over content and distribution. It is a system where intellectual journals are readily found nestled among pornographic magazines and where newspapers compete through "sexying" up news stories, using gender-biased language to win audiences and earn advertising revenues.

The purpose of this chapter is to look at what part gender plays in the portrayal of female politicians in Bulgarian media. In particular, we examine the press coverage of women politicians in the 2005 Parliament elections, asking whether the portrayals of women politicians circulate gender stereotypes and if so, what stereotypes tend to prevail in the coverage of female politicians in the Bulgarian press.

This is important because as John Corner suggested, the media have become the public sphere in which the identity of the politician as a "person of qualities" is constructed, and the strength of these media-performative criteria are often such as to disqualify certain candidates either from becoming public political figures at all or at least from competing for high office.[5] This is a particularly alarming trend in Eastern Europe where loss of state protections and welfare privileges combined with weak political representation of women might lead to a dramatic shift in the social positioning of women in the post-socialist transition. More importantly, how these trends are going to materialize for women across Eastern Europe will become the litmus test of the success of the post-socialist transition.

This chapter is based on a textual analysis to determine what type of press coverage Bulgarian female politicians receive. Textual analysis has evolved from a long tradition of literary and linguistic analyses of texts.[6] According to John Fiske, a media piece becomes a text "at the moment of reading, that is when its interaction with one of its many audiences activates some of the meanings/pleasures that it is capable of provoking."[7] A text, in this sense, can be polysemic, thus producing a multiplicity of meanings depending on the social conditions of reception.[8] The choice of a less "objective" methodology in comparison to quantitative content analysis was done with the intention to discern the implicit meanings, themes, and patterns used to describe women politicians. It is a technique that eschews quantification in favor of an inductive search of deep social and historical meanings and interpretations.

In order to develop a full understanding of how female politicians were portrayed, issues of the top Bulgarian newspaper *Trud* were collected and analyzed. The press was preferred over television because it tends to be the main venue for in-depth political information, especially in pre- and post-election periods and because Bulgarians are very avid newspaper readers—an astonishing 850,000 members of a population of less than eight million people read a newspaper on a daily basis. *Trud* alone was selected for this study because, as Madelene Danova points out, it is not only the newspaper with the largest circulation in Bulgaria, but is also foreign-owned and can be seen as representing the current process of globalization. "*Trud* represents also a very interesting 'glocal event,' combining the characteristics of a serious broadsheet with features of a sensational paper; very serious features and newsroom work appear alongside a barely dressed beauty on its 32nd page."[9]

The sample of articles analyzed in this study is comprised of all *Trud* issues for the period May 28, 2005, to July 23, 2005. The sampling period was selected to cover twenty-eight days before and after the 2005 parliamentary elections. Both authors read and analyzed the electronic versions of *Trud*, which are the exact reproductions of the full-color, print versions. The analysis included content from the entire newspaper, including headlines, articles, profiles, editorials, pictures, and cartoons. Content using gendered nouns or adjectives, metaphors, and descriptions of the candidates' psychological or physical characteristics or competency were underlined and, using an inductive approach, were gradually arranged into five emergent categories: physical appearance, credentials and performance, attributions, gender of the reporters, and photographs of women politicians.

MEDIA PORTRAYALS OF WOMEN POLITICIANS FROM AROUND THE WORLD

Although the women, politics, and communication dynamics has received considerable attention in recent years,[10] little has been written on press coverage of women politicians or even the media's role in covering female politicians in Eastern Europe. While different in methods and approaches, the existing studies foreground the importance of gender, but also underscore the paucity of research on how the press, as a core intermediary in contemporary politics, defines and presents women politicians.[11]

An important contribution to the study of media coverage of women politicians from around the world comes from Pipa Norris, who observed that although sex stereotyping was not always clearly delineated in news coverage, occasionally sexist remarks were made of women leaders as "conciliatory, compassionate, and sensitive while men were regarded as strong, ambitious, and tough."[12] Norris also found that women politicians were portrayed "as ambitious, effective, and often more confrontational than their rivals."[13]

In the United States, Kim Kahn's comparative examinations of the 1982 and 1986 Senate elections revealed that women candidates not only received less press attention than men, but that the type of coverage they received was qualitatively different, concentrating more on their political viability than their stance on political issues.[14] In an experimental study examining how press coverage and voter stereotypes influence the electability of women running in senatorial and gubernatorial races, Kahn found that the press does differentiate between male and female candidates, and that those differences are more pronounced in Senate races.[15] In both types of races, however, women candidates received more horserace coverage and less issue coverage, which in the case of Senate races augmented sex stereotypes and "lead people to view women as weaker leaders and less viable" candidates.[16]

Examinations of media portrayals of women politicians from around the world foreground, again, the importance of gender. In the United Kingdom, Karen Ross and Annabelle Sreberny analyzed media portrayals of British MPs only to observe media's obsession with the physicality of women politicians and their persistent domestication as part of "media's insistence on locating them only in feminine domains."[17] In Australia, and to a lesser degree in New Zealand, women politicians are often bestowed by the media the status of celebrities, which, however, upon their first mistake is marred by criticisms and judgmental evaluations.[18] In a study of female politicians in Singapore, Phyllis Chew examined how newspapers, through the use of gender stereotypes and language, constructed women politicians as anti-political.[19] And although female politicians in Hong Kong seem to receive more positive coverage by the press, their image of perfect women is codified by Confucian gender ethics and thus used to nullify any challenges to the status quo.[20] In a more recent study of women politicians in the United Kingdom, Australia, and South Africa, Karen Ross aptly summarized the overall state of media representations of women by pointing out that "the sadness and frustration is that after more than twenty years of documenting the media's representation of women so little has changed."[21]

The authors' extensive search of the literature revealed that very little has been written on the media's role in covering female politicians in Eastern Europe. While several studies have attempted to assess the factors affecting political representation of women in the former communist bloc,[22] none of them examines the role of the media in this process. A few studies have addressed the issue of gender in media coverage of women. For instance, Adla Isanovic explored gender representations in the daily newspapers of Bosnia, Herzegovina, Croatia, and Serbia to find out that women are hardly visible in stories that "make the news," but their visibility is much higher in stories of media, cultural, or artistic nature where they are often depicted in mostly decorative fashion.[23] As the author stated, "we can conclude by paraphrasing Snjezana Milivojevic—in all three countries the face of the serious news is male, and the body of the entertainment is female."[24] Another study that sheds light on the media coverage of female politicians in Eastern Europe is Madelene Danova's contribution to a recent report on stereotypes of women in Bulgarian media. In her critical comparison of two Bulgarian newspapers' coverage of female politicians, Danova argues that female politicians are presented as private consumers rather than public figures—a result of a post-modern globalizing discourse.[25]

Marusa Pusnik and Gregor Bulc also studied gender identity formation in Eastern Europe, albeit from a different perspective. Instead of focusing on the media itself, the authors examined how Slovenian women politicians' self-presentations in the press reflect the established hegemonic discourse through stereotypical expressions of femininity.[26] Denise Roman, on the other hand, has examined the role of professional norms in the biased media coverage of female politicians in Romania.[27] This bias, she argues, results from a male-dominated concept of the journalistic profession and the socialization of reporters into the predominantly misogynist ideology of the newsroom. Examples include newspapers featuring women's profiles mostly in the context of domesticity, not as directing a business or having political power. What is more, strong women are generally demonized, creating a fearful and often, hugely unattractive, image of women in power—one that is not human, or at least, not feminine. Indeed, to be a feminist is considered, even by strong women of political authority, shameful and offensive, and in many ways, immoral, or as a residue of the communist past.[28] Powerful women are also suspected of "being men" beyond metaphorical representations, or androgynous, such as the former Turkish premier, Tansu Ciller, former British Prime Minister, Margaret Thatcher, or former US Secretary of State, Madeleine Albright.[29]

THE GENDERED MEDIATION THESIS

Media play a crucial role in the formation of voters' opinions and perceptions, given that few people have the chance to meet in person candidates aspiring for political office. Most people learn about the political candidates from media reports, not first-hand experiences. Differential media coverage, as Kim Kahn observed, could carry "real consequences for voter information and candidate preference."[30] In this context, media's role in presenting or "framing" political candidates deserves special consideration.

The practice of assigning meaning and organizing reality is a central theme of a theoretical approach to news called framing analysis. The sociological underpinnings of the theory can be traced back to Erving Goffman, who argued that framing could be subject to all forms and levels of human experience.[31] In mass communication research, frames have been defined as "the central organizing idea for news content that supplies context and suggests what the issue is through the use of selection, emphasis, exclusion, and elaboration."[32] Framing, therefore, suggests that, as part of their daily routine of simplifying complex issues for audiences, journalists make decisions about what information to include or exclude from their stories, as well as how to present an issue.[33] Whether this process is conscious or not, the body of framing research suggests that the way an issue is framed bears a direct relation to the way audiences perceive it.[34]

Moreover, this assumption has given grounds to the theoretical thesis of gendered mediation.[35] The gendered mediation thesis rests on the assumption that "the way in which politics is reported is significantly determined by a male-oriented agenda that privileges the practice of politics as an essentially male pursuit. The image and language of mediated politics, therefore, supports the status quo (male as norm) and regards women politicians as novelties."[36] The gendered nature of news can be traced to the "gendered structure of news production."[37] Indeed, television news has been likened to a "masculine soap opera,"[38] using metaphors that often evoke the comparison of politics to a battle, a boxing match, or a horserace.[39] As such, the news is not simply reflecting the fact that politics is still very much a man's world; it is playing an active role in perpetuating a stereotypically masculine conception of politics and politicians.[40] This process is further amplified by the fact that the political economy of the newsroom and the professional rituals of the journalistic profession call for a masculine approach to reporting politics that includes adopting journalistic conventions, which by the nature of the trade are considered masculine by both female and male reporters.[41]

In order to gauge to what extent gendered mediation played a role in the treatment of women MPs in Bulgaria, the focus of this chapter falls on the 2005 Parliamentary election. While the elections registered the lowest voter turnout since the fall of the Berlin Wall (56 percent of registered voters participated), they brought 21 percent of women MPs to the 40th National Assembly. This number, although fairly high compared to other nations in Europe and the world, was nonetheless alarming, considering that the 2005 elections saw a dramatic increase in the number of women running for office—in 2001, 243 women were on the election ballots, compared to 713 female parliamentary candidates in 2005, an increase of 65 percent.[42]

BEAUTY AS A POLITICAL QUALIFICATION

One point stands out in the pre-election coverage of women candidates for MPs—coverage was scarce, and if present, it was invariably refracted through the prism of gender stereotypes. This is how one *Trud* article introduced the female candidate for one of the regions:

> The tax service specialist finally gathered the courage to participate in the elections as an independent candidate. The fifty-two-year-old Vesselina Bozhykova, mother of two, gave the start to her campaign in her apartment. In this way she wants to show that her house is open to everybody and she has nothing to hide from the voters.[43]

Not only that, but as Shannon Woodcock has argued, "'superwomen' are accepted as modern version of the traditional woman who raises the family at home as long as they are perceived as effortlessly taking on the public role only in addition to the primary task of motherhood and private care."[44]

The only extensive profile of a woman politician in the pre-election coverage of *Trud* featured the "beautiful girl" Denitza Dimitrova, who at twenty-seven, was personally invited by the prime minister to join him in the "election whirlpool."[45] The article described her as a disabled woman who would win the elections with the same "charm, intelligence and aura" that won her the title of "Miss Spring 2004" for disabled women. Denitza's qualifications, an accounting degree with honors and knowledge of four languages, were virtually drowned by detailed descriptions of her love for flowers, her ability to maintain an impeccably clean kitchen, and her weakness for Internet surfing. The "charming girl" had nothing to say about her stance on political issues besides that, if elected, she would like to work on social matters and better representation of people with disabilities.[46]

An article published after the elections spoke of Bulgarian female politicians as "the girls of parliament," downplaying the level of maturity, expertise, and political clout Bulgarian female politicians bring to the table. "There is going to be grace, charm and vanity, because gals from a wide range of occupations—from politicians to fashion models—are riding atop of many election tickets," the author wrote, trivializing not only the immense effort put forth by female candidates to enter the electoral race, but also clearly implying that women politicians win because of their attractiveness and charm and not because of their qualifications and preparation to guide domestic and international policy decisions.[47] A series of commentaries focusing mainly on the physical appearance and style of the new members of parliament titled "Vanity Fair" appeared in *Trud*, describing the reaction of the male members at the sight of their female counterparts—the men were described as "resting their eyes," "washing their faces in the sight of beauty," "pleasantly distracting themselves," and "stumbling over signs of beauty." Although the article did not identify an author, the style was clearly gender-biased—women MPs were described as "strutting on the red carpet," "super elegant," and having "delicate faces." As the article summed it up, "if beauty is said to save the world, then this year's parliament is certainly in safe hands."[48]

At the same time, if a female politician fails to exhibit what are deemed as highly desirable physical characteristics of femininity, the press takes immediate notice. An interesting case at hand is Ekaterina Mihaylova, who suffered a severe media backlash in her first term as one of the leaders of the Union for Democratic Forces (UDF). Mihaylova, who often stood shoulder to shoulder with Nadezhda Mihaylova, the head of the right-wing UDF and former foreign minister, was often ridiculed for her lack of grace, beauty, and style. In fact, the media coined a rather condescending nickname for Ekaterina Mihaylova—Klasnata—a derogative term used to describe a rigid, communist teacher, whose ideologue behavior and lackluster appearance would plague her leadership skills and political abilities. Interestingly, in the 2005 elections Ekaterina Mihaylova underwent a dramatic makeover of her image and demeanor, appearing more feminine and less threatening, which immediately attracted the attention of the media, placing her among the frontrunners for nomination in her political party. The press, following closely her remade image, noted that Mihaylova is finally looking "more human, more down to earth," "visibly beautified," thus implying that exhibiting male qualities is a risky move that could potentially damage one's political career.[49] Ironically, her political qualifications were legitimized by nothing short of a fashion makeover, topped with the appropriate media blitz.

A sidebar story in the same style section of the paper focused on the oldest female member of Parliament and leader of the People's Union, Anastasia Moser. In describing her personality and preferences for hairstyle and conservative clothing, the article makes a passing mention of the fact that as the only female member of this parliamentary group, she has also been its leader for the past six years, yet spends a disproportionate amount of time discussing her presence in the Union as the only sign of elegance and class. Moser's political wisdom and extensive experience, therefore, give way to a lengthy discussion of her conservative hairstyle and dress, implying that a clear connection must be established between a woman politician's appearance and her personal ideology and political agenda.

In a similar vein of sexual innuendos, female politicians themselves partake in the process of gender stereotyping. For example, Dora Yankova, the mayor of the city of Smolyan, who was one of the few women invited to participate in the negotiation of a ruling coalition between the King's movement and the CB, said, "it's natural to be courted by the member of parliament," likening the process of political negotiation with the opposing political factions to a dating game—a metaphor the press finds easily adaptable to its style of reporting.[50]

Chapter 5

CREDENTIALS AND PERFORMANCE

The analysis revealed that when women's credentials are discussed, *Trud* does make a mention of the educational and professional preparation of the female politicians. Indeed, all women candidates for parliament had more than satisfactory qualifications as lawyers, doctors, accountants, or engineers. Yet their qualifications, when included, seem to always appear in the context of their femininity. For example, in two consecutive articles that ran on Maria Kapon, voted as Miss Parliament (by a jury of four male journalists and one female political party speaker), the reporter makes a mention of her extensive line of professional credentials—an economist, production manager, and physics engineer, she has worked in a variety of important positions both in the business world and in industrial production. However, most of the report is focused on her important family affiliation of being married into a famous family and being a great wife and a mother. Kapon is described as "blonde but not in 'the blonde' joking sense of the words," "the fist in the velvet glove," "the blonde fury," and "having aristocratic taste."[51] Similarly, in an article discussing the political qualifications of the newly elected forerunner of the Union of Democratic Forces (UDF), Eleonora Nikolova, she is described as "window display case" of over twenty-eight years of successful marriage, implying that her ability to juggle both her professional responsibilities and the responsibilities of family life are significant indicators of her ability to perform on the political scene.[52]

Moreover, when female politicians' performance is discussed, their strengths are often closely linked to their ability to exhibit masculine qualities, implying that a successful woman politician is successful mainly because she is unfeminine. Thus, for instance, the former regional governor Maria Neikova was described as "fighting like a man" against the challenges of recent floods in the area, while at the same time she expressed as her greatest wish the chance to take a break, if time permits.[53] On another occasion, an analysis of the political viability of the leader of the Union of Democratic Forces, Nadezhda Mihaylova, gave her credit as the owner of the "most charming smile amongst the parliamentary ladies," but stated that one of her leadership weaknesses, "which are not unusual for women leaders," was her ability "to downplay rational arguments in favor of emotional ones, especially when it means forming a circle of favorites. Nadezhda likes to flirt. Allowing flirtations with her political partners, sometimes subjecting her political behavior to her intimate attractions, Nadezhda makes wrong assessments not only of their capabilities, but also about their realistic professional chances."[54] The analysis concluded, "In fact, it is not true that a female leader has significantly less chances at making it in the typically male world of big politics. Yet she has to be in the class of Margaret Thatcher, or possess the character and energy of the current [now former] Ukrainian Prime Minister Yulia Tymoshenko."[55]

The findings suggest that even when female politicians are asked to discuss issues of political importance, their responses are often trivialized and refracted through the prism of gender stereotyping. For example, when the negotiation process of establishing a ruling coalition after the elections was initiated, *Trud* speculated that the former deputy prime minister under NDSV's government, Lidia Shuleva, should be nominated by her party as the minister of defense, a post that has never been occupied by a female minister before. To turn this into a curious precedent, the newspaper ran a front page photo of Shuleva, holding a machine gun, appearing as inept in handling a weapon as Michael Dukakis appeared uncomfortable wearing a helmet and navigating a tank. Shuleva was never selected for this post, but a number of other female MPs were indeed nominated for inclusion in the structure of the newly proposed government, all occupying what have been seen as "natural" feminine areas of politics—EU integration, youth and sports, and labor and social relations, with one exception, foreign affairs.

ATTRIBUTIONS

One recurrent theme throughout *Trud*'s coverage of female politicians was the trivializing and familiarizing language used to refer to them. Female politicians were regularly referred to by first name only, as opposed to by first and last name, or by last name alone. For example, out of sixty-four mentions of the leader of the Union of Democratic Forces, Nadezhda Mihaylova, thirty-eight mentions, or 59 percent of all news reports after the elections referred to her as "Nadezhda," while two stories referred to her as "Hubavoto Nade," or "Pretty Nade," which is an abbreviated, diminutive version of the name Nadezhda, linguistically reserved for use only by relatives and very close friends. In fact, in a brief article on media coverage of the last elections, *Trud* reported that the Prime Minister Simeon Saxecoburgotski and Nadezhda Mihaylova were the top two politicians the press "likes to keep an intimate tone with," which the report concluded indicates "lack of distance and respect."[56] In Simeon's case, the first name attribution can be linked to the fact that, prior to his return to Bulgaria, most people knew him as the young king "Simeoncho," which is a diminutive of Simeon.

GENDER AND THE JOURNALISTIC PROFESSION

The textual analysis also revealed that the majority of articles written about female politicians were written and reported by female reporters or had no author with the assumption that a group of people contributed to that same piece. The elections coverage was usually marked by a specially created graphic "Parliamentary Elections 2005," further adorned with an appealing image of the Parliament building and the year 2005. In accordance with beat reporting practices, the names of four female reporters kept reappearing in the bylines of the election reports, which is not only indicative of the fact that the journalistic profession is popular among women in Bulgaria, but also points to the extent to which female journalists partake in the process of gender stereotyping. The tone of the reports and their gender-biased language were not mitigated by the fact that they were written by female reporters.

On the other hand, in some instances, it seemed that gender similarities allowed for added familiarization and trivialization. Two glaring examples are the profile of Denitza Dimitrova and the introduction of the tax specialist who "braved" politics. In both cases the pieces were written by two of the female beat reporters who contributed to most of *Trud*'s election coverage. In contrast, most of the analyses and commentaries were written by men and as such, support the trend toward continued gender discrimination in this profession even after the fall of communism. The analysis of Nadezhda Mihaylova's political credentials, for example, was written by a male reporter. While mixed teams of reporters were also present, there were no differences in the frames used to cover female politicians. The gender of the reporter seemed to exert no effect on the stereotypical mode of writing and reporting.

This observation foregrounds the prevalence of hegemonic ideologies that circulate widely in Bulgarian press newsrooms. The presence of gender-biased portrayals of women politicians only points to the fact that women journalists become universally socialized in the conventions of the profession.[57] They often accept their roles willingly, without critically examining or questioning the damaging effect of using such gender stereotyping language and portrayals.

PHOTOGRAPHS OF WOMEN POLITICIANS

The analysis also indicated that women politicians received significantly less photographic coverage than their male counterparts, and that when they did it was invariably framed within the standards of Western heterosexual femininity. In general, politicians who were more photogenic—that is, younger and better looking—received more than the usual mugshot. Photographs of women politicians performing their regular duties were a rarity unless they provided for a nice opportunity to reinforce the discrepancies between the two genders. Thus women politicians were usually shown as giving awards to college students, riding bikes with four-year-olds, wearing traditional Bulgarian outfits, dancing, making pottery, or playing the violin.

Out of the 110 photographs of women politicians, only four made it to the front page. The only front-page photograph before the elections was that of Nina Chilova, the Minister of Culture, and it was placed right next to a photo of Nikolai Svinarov, at the time, Acting Defense Minister. The big headline above the photos read "Two Chilovas are Equal to One Svinarov" suggesting not only that Chilova was half the weight of Svinarov, but also alluding that she was half the politician as well. The article on page two explained that Chilova's drastic weight loss of 5 kilograms (10 pounds) in the last three months was due to her hard work, suggesting that the job was probably too demanding for her. The reporters continued their speculations about the minister's weight as follows: "The weight loss of the already skinny minister is so obvious that even her colleague Nikolai Vassilev was swearing in front of our reporters that she had lost 7 kilograms. But he did not reveal how he knew her weight."[58]

The other three front-page photographs of women politicians followed the already established frame of reference—a cutout of Lidia Shuleva holding a gun and appearing inadequate, and two photographs of Anastasia Mozer "in action," one showing how she "receives orders from the Commander" (Kostov) and the other revealing her transgression when she attempted to cast a vote in the parliament with somebody else's voting card.

In some instances, the stereotypical coverage women politicians received was reinforced by striking choices of imagery. In a short article about the visit of two parliamentarian hopefuls to an agrarian exhibit, the readers were presented with a picture of a cow with a big ribbon coupled with a discussion of how there were "positive fluids" between the candidates and the "tame cow."[59] In sharp contrast, the rest of the page shows male candidates participating in marathons, driving sports cars, donning soccer t-shirts, or simply posing majestically.

THE FEMALE CANDIDATE SELLING HERSELF

The political realities of the transitions have indeed resulted in new challenges and opportunities for women's advancement in the political realm. More recently, while countries like Bulgaria have been frequently covered in the news as places where women's rise to power has been particularly notable and indicative of the positive climate that the transition has created for females who want to venture in the world of politics and business,[60] other countries have been faced with significant roadblocks on their path to achieving higher numbers of female representation at the levels of political power. One such country is Poland. In fact, in a 2011 report from the *Council of Europe's Steering Committee for Equality between Women and Men*, Poland was cited as one of the countries, where the reduced number of women in parliament and local government has necessitated the introduction of a quota system, which for the first time required political parties to include 30 percent of women on their lists of candidates for the parliamentary elections that were held in October 2011. Instead of embracing this quota as an opportunity to promote women's participation in the political process, journalists, who saw this as a golden opportunity to organize a game, invited readers to vote for the most beautiful candidate for the Sejm (the lower house of the Polish Parliament). "We invite you to participate in our poll. Together we choose a lady that deserves to be called the most beautiful candidate for the Sejm of Maloposka! Let's have some fun!"[61] The results were later published on the "current events" page, where the female candidates were featured by their respective headshot, plus the rating they were given.

This incident clearly exemplifies the media's tendency to reduce the relevance of women as legitimate political players, stressing physical appearance, specifically beauty, as the one distinctive attribute, and therefore, most qualifying characteristic, that female candidates can offer stepping into the realm of public governance. This attitude of treating women in the realm of politics as a spectacle, rather than a legitimate force, is also echoed in the chambers of power themselves, where male politicians far too frequently are overheard uttering derogatory remarks addressed at their female counterparts. To illustrate, consider Ukraine's Prime Minister's remarks concerning the role of women in legislature: "Some say our government is too large; others that there are no women. . . . There's no one to look at during cabinet sessions: they're all boring faces. With all respect to women, conducting reforms is not women's business."[62] Mykola Azarov's attack against women's suitability for high office was not simply a slip of the tongue as they reflect the Ukrainian's administration growing macho stance—early in 2010 Ukraine's President Viktor Yanukovych publicly "ordered" the leader of the opposition Yulia Tymoshenko to "demonstrate her whims in the kitchen," prompting Peter Williams of *Foreign Policy* to comment on his blog, "For anyone who just can't wait any longer for the premier of the next season of *Mad Men*, the next best thing might be following the Ukrainian political scene."[63]

Often dismissed both by journalists and editors alike as working under the common assumptions of the journalistic profession, the impact of gendered mediation on the female political candidates themselves and their style of campaigning is anything by trivial. Stereotyped by the news media for being female, and therefore, less able and qualified to do the "hard job" of running the country, female politicians themselves often play down their own political presence by internalizing and co-opting the image of what Julia Baird described as "media tarts."[64] As a result, female politicians in the region, particularly younger candidates, adopted a new strategy to make themselves "politically marketable." Armed with the help of brand managers turned political consultants, these young candidates transformed their candidacy into a new kind of spectacle, guaranteed to get them a spot on the news radar. In short, female candidates across the region in a post-feminist sense of empowerment have not only become "media tarts," but also "sex kittens," whose sexual power translates into a convincing and indisputably attractive novel contribution to a political realm tainted by the monolithic aftertaste of socialist grayness.

When the Polish singer turned political candidate Katarzyna Szczolek launched her campaign, she created a media buzz with her racy photo shoot, redefining the concept of the same old boring propaganda poster. On her billboard, Szczolek appears reclined on a beach, wearing nothing but a sexy bathing suit, fashioning an appearance suited for the pages of the Victoria's Secret catalog. Her slogan stated, "Beautiful, independent, competent," equating her most cherished physical attribute as empowering as her qualifications, which also include her youth and her education.

Similarly, another Polish female candidate for public office, Katarzyna Lenart, pushed the envelope of "political seduction" a step further by launching a YouTube video campaign advertisement, featuring her performing what is essentially a striptease. Tuned to the rhythm of seductive music, Lenart is seen provocatively removing an item of clothing at a time, as if symbolically shedding the conservative social norms of her surroundings. At the end, stripped down to her lingerie, she makes a final gesture removing her bra, when the camera fades to black and a red "Censored" sign appears over her pixelated bosom. The grand finale is offered by the tease line, "You want more? Vote for SLD [Lenart's party affiliation]. Only we can do more." Lenart's video is another example of how political empowerment is coded as having clear sexual overtones, creating the dubious association between seduction and political persuasion, as if the two are now legitimate counterparts. Lenart offered her own response to the media attention to her campaign: "I thought it was time to cause a stir. My campaign targets young people, and young people are only interested in controversial stuff, unfortunately," she told *Gazeta Wyborcza.*[65] Using the now conventional refrain that young people yearn for the controversial, even if that means sexualizing politics, Lenart exposes what she thinks is a new, modern identity for the young woman and the young female politician.

A similar process of sexy-ing politics by exposing one's most admirable body attributes is also taking place in places like Romania and Estonia. In Romania, Minister of Tourism Elena Udrea appeared on the November 2011 cover of *Taboo* fashion magazine, wearing a tightly fitting rubber dress, resembling a dominatrix outfit, knee-high leather boots, and sporting a bleached blonde "Charlie's Angels" hairdo. The magazine, appropriately named "taboo," used Udrea's image to promote its issue dedicated to the world's most powerful women, building a connection between her oozing sexual power, her exaggerated physical attractiveness, and her body posture, appearing as if she is carrying the weight of the globe on her shoulders. Udrea diffused the harsh criticism of her appearing in this manner by stating, "I would like very much to see that in Romania, one of the biggest political parties is open enough to propose a courageous and skillful woman in the most important state functions," describing herself as political "pariah" because of her gender.[66] Udrea further essentialized the stereotype that beauty is a woman's most powerful attribute, and therefore one that must be nurtured and encouraged, when she reportedly traveled to meet flood refugees with a truck loaded with high-heeled shoes for the affected women to make them feel "beautiful."

Not to be outdone in its ability to produce a cadre of young and beautiful female politicians, Estonia has also witnessed some unusual political campaigning. In this case, the female politician in question used the cover of the Estonian edition of *Playboy* to protest accusations that she has squandered EU funds for her own personal gain. Posing nude on the cover of the magazine, using only her arms to conceal her bare breasts, Anna-Maria Galojan used her body both as an instrument of political propaganda and a commodity for commercial gain. Stripping naked on the cover was her way of saying she had nothing to hide, while simultaneously repositioning political discourse into discourse through and about sex, thus masterfully divulging attention away of the dark cloud hanging over her political post. This trend, Helena Goscilo argued, leads to the perpetuation of a "malestream" that treats women entering spheres of public visibility usually reserved as male area of dominance, as novelty acts and as such, as either trivialized, or delegitimized through assigning women's roles and behavior properly situated within private activities where femininity is to be nurtured.[67] This, in turn, leads to normalizing gender stereotyping as a cultural mechanism, further desensitizing people to the encoded social and political inequality that is otherwise trivialized by reducing female political power only to the power embedded in their sex.

It is beyond doubt that women occupy far less prominent space than men in both political power and representation around the world. In Eastern Europe, this phenomenon has intensified with the collapse of the Berlin Wall, which brought about what has been called the "masculinization" of the democratic transition. The political trend has been accompanied by a widespread use of stereotypical images and representations of women in the popular press. As Sanya Sarnavka, Kristina Mihalec, and Nevenka Sudar point out, even when women achieve a measure of political success by joining the parliament, they are still not safe from insults and humiliation based upon their gender. Moreover, media stereotypical depictions perpetuate gender norms that deny the complexity of both women's issues and women's interests.[68] While women's interests and issues are extremely varied and complex, the media generally fail to capture this diversity and are often aided in this process by the female politicians themselves. As Jenna Mead contends, this is not an unusual phenomenon.[69] Rather, she argues, women are forced into clichés well past their use-by date and the media often ignore the discrimination women face today. It is more likely that media reporters will comment on women's personal appearance, discussing their hairstyles, weights, clothes, shoes, or glasses. Therefore, media portrayals continue to rely heavily on stereotypes and predictable gender conventions that do not allow for a well-rounded and thoughtful analysis of the role of women in the political discourse.

One exception to this trend has been the coverage of Meglena Kuneva who was the European Commissioner for Consumer Protection. Although the sampled *Trud* content did not include any extensive coverage of Kuneva, she is a founding member of the Tsarist Party and a leading scholar in legal affairs, and as such, has contributed extensively to the current political reforms in Bulgaria, earning the position of perhaps the most respected and recognized female MP in Bulgaria and across the European continent. Therefore, it is important to note that Kuneva has enjoyed a well-balanced relationship with the press, which partially might be attributed to her high-profile professional experience in law and politics as both a news editor and a law professor. Nevertheless, even under these circumstances, Kuneva was not spared subtle stereotypical comments in the press. For instance, when she was elected as the minister of European affairs, journalists were quick to point out that as a woman, she is well-balanced and an excellent negotiator, while also pointing out that the job will keep her so busy that she will have no time for her prominent husband financier and young son. As one journalist put it, "Now she has an official excuse not to go fishing with her husband."[70]

Thus far, the transition has not been overly kind to women. State paternalism and masculine democracies form the cultural-political framework within which identities are gendered in differently formed public and private spheres. Without fundamental restructuring of gender relations in both private and public discourses, and particularly so in political participation, women will continue to bear the burden of the pre-communist patriarchal oppression, the pseudo-communist emancipation, and the post-communist transitional illusion of political power. Democratization of gender relations in the political sphere is a sorely needed, but sadly neglected, aspect of social transformation that contributes to the shaping of gendered identities that get directly translated into media content as well.

Indeed, a fundamental shift in both gender norms and media conventions is needed to bring about the beginning of a new era of democracy—one in which equality of the sexes is more than a utopian idea or a remnant of a pseudo-emancipated communist past. While society's gender lens has been significantly blurred by intoxication with masculine power and determination, it is important to note that in the case of Bulgaria, women are equally responsible and silently contributing to the creation of the barriers of sexism and gender inequality. More importantly, the media, a significant number of which is represented by female reporters and editors, support sexism by portraying women politicians in a manner that discredits their political importance and influence. Thus, we often read interviews and see pictures in which women politicians speak about their favorite recipes, talk fashion and shopping tips, and share their wardrobe secrets and preferences in undergarments.[71] In order for a palpable change to ensue, women should cease to participate in the marginalization of their own representatives, first and foremost, by challenging and transforming media conventions and newsroom rituals in favor of a more balanced and impartial approach to covering both women politicians and women's issues.

NOTES

1. Daskalova, Krasimira, and Filipova, Pavlina, "Citizenship and Women's Political Participation in Bulgaria," Bulgarian country report for the Network for European Women's Rights, 2004, http://www.socialrights.org/spip/article494.html.

2. Einhorn, Barbara, "Imagining Women: Literature and the Media," in *Cinderella Goes to Market: Citizenship, Gender and Women's Movements in East Central Europe* (London: Verso Publishers, 1993), 151.

3. Ghodsee, Kristen, "It Takes a King? Simeon Saxecoburgotski and Women's Political Participation in Post-Communist Bulgaria," An IREX short-term travel grant report, 2003, http://www.irex.org/programs/stg/research/03/ghodsee.pdf.

4. Kahn, Kim, "The Distorted Mirror: Press Coverage of Women Candidates for Statewide Office," *The Journal of Politics*, 56, 1 (1994): 154–74; Kahn, Kim, "Does Gender Make a Difference? An Experimental Examination of Sex Stereotypes and Press Patterns in Statewide Campaigns," *American Journal of Political Science*, 38, 1 (1994): 162–95; Kahn, Kim, *The Political Consequences of Being a Woman* (New York: Columbia University Press, 1996); Herzog, Hannah, "More Than a Looking Glass: Women in Israeli Local Politics and the Media," *Press/Politics*, 3, 1 (1998): 26–47; Ross, Karen, *Women, Politics and Media: Uneasy Relations in Comparative Perspective* (Cresskill, NJ: Hampton Press 2002); Robinson, Gertrude, and Saint-Jean, Armande, "Women Politicians and Their Media Coverage: A Generational Analysis," in *Women in Canadian Politics* (vol. 6), ed. K. Megyery (Toronto: Dundurn Press, 1991), 127–69; Ross, Karen, and Sreberny, Annabelle, "Women in the House: Media Representation of British Politicians," in *Gender, Politics and Communication*, eds. Annabelle Sreberny and Lisbet van Zoonen (Cresskill, NJ: Hampton Press, 2000), 79–99.

5. Corner, John, "Mediated Persona and Political Culture. In *Media and the Restyling of Politics*, eds. John Corner and Dick Pels (London: Sage, 2003), 75.

6. McQuail, Dennis, *McQuail's Mass Communication Theory* (London: Sage Publications, 2005).

7. Fiske, John, *Television Culture* (New York: Methuen, 1987), 14.

8. Ibid.

9. Danova, Madelene, "Women in Politics in Bulgarian Newspapers: Post-Feminism in a Post-Totalitarian Society," in *Stereotyping: Representation of Women in Print Media in Southeast Europe* (2006), 121, accessed March 13, 2006, http://kilden.forskningsradet.no/c16877/publikasjon/vis.html?tid=43074.

10. Sreberny, Annabelle, and Van Zoonen, Liesbet, *Gender, Politics and Communication* (Cresskill, NJ: Hampton Press, 2000); Ross and Sreberny, "Women in the House"; Ross, *Women, Politics and Media*; Carilli, Theresa, and Campbell, Jane, *Women and the Media: Diverse Perspectives* (Lanham, MD: University Press of America, 2005).

11. Ross, *Women, Politics and Media*.

12. Norris, Pippa (ed.), *Women, Media and Politics* (New York: Oxford University Press, 1997), 159.

13. Ibid.

14. Kahn, Kim, "The Distorted Mirror"; Kahn, Kim, "Does Gender Make a Difference?"; Kahn, Kim, *The Political Consequences of Being a Woman*.

15. Kahn, Kim, "Does Gender Make a Difference?"

16. Ibid., 178.

17. Ross and Sreberny, "Women in the House," 95.

18. Van Acker, Elizabeth, "Media Representations of Women Politicians in Australia and New Zealand: High Expectations, Hostility or Stardom," *Policy, Organization and Society*, 22, 1 (2003): 116–36.

19. Chew, Phyllis, "Political Women in Singapore: A Socio-Linguistic Analysis," *Women's Studies International Forum*, 24, 6 (2001): 727–36.

20. Lee, Francis L., "Constructing Perfect Women: The Portrayals of Female Officials in Hong Kong," *Media, Culture & Society*, 26, 2 (2004): 207–25.

21. Ross, *Women, Politics and Media*, 79.

22. Matland, R. E., and Bojinkova, D., "The Representation of Women in Political Parties in Central and Eastern Europe," paper presented at the annual meeting of the American Political Science Association, Chicago, IL, 2004; Sloat, Amanda, "Engendering European Politics: The Influence of the European Union on Women in Central and Eastern Europe," paper presented at the Midwest Political Science Association, Chicago, IL, 2005; Chiva, Cristina, "Women in Post-Communist Politics: Explaining Under-Representation in the Hungarian and Romanian Parliament," *Europe-Asia Studies*, 57, 7 (2005): 969–94.

23. Isanovic, Adla, "Media Discourse as a Male Domain: Gender Representation in the Daily Newspapers of Bosnia, Herzegovina, Croatia, and Serbia," in *Stereotyping: Representation of Women in Print Media in Southeast Europe* (2006), 43–79. A report issued by Mediacentar, accessed March 13, 2006, http://kilden.forskningsradet.no/c16877/publikasjon/vis.html?tid=43074.

24. Ibid., 76.

25. Danova, "Women in Politics in Bulgarian Newspapers."

26. Pusnik, Marusa, and Bulc, Gregor, "Women in Their Own Reflections: Self-Representation of Women Politicians in the Slovenian Press," *Journal of Communication Inquiry*, 25, 4 (2001): 396–413.

27. Roman, Denise, "Gendering Eastern Europe: Pre-Feminism, Prejudice, and East-West Dialogues in Post-Communist Romania," *Women's Studies International Forum*, 24, 1 (2001): 55–66.

28. Ibid.

29. Ibid.

30. Kahn, Kim, "Does Being Male Help? An Investigation of the Effects of Candidate Gender and Campaign Coverage on Evaluations of U.S. Senate Candidates," *The Journal of Politics*, 54, 2 (1992): 498.

31. Goffman, Erving, *Frame Analysis: An Essay on the Organization of Experience* (New York: Harper and Row, 1974).

32. As quoted in Sparks, Glenn, *Media Effects Research* (Belmont, CA: Wadsworth Thomson, 2002), 156.

33. Gans, Herbert, *Deciding What's News* (New York: Pantheon, 1979).

34. McQuail, *McQuail's Mass Communication Theory*; Scheufele, Dietram, and Tewksbury, David, "Framing, Agenda Setting, and Priming: The Evolution of Three Media Effects Models," *Journal of Communication*, 57, 1 (2007): 9–20; Rosenberry, Jack, and Vicker, Lauren A., *Applied Mass Communication Theory* (Boston: Pearson, 2009).

35. Sreberny-Mohammadi, Annabelle, and Ross, Karen, "Women MPs and the Media: Representing the Body Politic," *Parliamentary Affairs*, 49 (1996): 103–15.
36. Ross and Sreberny, "Women in the House," 93.
37. Van Zoonen, Liesbet, *Feminist Media Studies* (London, Sage Publications, 1994), 43.
38. Fiske, John, *Television Culture* (New York: Methuen, 1987), 308.
39. Gidengil, Elisabeth, and Everitt, Joanna, "Talking Tough: Gender and Reported Speech in Campaign News Coverage," *Political Communication*, 20 (2003): 209–32.
40. Rakow, Lana, and Kranich, Kimberlie, "Women as Sign in Television News," *Journal of Communication*, 41(1991): 8–23; Peake, Lucy, "Press Coverage of Women Candidates for the UK Parliament." Paper presented at the ECPR 25th Joint Sessions of Workshops, Universität Bern, Switzerland, 1997.
41. Meehan, Eileen R., and Riordan, Ellen (eds.), *Sex and Money: Feminism and Political Economy in the Media* (Minneapolis: University of Minnesota Press, 2002); Bourdieu, Pierre, *On Television and Journalism* (London: Pluto Press, 1998).
42. UN Human Development Report, 2005, accessed September 2005, http://hdr.undp.org/reports/global/2005/.
43. Nikolova, R., "Who Will Be the New Freedom Fighters in Sliven," *Trud*, June 11, 2005, 14, accessed March 15, 2006, http://www.trud.bg.
44. Woodcock, Shannon, "Romanian Women's Discourses of Sexual Violence: Othered Ethnicities, Gendered Spaces," in *Living Gender After Communism*, eds. Janet Elise Johnson and Jean C. Robinson (Bloomington: Indiana University Press, 2007), 156.
45. Dimitrova, R., "One Hand Distance," *Trud*, June 14, 2005, 17, accessed March 15, 2006, http://www.trud.bg.
46. Ibid.
47. Apostolova, Y., Krusteva, K., and Avramova, M., "Female Mps Strut in a Vanity Fair," *Trud*, July 21, 2005, 16–17, accessed March 15, 2006, http://www.trud.bg.
48. Ibid.
49. Ibid, 16.
50. Veleva, Violeta, Interview with Dora Yankova. *Trud*, July 2, 2005, 10–11, accessed March 15, 2006, http://www.trud.bg.
51. Todorova, R., "Miss Parliament," *Trud*, July 15, 2005, 12, accessed March 15, 2006, http://www.trud.bg.
52. Veleva, Violeta, "Even in Walking Against the Wind, I Always Succeed," interview with Eleonora Nikolova, *Trud*, July 23, 2005, 15, accessed March 15, 2006, http://www.trud.bg.
53. "The Governor Entertains Her Colleagues With Folk Songs," *Trud*, July 6, 2005, 4, accessed March 16, 2006, http://www.trud.bg.
54. Gradinarov, B., "For one honor and . . . Nadezhda (Hope)," *Trud*, June 1, 2005, 10, accessed March 15, 2006, http://www.trud.bg.
55. Ibid.
56. "Who Are They Familiarizing With? With Simeon and Nadezhda," *Trud*, May 29, 2005, 7, accessed March 11, 2006, http://www.trud.bg.
57. McQuail, *McQuail's Mass Communication Theory.*
58. Avramova, M., and Dimov, I., "The Leadership Is Melting," *Trud*, June 3, 2005, 1–2, accessed March 11, 2006, http://www.trud.bg.
59. "Parliament Hopefuls Like a Cow," *Trud*, May 29, 2005, 5, accessed March 11, 2006, http://www.trud.bg.
60. See, for example, Julian Popov's commentary "Do Women Rule Bulgaria?"*Al-Jazeera*, December 15, 2011, accessed May 2, 2012, http://www.aljazeera.com/indepth/opinion/2011/12/20111210122330666785.html.
61. Quoted in "Women and Journalists First," Report by the Steering Committee for Equality between Women and Men (CDEG), December 11, 2011, Council of Europe, Strasbourg.
62. *Peter Williams Foreign Policy Blog*, March 2011, accessed January 28, 2013, http://blog.foreignpolicy.com/blog/21416.
63. Ibid.

64. Baird, Julia, *Media Tarts: How the Press Frames Female Politicians* (Melbourne: Scribe Publications, 2004).
65. Quoted in the *Herald Sun*, October 7, 2011.
66. Quoted by Nada Gillani, *Daily Mail*, November 2, 2011.
67. Goscilo, Helena, *Dehexing Sex: Russian Womanhood During and After Glasnost* (Ann Arbor: University of Michigan, 1996).
68. Sarnavka, Sanya, Mihalec, Kristina, and Sudar, Nevenka, "Croatian Feminists Stave Off Onslaught of Sexist Media," *Off Our Back*, xxxiii, 3–4 (2002): 13–17.
69. Mead, Jenna, *Bodyjamming: Sexual Harassment, Feminism, and Public Life* (Milson Point: Vintage, 1997).
70. Hristova, R., "Kuneva Makes the A Grade." *Sofiaecho*, May 30, 2002, accessed February 8, 2008, http://www.sofiaecho.com/article/kuneva-makes-the-a-grade/id_4554/catid_30.
71. Sarnavka, Mihalec, and Sudar, "Croatian Feminists Stave Off Onslaught."

Conclusion

The post-communist transition has affected not only the way in which Eastern European men and women live, but also the way in which Eastern European men and women think about each other. In the atmosphere of confusion and political disarray characterizing the collapse of the socialist system, gender identities were caught in a limbo. And while it is hard to deny that this limbo has led to fundamental social and cultural changes in conceptualizing gendered selves, we must also acknowledge that the core reasons for this shift were closely connected to the market, where a new post-socialist consumer consciousness was burgeoning. The goal of this book was to capture how this new way of thinking of the socialist subject as a consumer also signaled a shift in thinking about sex and gender as reflected in the changing images of women and notions of femininity in media advertising. This, in turn, has also produced a reconfiguration of post-socialist gender hierarchies that have the potential to determine the success or failure of women's future positioning in the structure of social and political power, especially so in the Balkan region—the focus of this book—where the prevailing "macho" culture and the recent "masculinization" of democracy have become fixtures of the cultural narrative of the transition.

Commercial advertising as an industry that also shapes cultural beliefs emerged in the Eastern bloc after the collapse of communism. Prior to that, advertising was seen as an unnecessary and unhealthy promotion of excessive consumerism and decadent social values. It was thought to be "a particularly capitalist phenomenon incompatible with socialism,"[1] and therefore was used scarcely, only in its propaganda function, promoting a very deliberate and engineered view of consumption that virtually had no bearing on the reality of everyday life. Even when advertising's power to influence the thoughts and desires of the socialist subject, as this book has demonstrated, was acknowledged by the ideologues of socialist consumption, its fundamental function to move products off the market through the magic of desire was lost on the socialist "Mad Men," who ironically preferred to focus their effort on the ideological task of educating the worker in the spirit of socialism.

Despite the fact that this essentially sounded like a lofty idea, it also led to the creation of a style of commercial propaganda that in its pursuit of functionality and purpose became completely devoid of style, attractive presentation, and playfulness. Western advertisements clearly outrivaled its socialist brethren in creating a world of quality products, where the individual reigned supreme and where choice was a human right, not a privilege reserved for the chosen few. As Ivaylo Ditchev argued, "the aspiration towards the standards of the normal countries was no longer motivated by the wish to be free or to produce like them, but to consume like they do."[2]

The fundamental move to foster a consumer mentality in the post-socialist citizen, which was intrinsically tied to the penetration of capitalism in the transition and visually manifested in advertising, brought about very deliberate images of gender, class, and social status, which were seen by the majority of men and women as a sign of westernization and breaking away from the past. As a result, images of the female body accompanied by gender-stereotypical comments and combined with a market ideology represented the woman and her sexuality as yet another available commodity.[3] Partially clad women and nude models on the inside pages of the daily papers have now become a regular diet for the Bulgarian reader and accepted as routine. More importantly, this trend became a commonly recognized symbol of the post-socialist transition across the region, as Borenstein contended, mostly because "the discourse of sex became inextricably linked with the discourse of economics."[4]

The result is a commodification of women's bodies and female sexualities unseen in this scope and scale during the communist regime. This is perhaps best exemplified in a recent TV ad for a Bulgarian cheese-like product conspicuously named "bulka" (the Bulgarian word for bride). In the commercial, a young woman dressed in a tight, low-cut red dress carries around a tray of cheese treats when she is confronted by a male "Romeo," in the ambiance of the *chalga* club music. "Julieta" leans forward and drops a cheese cube in between her breasts, teasing her male admirer in a highly sexualized way. The ad continues on in a "cheesy," yet equally crass, dialogue between the two, essentially, putting the man in control of getting what he wants—the dairy treat—while reducing the young woman to nothing more than a milk-producing pair of breasts. The tagline at the end of the thirty-second commercial reveals the woman's response to the young man's inquiry: "It's not cheese, it's a delicatessen," playing a pun on both the ingredients of the product (not real cheese) and the nature of her bosoms (tasty as the real cheese would be). The TV commercial caused a wave of criticism among the Bulgarian viewing audiences; however, the discontent and much of the debate surrounding the ad were not about the crass treatment of women, but about the misleading product information. Trivializing women as domestic cattle and domestic servers is not the problem, paying for cheese that isn't real cheese is.

It is precisely because of its ability to "normalize" cultural notions that advertising must be recognized not only as a vehicle for commercial success, but also as a forum for cultural pedagogy, where new ideas of what it means to be a "modern" woman, what it means to be a successful business entrepreneur, and many other new cultural symbols and their significations could be learned. This pedagogical aspect of advertising has become particularly gendered and alluring with images of beauty, luxury, and social norms often in direct clash with established patriarchal traditions of the past. It is this cultural shift in identity formation, triggered by advertising images and messages and combined with the economic hardships and social pressures of the transition, that has resulted in what Donna Hughes argued are profound psychological changes in the self-esteem and self-worth of women across the former Soviet Union and the countries of the Eastern bloc.[5] Even more, the idea of the sexual pseudo-liberation that the post-socialist indulgence in female sexuality so blatantly displays was nothing more than an attempt to co-opt the transformation of gender ideologies into political ones. As Eliot Borenstein pointed out, "the only thing more naked than the women plastered on so many publications and advertisements was the ideology that put them there: a naïve, largely masculine 'liberation sexology' that identified sexual expression with democracy."[6]

The hypersexualization of women could indeed be seen as a reaction, albeit a fairly drastic one, to the stifling sexual politics of the socialist ideology. However, it is also important to note that the market economy that stimulates the growth of advertising and the perpetuation of these hypersexual images of women emerged at the time when female images turned out to provide a most profitable commodity in the conditions of unbridled capitalism. After all, "The body is a profitable commodity which satisfies all manner of fantasies in all manner of ways."[7] Advertising media conglomerates were among the first to test out this notion. And while the production value of print and outdoor advertisements at the onset of the transition was questionable, ads did not shy away from featuring sexualized females, hoping to grab the attention of the eager consumers, selling anything and everything— from air-conditioners to vitamins—with a sexy twist. The very idea of promoting goods for the sake of consuming out of pleasure and choice, rather than out of necessity and force, posed a novel challenge to Bulgarian advertising companies, which had a lot to learn from their Western counterparts. In this vein, it is important to note that at the initial stages of introducing advertising to the Bulgarian market, there was a general lack of creative approaches to promote consumer goods. The sexy female model (there were many eager young women who wanted to see their faces on giant billboard) was the simplest, cheapest, and most immediate solution.

Whether it was the lack of professional norms among advertising executives or the lack of original creative approaches that led the Bulgarian advertising industry to an overreliance on the classic saying "sex sells" in the early days of the industry coming of age still remains open for debate. However, it appears that for the Bulgarian woman, the transformation into an over-sexed, hyperfeminine body produces a feeling of empowerment, a feeling of having set out on the road of a different kind of life, a life devoid of hardships and struggles of the likes their mothers and grandmothers endured. That, in turn, also promotes and mainstreams the sexualization of the female body as the "norm," as both expected, and in fact, desired mode of identifying a woman's worth. As Daskalova aptly pointed out, "while pornography is a universal modern phenomenon, it seems to me that its warm reception in present-day Bulgarian society is due in part to the fact that it reinforces fundamental notions of women's inferiority that were present before, during, and after the communist period."[8]

It is difficult to predict whether these persisting notions of women's diminished worth will continue to occupy a prominent place in Bulgarian culture. And while they might not be a direct consequence of the sexualization of advertising, it must be acknowledged that the allure of consumption and the commodification of the female body it engendered will remain a staple of what we celebrate as the liberation from communist control and embrace as a sign of a new social order. The problem here also lies, as I have argued elsewhere, "in the political economy underlying the import of Western images of the perfect, sexed-up body, which creates in turn a new type of stereotype of the Eastern European women—sexy, hungry for attention, frail and waiting to be rescued (or discovered) by a rich, powerful man, producing new masked politics of domination and subordination."[9]

The notion of liberty as inscribed in the unwritten rules of consumerism was undoubtedly intoxicating. The "democratic" illusion of Western advertising masterfully blended personal freedom and the right to choose in a magically irresistible fashion, or as Helena Goscilo argued, "finely tuned strategies of 'consumer engineering' have enabled manufacturers to sell everything from cars and furniture to clothes, cosmetics, and alcohol by projecting flattering, illusionary self-images onto the potential buyer—as someone subject to that special sexual hunger that, not coincidentally, will be appeased through the acquisition of whatever product is being featured."[10] In the East, choice was neither individualized nor paraded as a virtue as its essentially self-serving function contradicted the communal nature of the socialist project. "Consumerism provided a much-needed new framework for developing personal and collective identities; it liberated hidden desires; and it offered an alternative form of expression to the poeticized discourse of the past."[11]

For the women of the socialist states, the illusionary freedom of advertising was particularly appealing as it offered a wish-fulfillment script unimaginable within the ideological straitjacket of the socialist gender dogma. Advertising, with all of its allure and promises, appear to offer a collective fantasy that women could now invest and populate with their own individual meaning. Gilles Lipovetsky described this allure as the empire of seduction, stating that "The empire of seduction has been an euphoric grave-digger for the great ideologies. Taking into account neither the singular individual nor the requirement of freedom to love hic and nunc, those ideologies found themselves poles apart from temporary individual aspiration."[12]

The breakdown of the constraining order of socialism that caved in under the pressure of consumer discontent presented men and women alike for the first time in decades with the concept of choice, including the choice of expressing their sexuality. As a result, the visual space of the post-socialist transition suddenly was flooded with simultaneously erotic and politicized images of women. These highly suggestive images of women, presented in a cultural context where hypersexuality is not only sought after as a quality of character, but also had achieved the status of a legitimate form of reputation, have curiously taken place parallel to the growing sense of consumer awareness and the ability to spend money on oneself—an act of self-indulgence not only decried as immoral behavior by socialist ideologues, but also depicted as a shameful display of lack of communal commitment to the ideas of socialism itself. As Kristen Ghodsee has masterfully captured in her recent ethnographic retrospect on everyday life under socialism in Bulgaria:

> Over the years, I have watched Bulgaria evolve from a veritable wasteland, where procuring essential goods and services was a feat requiring all the perseverance and tracking skills of a Louisiana bloodhound, into a country brimming with luxurious retail oases where opulent, new shopping malls spring forth from the earth like magic beanstalks and where compact islands of consumerism are surrounded by oceans of abject poverty.[13]

In this sea of economic contradictions and raving-mad consumerism, women have been directly and indirectly implicated as a responsible culprit and a naive casualty. And it does not come as a surprise that it is exactly advertising as the engine that fuels consumption that delivered the most enchanting way of blurring the distinction between the realities of everyday life and the dream world in which we as consumers are invited to partake. As Alise Tīfentāle pointed out, "the tentative version of capitalism [in today's Latvia] aggressively appeals to the most basic human drives, offering an egocentric world view and continually inviting one to transgress the tenth commandment [Thou shalt not covet] in the name of personal well-being and happiness."[14]

On the other hand, the promises of the "imagined West" did not deliver the coveted dreams that inspired the dismantling of the socialist project. As Paulina Bren and Mary Neuburger poignantly argued, "Just as 'real socialism' proved to be less than its promise, the post-1989 confrontation with 'real capitalism' was (and in many cases continues to be) complicated and in some cases downright disappointing."[15] This idea is further supported by philosopher and sociologist Renata Salecl, who contends that capitalism functionally transformed the proletariat-slave into a free consumer and has done so by what she calls the "tyranny of choice"—the illusive idea that choice offers an instantaneous appeasement of our internal insecurities. Consequently, she argued, the problem is not really with choice itself, but rather, "the problem is that the idea of rational choice, transferred from the domain of economics, has been glorified as the only kind of choice we have."[16]

In the conditions of post-socialism, I argue, the idea of choice for socialist women was particularly alluring because it allowed women to construct a new way of expressing their essence, the language of which was encoded in the dreams presented by advertising. However, as Angela McRobbie has argued, "choice is surely, within lifestyle culture, a modality of constraint," yet choice is essential in creating the illusion of freedom even though it delivers very little in arming women with actual agency.[17] Similarly, Rosalind Gill has also articulated her view of advertising as the one place where the ideas of choice and autonomy have done very little to empower women: "The notions of choice and autonomy as they are articulated within advertising are systemically eradicating any space within which we might think about ourselves as social being. In short, any notion of cultural and political influence is disavowed."[18]

For the overtired, over-preached, and over-sanctioned socialist woman, however, the sense of choice, whether engineered by the empire of seduction or imposed from an invisible cultural elite, was a welcome breath of fresh air—so much so that that even political action can now be infused with ideas of sexual expression, serving as the most unique and most genuine form of argumentation that felt simultaneously genuine and empowering. However, that very sexual expression was quickly realized and converted into a commodity for sale, where the language of sexual post-socialist revolution was co-opted by the "marketeers of the global prostitution industry," acting like great illusionists, "who sell not only products but also a new lifestyle."[19] Using the very same gender codes embedded in the commercial language of capitalism, Loretta Napoleoni argued that the "global pimps" of the new economic orders were able to apply the same exact technique to lure unsuspected Slav women in sex slavery and other forms of forced labor exploitation.[20]

While one might argue that making a connection between the boom in the sexualization of women in advertising and the boom in the sex trade in Eastern Europe is just a coincidence, it is also hard to ignore the potentially dangerous consequences of this cultural trend. On the other hand, scholars have also argued that the transformations of female identity as signaled in the visuals of consumer advertising can be seen as a form of subversive liberation, and indeed as David Berry contended, "magazines do portray new images of women who are both confident of their position and economically independent, which empowers, or at least has provided the potential for, women to make autonomous choices over lifestyle."[21]

This sense of empowerment, however, at minimum rests on shaky grounds—among other things, it is based on an archaic, patriarchal definition of femininity, which reinforces rather than transforms the relations of gender inequality in the Balkans. Moreover, I argue, these sexually provocative depictions of women feed into a cookie-cutter routine of exploitive imagery that regularly portrays women's bodies as commodified objects. This is a particularly dangerous trend in post-communist societies like Bulgaria because Bulgarian women are now exposed to a steady diet of exploitative, sexually provocative depictions of women that in turn feeds a poisonous trend in women's and girls' perceptions of their bodies and their sense of self-worth in the absence of alternative role models.[22] In a culture where young girls model their appearance after the exaggerated, oozing sexuality of the *chalga* bombshells while viewing their careers as the professional aspiration, it is hard to overlook the ubiquity of these images and the outcomes they might produce.

These concerns are even more pressing when the treatment of female sexuality as a genuine product of the market is legitimized by the economic realities of the new EU member states, such as Bulgaria and Romania. Consider the recent success of Payner Media, Bulgaria's largest *chalga* music house and a media broadcaster, in securing a non-refundable grant of one million euros from the European Regional Development Fund. The grant was awarded, as local and international media reported, to purchase new recording equipment and promote further growth in the creative industries, entirely oblivious of the problematic cultural norms and questionable content that this very same equipment will eventually produce. In a way, Payner's success in securing these EU monies demonstrates the triumphant logic of the market. The *Economist's Eastern Approaches* blog illustrated this in the following comment by Georgi Ivanov, a film and TV producer: "It's all about business viability: If they proposed a good business plan, why shouldn't they get the money?"[23] In more important ways, however, it also promotes and mainstreams the sexualization of the female body as the "norm," and as "commonplace," a legitimate, marketable product, now also accepted, and in fact, financially supported, by the coffers of the European Union.

Whether one chooses to position the argument about the growing mainstreaming of "porno-chic" in advertising as a passing phase or a peculiarity of the Balkan culture and the Eastern Europeans' seemingly relaxed attitude about sex and eroticism, it is certainly dictated and supported by the inevitable logic of the market and its unquestionably validating renditions of "normal" gendered behavior. As Helen Kelly-Holmes stated, "this is perhaps, the true triumph of market ideology and its discourse: its assumed normalcy, its status as the given way of life from which there may be minor deviations, but not serious alternative."[24] For the post-socialist female consumer, who oozes sexuality and owns it as her true marker of success and separation from the past, this incantation has never sounded more convincing.

NOTES

1. Markham, James, "Is Advertising Important in the Soviet Economy?" *Journal of Marketing*, 28, 2 (1994):31.
2. Ditchev, Ivaylo, "The Eros of Identity," in *Balkan as Metaphor: Between Globalization and Fragmentation*, eds. Dušan I. Bjelic and Obrad Savic (Cambridge, MA: The MIT Press, 2002), 246.
3. Kronja, Ivana, "Politics and Porn: The Pornographic Representation of Women in Serbian Tabloids and Its Role in Politics," in *Stereotyping: Representations of Women in Print Media in Southeast Europe*, report issued by Mediacentar (2006), 187–216.
4. Borenstein, Eliot, *Overkill: Sex and Violence in Contemporary Russian Popular Culture* (Ithaca and London: Cornell University Press, 2008), 88.
5. Hughes, Donna, "Supplying Women for the Sex Industry: Trafficking from the Russian Federation," in *Sexuality and Gender in Post-Communist Eastern Europe and Russia*, eds. Alesksandar Stulhofer and Theo Sandfort (New York: Haworth Press, 2005), 209–30.
6. Borenstein, *Overkill*, 59.
7. Kligman, Gail, "Women and the Negotiation of Identity in Post-Communist Eastern Europe," in *Identities in Transition: Eastern Europe and Russia after the Collapse of Communism*, ed. Victoria E. Bonnell (Berkeley: University of California Press/University of California International and Area Studies Digital Collection, Research Series # 93, 1996), 77.
8. Daskalova, Krasimira, "Women's Problems, Women's Discourses in Post-Communist Bulgaria," in *Reproducing Gender: Politics, Publics and Everyday Life After Socialism*, eds. Susan Gal and Gail Kligman (Princeton: Princeton University Press, 2000), 349.
9. Ibroscheva, Elza, "From 'Babuski' to 'Sexy Babes': The Sexing Up of Bulgarian Women in Advertising," in *Challenging Images of Women in the Media: Reinventing Women's Lives* (Lanham, MD: Lexington Books, 2012), 117.
10. Goscilo, Helena, *Dehexing Sex: Russian Womanhood During and After Glasnost* (Ann Arbor: University of Michigan, 1996), 140.
11. Kaneva, Nadia, and Ibroscheva, Elza, "Media and the Birth of the Post-Communist Consumer," in *Media Transformations in the Post-Communist World*, eds. Peter Gross and Karol Jakubowicz (Lanham, MD: Lexington Books, 2012), 82.
12. Lipovetky, Gilles, *The Empire of Fashion: Dressing Modern Democracy* (Princeton: Princeton University Press, 1994), 210.
13. Ghodsee, Kristen, *Lost in Transition. Ethnographies of Everyday Life After Communism* (Durham and London: Duke University Press, 2011), 83.
14. Tīfentāle, Alise, "The Language and Value of Things Under Communism and Capitalism," *Dizaina Studija*, 2008, accessed March 31, 2012, http://www.dizainastudija.eu/index.php/en/0/2/188/316/318/index.html.

15. Bren, Paulina, and Neuburger, Mary, *Communism Unwrapped: Consumption in Cold War Eastern Europe* (Oxford: Oxford University Press, 2012), 14.
16. Salecl, Renata, *The Tyranny of Choice* (London: Profile Books, 2010), 42.
17. McRobbie, Angela, "Post-Feminism and Popular Culture," *Feminist Media Studies*, 4, 3 (2004): 26.
18. Gill, Rosalind, "Supersexualize Me! Advertising and the Midriffs," in *Mainstreaming Sex: The Sexualization of Culture*, ed. Feona Attwood (London: IB Tauris, 2009), 106.
19. Napoleoni, Loretta, *Rogue Economics. Capitalism's New Reality* (New York: Seven Stories Press, 2008), 19.
20. Ibid.
21. Berry, David, "Is Popular Culture Subversive in Romania? An Assessment of Teenage Girls' and Women's Magazines," *Slovo*, 16, 2 (2004): 134.
22. Ibroscheva, "From 'Babuski' to 'Sexy Babes.'"
23. "Dance it or hate it," *Eastern Approaches Blog*, January 23, 2013, accessed January 28, 2013, http://www.economist.com/blogs/easternapproaches/2013/01/eu-funds-bulgaria.
24. Kelly-Holmes, Helen, "The Discourse of Western Marketing Professionals in Central and Eastern Europe: Their Role in the Creation of a Context for Marketing and Advertising Messages," *Discourse and Society*, 9, 3 (1998): 349.

Bibliography

Aday, Sean, and Devitt, James. "Style over Substance: Newspaper Coverage of Elizabeth Dole's Presidential Bid." *Harvard International Journal of Press/Politics*, 6, 2 (2001): 52–73.

Apostolov, Georgi. "The thoughts of a young man." *Zhenata Dnes*, 7 (1979): 12.

Apostolova, Y., Krusteva, K., and Avramova, M. "Female Mps Strut in a Vanity Fair." *Trud* (July 21, 2005): 16–17. Retrieved March 15, 2006, from http://www.trud.bg.

Attwood, Feona. *Mainstreaming Sex: The Sexualization of Western Culture*. London: I. B. Tauris, 2009.

Avramova, M., and Dimov, I. "The Leadership is Melting." *Trud* (June 3, 2005): 1–2. Retrieved March 11, 2006, from http://www.trud.bg.

Azhgikhina, Nadezhda. "Women as Presented by the Russian Media." A report for the *United Nations Department of Economic and Social Affairs (DESA)*, 1995. Available online at http://un.org/documents/ecosoc/cn6/1996/media/rmediaen.htm (July 13, 2008).

Baban, Adriana. "Women's Sexuality and Reproductive Behavior in Post-Ceausescu Romani: A Psychological Approach." In *Reproducing Gender: Politics, Publics and Everyday Life After Socialism*, edited by Susan Gal and Gail Kligman, 225–57. Princeton: Princeton University Press, 2000.

Babbie, Earl. *The Practice of Social Research*. Belmont, CA: Wadsworth Publishing Company, 2010.

Baird, Julia. *Media Tarts: How the Press Frames Female Politicians*. Melbourne: Scribe Publications, 2004.

Balockaite, Rasa. "'Go West . . .': Myths of Femininity and Feminist Utopias in East and West." *Eurozine* (2009). Retrieved June 11, 2012, from http://www.eurozine.com/articles/2009-08-14-balockaite-en.html.

Bankov, Nikolay. "The Thoughts of a Young Man." *Zhenata Dnes*, 9 (1979): 20.

Barker, Adele Marie. "Rereading Russia." In *Consuming Russia: Popular Culture, Sex, and Society*, edited by Adele M. Barker, 1–9. Durham: Duke University Press, 1999.

Bartlett, Djurdja. *FashionEast: The Spectre that Haunted Socialism*. Cambridge, MA: MIT Press, 2010.

Berry, David (2004). "Is Popular Culture Subversive in Romania? An Assessment of Teenage Girls' and Women's Magazines." *Slovo*, 16, 2 (2004): 131–42.

Berstein, Frances. *The Dictatorship of Sex: Lifestyle Advice for the Soviet Masses*. DeKalb: Northern Illinois University Press, 2007.

Blum, Martin. (2000). "Remaking the East German Past: Ostalgie, Identity, and Material Culture." *Journal of Popular Culture*, 34, 3 (2000): 229–53.

Bokov, Georgi. "The Great Responsibility of Bulgarian Journalism [in Bulgarian]." *Kultura*, 10, 8: (1976).
Borenstein, Eliot. *Men with Women: Masculinity and Revolution in Russian Fiction, 1917–1929*. Durham and London: Duke University Press, 2000.
Borenstein, Eliot. *Overkill: Sex and Violence in Contemporary Russian Popular Culture*. Ithaca and London: Cornell University Press, 2008.
Bostandjiev, Todor. "Are our Women Frigid?" *Zhenata Dnes*, 5 (1968): 17.
Bourdieu, Pierre. *On Television and Journalism*. London: Pluto Press, 1998.
Braikova, Vasila. "Fashion for the Chubby Woman." *Zhenata Dnes*, 5 (1968): 17.
Bren, Paulina, and Neuburger, Mary. *Communism Unwrapped: Consumption in Cold War Eastern Europe*. Oxford: Oxford University Press, 2012.
Brunnbauer, Ulf. "Making Bulgarians Socialist: The Fatherland Front in Communist Bulgaria." *East European Politics and Societies*, 22, 1 (2008): 44–79.
Bryan, Carter. "Communist Advertising: Its Status and Functions." *Journalism Quarterly* (1962): 500–506.
Carilli, Theresa, and Campbell, Jane. *Women and the Media: Diverse Perspectives*. Lanham, MD: University Press of America, 2005.
Carleton, Gregory. *Sexual revolution in Bolshevik Russia*. Pittsburgh: University of Pittsburgh Press, 2005.
Carter, C., Branston, G., and Allan, S., eds. *News, Gender and Power*. London: Routledge, 1998.
Carter, Cynthia, and Weaver, C. Kay. *Violence and the Media*, Buckingham, UK: Open University Press, 2003.
Chew, Phyllis Ghim Lian. "Political Women in Singapore: A Socio-Linguistic Analysis." *Women's Studies International Forum*, 24, 6 (2001): 727–36.
Chiva, Cristina. "Women in Post-Communist Politics: Explaining Under-Representation in the Hungarian and Romanian Parliament." *Europe-Asia Studies*, 57, 7 (2005): 969–94.
Collins, Patricia Hill. *Black feminist thought*. London: Routledge, 2000.
Corner, John. "Mediated Persona and Political Culture." In *Media and the Restyling of Politics*, edited by John Corner and Dick Pels, 67–85. London: Sage, 2003.
Corrin, Chris, ed. *Superwomen and the Double Burden: Women's Experience of Change in Central and Eastern Europe and the Former Soviet Union*. London: Scarlet Press, 1992.
Cox, Randi. "'NEP without Nepmen!': Soviet Advertising and the Transition to Socialism." In *Everyday Life in Early Soviet Russia: Taking the Revolution Inside*, edited by C. Kiaer and E. Naiman, 119–53. Bloomington: Indiana University Press, 2006.
Cronin, Anne. "Regimes of Mediation: Advertising Practitioners as Cultural Intermediaries?" *Consumption Markets & Culture*, 4 (2004): 349–69.
"Dance It or Hate It." *Eastern Approaches Blog* (January 23, 2013). Retrieved January 28, 2013, from http://www.economist.com/blogs/easternapproaches/2013/01/eu-funds-bulgaria.
Danova, Madelene. "Women in Politics in Bulgarian Newspapers: Post-Feminism in a Post-Totalitarian Society." In *Stereotyping: Representation of Women in Print Media in Southeast Europe*, 2006, 111–32. A report issued by Mediacentar. Retrieved March 13, 2006, from http://kilden.forskningsradet.no/c16877/publikasjon/vis.html?tid=43074.
Daskalova, Krasimira. "Women's Problems, Women's Discourses in Post-Communist Bulgaria." In *Reproducing Gender: Politics, Publics and Everyday Life after Socialism*, edited by Susan Gal and Gail Kligman, 331–80. Princeton: Princeton University Press, 2000.
Daskalova, Krasimira, and Filipova, Pavlina. *Citizenship and Women's Political Participation in Bulgaria*. Bulgarian country report for the Network for European Women's Rights, 2004. Available online at http://www.socialrights.org/spip/article494.html, retrieved October 3, 2005.
Deltcheva, Roumiana. "New Tendencies in Post-Totalitarian Bulgaria: Mass Culture and the Media." *Europe-Asia Studies*, 48, 2 (1996): 305–16.
Devitt, James. "Framing Gender on the Campaign Trail: Female Gubernatorial Candidates and the Press." *Journalism and Mass Communication Quarterly*, 78 (2002): 445–63.
Dimitrova, R. "One Hand Distance." *Trud* (June 14, 2005): 17. Retrieved March 15, 2006, from http://www.trud.bg

Dinkova, Maria. "Women Today and Tomorrow." *Zhenata Dnes*, 5 (1969): 5.
Dinkova, Maria. "Could You Carry Two Watermelons under One Arm?" *Zhenata Dnes*, 4 (1971): 5–6.
Ditchev, Ivaylo. "The Eros of Identity." In *Balkan as Metaphor: Between Globalization and Fragmentation*, edited by Dušan I. Bjelic and Obrad Savic, 235–50. Cambridge, MA: The MIT Press, 2002.
Ditchev, Ivaylo. "Die Konsumentenschmiede: Versuch über das kommunistische Begehren." In *Zurück aus der Zukunft. Osteuropäische Kulturen in Zeitalter des Poskommunismus*, edited by B. Groys. Frankfurt: Suhrkamp, 2007. (An abbreviated version of this article was published in *Kultura*, February 22, 2007, in Bulgarian.)
Dölling, Irene. "'But the Pictures Stay the Same': Images of Women in the *Journal Fur Dich* Before and After the Turning Point." In *Gender Politics and Post-Communism*, edited by Nanette Funk and Magda Mueller. New York: Routledge, 1994.
Dölling, Irene, Hahn, Daphne, and Scholz Sylka. "Birth Strike in the New Federal States: Is Sterilization an Act of Resistance?" In *Reproducing Gender: Politics, Publics and Everyday Life After Socialism*, edited by Susan Gal and Gail Kligman, 118–49. Princeton: Princeton University Press, 2000.
Ehrenreich, Barbara. "Laden with Lard." *ZETA* (July/August 1990).
Einhorn, Barbara. "Imagining Women: Literature and the Media." In *Cinderella Goes to Market: Citizenship, Gender and Women's Movements in East Central Europe*, 216–56. London: Verso Publishers, 1993.
Ewen, Stuart. *Captains of Consciousness: Advertising and the Social Roots of the Consumer Culture*. New York: McGraw-Hill, 1976.
Fairclough, Norman. *Language and Power*. London and New York: Longman, 1989.
Faraday, George. *Revolt of the Filmmakers: The Struggle for Artistic Autonomy and the Fall of the Soviet Film Industry*. University Park: Pennsylvania State University Press, 2000.
Fehervary, Krisztina. "Goods and States. The Political Logic of State-Socialist Material Culture." *Comparative Studies in Society and History*, 51 (2006): 426–59.
Fiske, John. *Television culture*. New York: Methuen, 1987.
Fodor, Eva. *Working Difference: Women's Working Lives in Hungary and Austria, 1945–1995*. Durham: Duke University Press, 2003.
Foucault, Michel. *History of Sexuality: An Introduction, Volume 1*. London: Penguin Books, 1976.
Fox, Karen F. A., Skorobogatykh, Irina I., and Saginova, Olga V. "The Soviet Evolution of Marketing Thought, 1961–1991: From Marx to Marketing." *Marketing Theory*, 5 (2005): 283–307.
French, Marilyn. *The War Against Women*. New York: Ballantine Books, 1993.
Funk, Nanette, and Muller, Magda, eds. *Gender, Politics and Post-Communism: Reflection from Post-Communism and the Former Soviet Union*. New York: Routledge, 1993.
Gal, Susan, and Kligman, Gail. *The Politics of Gender After Socialism: A Comparative Historical Essay*. Princeton: Princeton University Press, 2000.
Gal, Susan, and Kligman, Gail. *Reproducing Gender: Politics, Publics and Everyday Life After Socialism*. Princeton: Princeton University Press, 2000.
Gallagher, Margaret. "Velvet Revolution, Social Upheaval, and Women in European Media." In *Women Empowering Communication: A Resource Book on Women and the Globalization of Media*, edited by Margaret Gallagher and Lilia Quindoza-Santiago, 95–127. London: World Association for Christian Communication, 1993.
Gamson, William. *Talking Politics*. New York: Cambridge University Press, 1992.
Gans, Herbert. *Deciding What's News*. New York: Pantheon, 1979.
Geertz, Clifford. *The Interpretation of Cultures*. New York: Basic Books, 1973.
Germogenova, L. J. *Èffektivnaja reklama v Rossii. Praktika I rekomendacii* [The Effectiveness of Advertising in Russia: Practices and Recommendations]. Moscow: RusPartner Ltd., 1994.
Gessen, Masha. "Sex in Media and the Birth of the Sex Media in Russia." In *Post-Communism and the Body Politics*, edited by Ellen Berry, 197–228. New York: New York University Press, 1995.

Ghodsee, Kristen. *The Red Riviera: Gender, Tourism and Post-Socialism on the Black Sea.* Durham: Duke University Press, 2005.

Ghodsee, Kristen. "Potions, Lotions and Lipstick: The Gendered Consumption of Cosmetics and Perfumery in Socialist and Post-Socialist Urban Bulgaria," *Women's Studies International Forum*, 30, 1 (2007): 26–39.

Ghodsee, Kristen. "It Takes a King? Simeon Saxecoburgotski and Women's Political Participation in Post-Communist Bulgaria." An IREX Short-term Travel Grant Report (2003), available at http://www.irex.org/programs/stg/research/03/ghodsee.pdf, retrieved October 13, 2005.

Ghodsee, Kristen. *Lost in Transition. Ethnographies of Everyday Life After Communism.* Durham and London: Duke University Press, 2011.

Gidengil, Elisabeth, and Everitt, Joanna. "Talking Tough: Gender and Reported Speech in Campaign News Coverage." *Political Communication*, 20 (2003); 209–32.

Gill, Rosalind. "Supersexualize Me! Advertising and the Midriffs." In *Mainstreaming Sex: The Sexualization of Culture*, edited by Feona Attwood, 93–111. London: I. B. Tauris, 2000.

Goffman, Erving. *Frame Analysis: An Essay on the Organization of Experience.* New York: Harper and Row, 1974.

Goldman, Marshall I. "Product Differentiation and Advertising: Some Lessons from Soviet Experience." *The Journal of Political Economy*, 68 (1960): 346–57.

Goscilo, Helena. *Dehexing Sex: Russian Womanhood During and After Glasnost.* Ann Arbor: University of Michigan, 1996.

"The Governor Entertains her Colleagues with Folk Songs." *Trud* (July 6, 2005): 4. Retrieved March 16, 2006, from http://www.trud.bg.

Gradinarov, B. "For One Honor and . . . Nadezhda (Hope)." *Trud* (June 1, 2005): 10. Retrieved March 15, 2006, from http://www.trud.bg.

Gricenko-Wells, Ludmilla. "Western Concepts, Russian Perspectives: Meanings of Advertising in the Former Soviet Union." *Journal of Advertising* 23, 1 (1994): 83–95.

Gronow, Jukka. *Caviar with Champagne: Common Luxury and the Ideals of the Good Life in Stalin's Russia.* Oxford: Berg, 2003.

Guineva, Maria. "Sex, Chalga and Alcohol: Sexual Harassment or Bulgaria's Best Selling Mix (August 26, 2009). Retrieved February 8, 2008, http://www.novinite.com/view_news.php?id=107166.

Hall, Stuart. "Introduction." In *Paper Voices: The Popular Press and Social Change, 1935–1965*, edited by A. C. H. Smith, 11–24. Totowa: NJ: Rowman & Littlefield, 1975.

Hall, Stuart. "The Rediscovery of 'Ideology': Return of the Oppressed in Media Studies." In *Culture, Society and the Media*, edited by M. Gurevitch, T. Bennett, and J. Woollacott, 56–90. New York: Methuen, 1982.

Haney, Lynne. *Inventing the Needy: Gender and the Politics of Welfare in Hungary.* Berkeley: University of California Press, 2002.

Hanson, Phillip. *Advertising and Socialism: The Nature and Extent of Consumer Advertising in the Soviet Union, Hungary and Yugoslavia.* White Plains, NY: International Arts and Sciences Press, 1974.

Hashamova, Yana (2004). Post-Soviet Russian film and the trauma of globalization. *Consumption Markets & Culture* 1: 53-68.

Herzog, Hannah. "More Than a Looking Glass: Women in Israeli Local Politics and the Media." *Press/Politics*, 3, 1 (1998): 26–47.

Holmgren, Beth. "Bug Inspectors and Beauty Queens: The Problem of Translating Feminism in Russian." In *Post-Communism and the Body Politic*, edited by Ellen Berry, 15–32. New York: New York University Press, 1995.

Hristova, Julia. "A Man in the Kindergarten." *Zhenata Dnes*, 2 (1989): 18–19.

Hristova, R. "Kuneva Makes the A Grade." *Sofiaecho* (May 30, 2002). Retrieved February 8, 2008, from http://www.sofiaecho.com/article/kuneva-makes-the-a-grade/id_4554/catid_30.

Hughes, Donna M. "Supplying Women for the Sex Industry: Trafficking From the Russian Federation." In *Sexuality and Gender in Post-Communist Eastern Europe and Russia*, edited by A. Stulhofer and T. Sandfort, 209–30. New York: Haworth Press, 2005.

Ibroscheva, Elza. "The New Eastern European Woman: A Gold-digger or an Independent Spirit?" *Global Media Journal*, 5, 9 (2006): article 2.
Ibroscheva, Elza. "Caught Between East and West? Portrayals of Women and Gender in Bulgarian Television Advertisements." *Sex Roles: Journal of Research*, 57, 5–6 (2007): 409–18.
Ibroscheva, Elza. "From 'Babuski' to 'Sexy Babes': The Sexing Up of Bulgarian Women in Advertising." In *Challenging Images of Women in the Media: Reinventing Women's Lives*, edited by Theresa Carilli and Jane Campell, 107–19. Lanham, MD: Lexington Books, 2012.
Ilieva, Paloma. "Who Are We, Women?" *Bhozur*, 7 (1995): 38.
Imre, Aniko. *Identity Games: Globalization and the Transformation of Media Cultures in the New Europe*. Cambridge, MA: MIT Press, 2009.
Imre, Aniko. Sex and the Postsocialist City. *FlowTV* (2009). Retrieved on June 9, 2012, from http://flowtv.org/2009/07/sex-and-the-postsocialist-city.
Isanovic, Adla. "Media Discourse as a Male Domain: Gender Representation in the Daily Newspapers of Bosnia, Herzegovina, Croatia, and Serbia." In *Stereotyping: Representation of Women in Print Media in Southeast Europe*, 43–79. A report issued by Mediacentar (2006). Retrieved March 13, 2006, from http://kilden.forskningsradet.no/c16877/publikasjon/vis.html?tid=43074.
Jhally, Sutt. "Advertising at the Edge of the Apocalypse." In *The Advertising and Consumer Culture Reader*, edited by Joseph Turow and Matthew Mcallister, 416–29. New York: Routledge, 2009.
Jhally, Sutt. "Advertising, Gender and Sex: What's Wrong with a Little Objectification?" (n.d.). Retrieved June 20, 2012, from http://www.sutjhally.com/articles/whatswrongwithalit/
Johnson, Janet Elise, and Robinson, Jean C., eds. *Living Gender After Communism*. Bloomington: Indiana University Press, 2007.
Kahn, Kim Fridkin. "Does Being Male Help? An Investigation of the Effects of Candidate Gender and Campaign Coverage on Evaluations of U.S. Senate candidates." *The Journal of Politics*, 54, 2 (1992): 497–517.
Kahn, Kim Fridkin. "The Distorted Mirror: Press Coverage of Women Candidates for Statewide Office." *The Journal of Politics*, 56, 1 (1994a): 154–74.
Kahn, Kim Fridkin. "Does Gender Make a Difference? An Experimental Examination of Sex Stereotypes and Press Patterns in Statewide Campaigns," *American Journal of Political Science*, 38, 1 (1994b): 162–95.
Kahn, Kim Fridkin. *The Political Consequences of Being a Woman*. New York: Columbia University Press, 1996.
Kaier, Christina. *Imagine No Possessions: The Socialist Objects of Russian Constructivism*. Cambridge, MA: MIT Press, 2005.
Kaneva, Nadia, and Ibroscheva, Elza. "Hidden in Public View: A Critical Analysis of Visual Representations of Women in the Communist Bulgarian Press." *Feminist Media Studies* iFirst (2012) (online).
Kaneva, Nadia, and Ibroscheva, Elza. "Media and the Birth of the Post-Communist Consumer." In *Media Transformations in the Post-Communist World*, edited by Peter Gross and Karol Jakubowicz, 67–85. Lanham, MD: Lexington Books, 2012.
Kasic, Biljana. "The Spatiality of Identities and Sexualities: Is 'Transition' a Challenging Point at All?" In *Sexuality and Gender in Post-Communist Eastern Europe and Russia*, edited by Alesandar Stulhofer and Theo Sanfort, 95–102. New York: The Haworth Press, 2005.
Kelly-Holmes, Helen. "The Discourse of Western Marketing Professionals in Central and Eastern Europe: Their Role in the Creation of a Context for Marketing and Advertising Messages. *Discourse and Society*, 9, 3 (1998): 339–62.
Kipnis, Laura. *Bound and Gagged: Pornography and the Politics of Fantasy in America*. New York: Grove Press, 1996.
Kligman, Gail. "Women and the Negotiation of Identity in Post-Communist Eastern Europe." In *Identities in Transition: Eastern Europe and Russia after the Collapse of Communism*, edited by Victoria E. Bonnell, 68–91. University of California Press/University of California International and Area Studies Digital Collection, Research Series # 93, 1996.
Kochen, Lionel, and Keep, John. *The Making of Modern Russia*. London: Penguin, 1990.

Kolesnik, Svetlana. "Advertising and Cultural Politics." *Journal of Communication*, 41, 2 (1991): 46–54.
Kon, Igor. "The Appeal of Commercial Eroticism [in Bulgarian]." *Kultura*, 51 (1971): 3.
Kon, Igor. "Sexuality and Culture." In *Sex and Russian Society*, edited by Igor Kon and James Riordian, 15–45. London: Pluto Press, 1993.
Kon, Igor. *The Sexual Revolution in Russia: From the Age of the Czars to Today*. Translated by James Riordian. New York: Free Press, 1995.
Kotzeva, Tatyana. "Reimagining Bulgarian Women: The Marxist Legacy and Women's Self-Identity." In *Gender and Identity in Central and Eastern Europe*, edited by Chris Corrin, 83–99. London: Frank Cass Publishers, 1999.
Koznetsova, Larisa. "Mini, Midi, Maxi" [in Bulgarian]. *Kultura* 8 (1971): 3.
Kronja, Ivana. "Politics and Porn: The Pornographic Representation of Women in Serbian Tabloids and Its Role in Politics." In *Stereotyping: Representations of Women in Print Media in Southeast Europe*, 187–216. Report issued by Mediacentar, 2006.
Kuntsche, Emmanuel, Kuntsche, Sandra, Knibbe, Ronald, Simons-Morton, Bruce, Tilda, Farhat, Hublet, Anne, Bendtsen, Pernille, Godeau, Emmanuelle, and Demetrovics, Zsolt. "Cultural and Gender Convergence in Adolescent Drunkenness: Evidence From 23 European and North American Countries." *Archives of Pediatrics and Adolescent Medicine*, 165, 2 (2011): 152–58.
Kurkela, Vesa. "Bulgarian *Chalga* on Video: Oriental Stereotypes, Mafia Exoticism, and Politics," In *Balkan Popular Culture and the Ottoman Ecumene*, edited by Donna A. Buchanan, 143–75. Lanham, MD: The Scarecrow Press, 2007.
LaFont, Suzanne. *Women in Transition: Voices from Lithuania*. Albany, NY: State University of New York Press, 1998.
Lampe, John. *The Bulgarian Economy in the Twentieth Century*. London: Croom Helm, 1986.
Lee, Francis L. "Constructing Perfect Women: The Portrayals of Female Officials in Hong Kong." *Media, Culture & Society*, 26, 2 (2004): 207–25.
Lipovetky, Gilles. *The Empire of Fashion: Dressing Modern Democracy*. Princeton: Princeton University Press, 1994.
Lippmann, Walter. *Public Opinion*. New York: Macmillan, 1956/1922.
Ljaxov, V. N. *Sovetskij Reklamnyj Plakat 1917–1932* [The Soviet Advertising Poster 1917–1932]. Moscow: Sovetskij Xudožnik, 1972.
Lukic, Jasmina. "Media Representation of Men and Women in Times of War and Crisis: The Case of Serbia." In *Reproducing Gender: Politics, Publics and Everyday Life After Socialism*, edited by Susan Gal and Gail Kligman, 393–424. Princeton: Princeton University Press, 2000.
Magó-Maghiar, Ana. "Representations of Sexuality in Hungarian Popular Culture of the 1980s." *Medij. Istraz*, 16, 1 (2009): 73–95.
Malfatto, Monica. "In the Footsteps of Pornography." *Zhenata Dnes*, 8 (1980): 33.
Mamonova, Tatyana. *Russian Women's Studies: Essays on Sexism in Soviet Culture*. Oxford: Pergamon Press, 1994.
Marciniak, Katarzyna (2006). *Alienhood, Citizenship, and the Logic of Difference*, Minneapolis: University of Minnesota Press.
Marciniak, Katarzyna, Imre, Aniko, and O'Healy, Áine. "Transcultural Mediations and Transnational Politics of Difference." *Feminist Media Studies*, 9, 4 (2009): 385–90.
Marciniak, Katarzyna, Imre, Aniko, and O'Healy, Áine, eds. *Transnational Feminism in Film and Media*. New York: Palgrave, 2007.
Markham, James W. "Is Advertising Important in the Soviet Economy?" *Journal of Marketing*, 28 (1964): 31–37.
Marody, Mira, and Giza-Poleszczuk, Anna. "Changing Images of Identity in Poland: From the Self-Sacrificing to the Self-Investing Woman?" In *Reproducing Gender: Politics, Publics and Everyday Life After Socialism*, edited by Susan Gal and Gail Kligman, 151–76. Princeton: Princeton University Press, 2000.
Massino, Jill. "From Black Caviar to Blackouts: Gender, Consumption, and Lifestyle in Ceausescu's Romania." In *Communism Unwrapped: Consumption in Cold War Eastern Europe*, edited by P. Bren and M. Neuburger, 226–54. Oxford: Oxford University Press, 2012.

Matland, R. E., and Bojinkova, D. "The Representation of Women in Political Parties in Central and Eastern Europe." Paper presented at the annual meeting of the American Political Science Association, Chicago, IL, 2004.
McNair, Brian. *Mediated Sex: Pornography and Postmodern Culture*. London: Arnold, 1996.
McNair, Brian. *Striptease Culture: Sex, Media and the Democratization of Desire*. London and New York: Routledge, 2002.
McQuail, Dennis. *McQuail's Mass Communication Theory*. London: Sage Publications, 2005.
McRobbie, Angela. "Post-Feminism and Popular Culture" *Feminist Media Studies*, 4, 3 (2004): 255–64.
Mead, Jenna. *Bodyjamming: Sexual Harassment, Feminism, and Public Life*. Milson Point: Vintage, 1997.
Meehan, Eileen R., and Riordan, Ellen, eds. *Sex and Money: Feminism and Political Economy in the Media*. Minneapolis: University of Minnesota Press, 2002.
Mineva, Mila. "Stories and Images of Socialist Consumption" [in Bulgarian]. *Sociologicheski Problemi*, 1–2 (2003): 143–65.
Mineva, Mila."Made in Bulgaria: The National as Advertising Repertoire." *Eurozine* (2008), originally published in *Critique & Humanism* 25 [in Bulgarian].
Muzlekov, Marin. "Facts That Worry Us." *Zhenata Dnes*, 4 (1974): 19.
Naiman, Eric. *Sex in Public: The Incarnation of Early Soviet Ideology*. Princeton: Princeton University Press, 1997.
Napoleoni, Loretta. *Rogue Economics. Capitalism's New Reality*. New York: Seven Stories Press, 2008.
Neuburger, Mary. "Pants, Veils, and Matters of Dress: Unraveling the Fabric of Women's Lives in Communist Bulgaria." In *Style and Socialism: Modernity and Material Culture in Post-War Eastern Europe*, edited by D. Rowley and S. Reid, 169–87. Oxford: Berg Publishing, 2000.
Nikolic, Tea. "Serbian Sexual Response: Gender and Sexuality in Serbia during the 1990s." In *Sexuality and Gender in Post-Communist Eastern Europe and Russia*, edited by Alesandar Stulhofer and Theo Sanfort, 125–40. New York: The Haworth Press, 2005.
Nikolova, R. "Who Will Be the New Freedom Fighters in Sliven." *Trud* (June 11, 2005): 14. Retrieved March 15, 2006, from http://www.trud.bg.
Nord, David P. "The Nature of Historical Research." In *Research Methods in Mass Communication*, edited by Guido Stempel and B. H. Westley, 290–315. Upper Saddle River, NJ: Prentice-Hall, 1989.
Norman, Beret. "'Test the West': East German Performance Art Takes on Western Advertising." *The Journal of Popular Culture*, XXXIV (2000): 255–67.
Norris, Pippa, ed. *Women, Media and Politics*. New York: Oxford University Press, 1997.
Nove, Alec. *An Economic History of the USSR, 1917–1991*. London: Penguin, 1992.
Oakley, Ann. "Sexuality." In *Feminism and Sexuality: A Reader*, edited by S. Stevi Jackson and Sue Scott, 35–40. New York: Columbia University Press, 1996.
"Open Letter to the Ministry of Light Industry." *Zhenata Dnes*, 2 (1963): 14.
"Overhead in the Hallway." *Trud* (July 12, 2005): 3. Retrieved March 11, 2006, from http://www.trud.bg.
Papazova, Zlatka. "Venus's Weapon." *Bhozur*, 3 (1991): 38.
"Parliament Hopefuls Like a Cow." *Trud* (May 29, 2005): 5. Retrieved March 11, 2006, from http://www.trud.bg.
Pasca-Harsanyi, Doina. "Women in Romania." In *Gender, Politics, and Post-Communism. Reflections from Eastern Europe and the Former Soviet Union*, edited by Nannette Funk and Magda Mueller, 42–52. London: Routledge, 1993.
Patterson, Patrick H. "Truth Half Told: Finding the Perfect Pitch for Advertising and Marketing in Socialist Yugoslavia, 1950–1991." *Enterprise and Society*, 4 (2003): 179–225.
Patterson, Patrick H. "Just rewards? Communism's Hard Bargain with the Citizen-Consumer." A National Council for Eurasian and East European Research Report, 2008.
Peake, Lucy. "Press Coverage of Women Candidates for the UK Parliament." Paper presented at the ECPR 25th Joint Sessions of Workshops, Universität Bern, Switzerland, 1997.
Peshev, Georgi. "An Experiment: Girls in the Line of Duty." *Zhenata Dnes*, 2 (1989): 30–31.

Peter Williams Foreign Policy Blog (March 2011). Retrieved January 28, 2013, from http://blog.foreignpolicy.com/blog/21416.
Popkostadinova, Nikoleta. "Bulgarian Vogue: Socialist or Not, Lada is the Coolest Bulgarian Fashion Magazine" (n.d.). Retrieved May 11, 2011, from http://www.viceland.com/bg/v2n4/htdocs/bbjta-365.php.
Popov, Julian. "Do Women Rule Bulgaria?" *Al-Jazeera* (December 15, 2011). Retrieved May 2, 2012, from http://www.aljazeera.com/indepth/opinion/2011/12/20111210122330666785.html
Popova, Pavlina. "Stop, Julieta, Stop." *Zhenata Dnes*, 9 (1972): 14–15.
Popova, Velislava. "Bulgaria." In *Media Ownership and its Impact on Media Independence and Pluralism* (2004): 94–116. Retrieved September 21, 2004, from http://www.mirovni-institut.si/media_ownership/bulgaria.htm.
Pusnik, Marusa, and Bulc, Gregor. "Women in Their Own Reflections: Self-Representation of Women Politicians in the Slovenian Press." *Journal of Communication Inquiry*, 25, 4 (2001): 396–413.
Rakow, Lana, and Kranich, Kimberlie. "Women as Sign in Television News." *Journal of Communication*, 41 (1991): 8–23.
Ranova, Elitza. "Of Gloss, Glitter and Lipstick: Fashion, Femininity and Wealth in Post-Socialist Urban Bulgaria." *Anthropology of East Europe Review*, 24, 2 (2006): 25–34.
Reid, Susan. "Cold War in the Kitchen: Gender and the De-Stalinization of Consumer Taste in the Soviet Union under Khrushchev." *Slavic Review*, 61, 2 (2002): 211–52.
Reid, Susan, and Crowley, David. *Style and Socialism: Modernity and Material Culture in Post-War Eastern Europe.* New York: Berg, 2000.
Remmler, Karen. "Deciphering the Body of Memory: Writing by Former East German Women Writers." In *Postcommunism and the Body Politic*, edited by Ellen Berry, 134–63. New York: New York University Press, 1995.
"Remnants of a Barbaric Past." *Zhenata Dnes*, 10 (1969): 9.
Rice, Timothy. "Bulgaria or Chalgaria: The Attenuation of Bulgarian Nationalism in Mass-Mediated Popular Music. *Yearbook of Traditional Music*, 34 (2002): 25–46.
Robinson, Gertrude, and Saint-Jean, Armande. "Women Politicians and Their Media Coverage: A Generational Analysis." In *Women in Canadian Politics* (vol. 6), edited by K. Megyery, 127–69. Toronto: Dundurn Press, 1991.
Roman, Denise. "Gendering Eastern Europe: Pre-Feminism, Prejudice, and East-West Dialogues in Post-Communist Romania." *Women's Studies International Forum*, 24, 1 (2001): 55–66.
Roman, Denise. *Fragmented Identities: Popular Culture, Sex, and Everyday Life in Post-Communist Romania.* Lanham, MD: Lexington Books, 2003.
Rosenberry, Jack, and Vicker, Lauren A. *Applied Mass Communication Theory.* Boston: Pearson, 2009.
Ross, Karen. *Women, Politics and Media: Uneasy Relations in Comparative Perspective.* Cresskill, NJ: Hampton Press, 2002.
Ross, Karen, and Sreberny, Annabelle. "Women in the House: Media Representation of British Politicians." In *Gender, Politics and Communication*, edited by A. Sreberny and L. van Zoonen, 79–99. Cresskill, NJ: Hampton Press, 2000.
Rotkirch, Anna. "Women's Agency and the Sexual Revolution in Russia." Paper presented at the research seminar on Women's Active Citizenship University of Joensuu, Department of Social Policy and Philosophy, Helsinki, Finland, September 11, 1997.
Said, Edward. *Orientalism.* New York: Penguin, 2003/1978.
Salecl, Renata. *The Tyranny of Choice.* London: Profile Books, 2010.
Samardjieva, Violeta. "Women and the Scientific Technical Revolution." *Zhenata Dnes*, 7 (1970): 14–15.
Sarnavka, Sanya, Mihalec, Kristina, and Sudar, Nevenka. "Croatian Feminists Stave Off Onslaught of Sexist Media." *Off Our Back*, xxxiii (2002): 3–4, 13–17.
Scheufele, Dietram. "Framing as a Theory of Media Effects." *Journal of Communication*, 49, 1, (1999): 103–22.

Scheufele, Dietram, and Tewksbury, David. "Framing, Agenda Setting, and Priming: The Evolution of Three Media Effects Models." *Journal of Communication*, 57, 1 (2007): 9–20.
Schippers, Mimi. "Recovering the Feminine Other: Masculinity, Femininity, and Gender Hegemony." *Theory and Society*, 36, 1 (2007): 85–102.
Schudson, Michael. *Advertising, the Uneasy Persuasion: Its Dubious Impact on American Society*. London: Routledge, 1984.
Sender, Katherine. "Sex Sells: Sex, Taste, and Class in Commercial Gay and Lesbian Media." *GLQ*. 9, 9 (2003): 331–65.
Siebert, Fred S., Peterson, Theodore, and Schramm, Wilbur W. *Four Theories of the Press*. Urbana: University of Illinois Press, 1963.
Sieg, Katrin. "Sex, Subjectivity, and Socialism: Feminist Discourse in East Germany." In *Post-Communism and the Body Politic*, edited by Ellen Berry, 105–34. New York: New York University Press, 1995.
Simeonov, Vasil. "Affair at the Office." *Bhozur*, 7 (1995): 37.
Slavov, Ivan. "Against the Consumerist Psychology" [in Bulgarian]. *Kultura*, 48 (1971): 3.
Slavova, Kornelia. "Looking at Western Feminisms through the Double Lens of Eastern Europe and the Third World." In *Women and Citizenship in Central and Eastern Europe*, edited by Jasmina Lukic, Joanna Regulska, and Darja Zavirek, 245–63. Aldershot, UK: Ashgate, 2006.
Sloat, Amanda. "Engendering European Politics: The Influence of the European Union on Women in Central and Eastern Europe." Paper presented at the Midwest Political Science Association, Chicago, IL, 2005.
Slobin, Greta. "Revolution Must Come First: Reading V. Aksenov's *Island of Crimea*." In *Nationalism and Sexualities*, edited by A. Parker, M. Russo, and P. Yaeger. London: Routledge, 1992.
Sparks, Glenn. *Media Effects Research*. Belmont, CA: Wadsworth Thomson, 2002.
Spence, Janet T., and Buckner, Camille. "Masculinity and Femininity: Defining the Undefinable." In *Gender, Power, and Communication in Human Relationships*, edited by Pamela Kalbfleisch and Michael J. Cody, 105–38. Hillsdale, NJ: Lawrence Erlbaum Associates, 1995.
Sreberny-Mohammadi, Annabelle, and Ross, Karen. "Women MPs and the Media: Representing the Body Politic." *Parliamentary Affairs*, 49 (1996): 103–15.
Sreberny, Annabelle, and Van Zoonen, Liesbet. *Gender, Politics and Communication*. Cresskill, NJ: Hampton Press, 2000.
Stitziel, Judd. *Fashioning Socialism: Clothing, Politics, and Consumer Culture in East Germany*. Oxford: Berg, 2005.
Svab, Alenka. "Consuming Western Image of Well-Being: Shopping Tourism in Socialist Slovenia." *Cultural Studies*, 16, 1 (2002): 63–79.
Svendsen, Mette Nordahl. "The Post-Communist Body: Beauty and Aerobics in Romania." *Anthropology of East Europe Review*, 14, 1 (1996): 8–15.
Swayne, Linda E. "Soviet Advertising: Communism Imitates Capitalism to Survive." In *The Role of Advertising*, edited by Charles H. Sandage and Vernon Fryburger, 93–104. Homewood, IL: R. D. Irwin, 1960.
Tankova, Diamana. "In Bad Need of A Good Image," *Vagabond* (n.d). Retrieved September 2009, http://old.vagabond.bg/?page=live&sub=37&open_news=1047.
Thornham, Sue. *Women, Feminism and Media*. Edinburgh: Edinburgh University Press, 2007.
Tīfentāle, Alise. "The Language and Value of Things under Communism and Capitalism." *Dizaina Studija* (2008). Retrieved March 31, 2012, from http://www.dizainastudija.eu/index.php/en/0/2/188/316/318/index.html.
Todorov, Bozhan. "The Problems of Visual Propaganda" [in Bulgarian]. *Kultura*, 18 (1971): 3.
Todorov, Konstantin. "The Need for Advertising" [in Bulgarian]. *Kultura*, 4 (1989): 1.
Todorova, Maria. *Imagining the Balkans*. New York: Oxford University Press, 1997.
Todorova, R. "Miss Parliament." *Trud* (July 15, 2005): 12. Retrieved March 15, 2006, from http://www.trud.bg.
Tolstikova, Natasha. "Early Soviet Advertising: We Have to Extract all the Stinking Bourgeois Elements." *Journalism History*, 33, 1 (2007): 42–50.

"Travel Tips for the Wife." *Zhenata Dnes*, 10 (1971): 25.
True, Jacqui. *Gender Globalization and Post-Socialism: The Czech Republic after Communism*. New York: Columbia University Press, 2003.
Tuchman, Gaye. *Making the News: A Study in the Construction of Reality*. New York: The Free Press, 1978.
"UN Human Development Report" (2005). Retrieved September 2005, from http://hdr.undp.org/reports/global/2005/.
Vacheva, Dimitria. "Things That Worry Us." *Zhenata Dnes*, 3(1968): 7.
Vaknin, Sam. "Women in Transition: From Post-Feminism to Post-Femininity." *Central Europe Review*, 3, 22 (2001). Retrieved June 20, 2011, from http://www.ce-review.org/01/3/vaknin3.html.
Van Acker, Elizabeth. "Media Representations of Women Politicians in Australia and New Zealand: High Expectations, Hostility or Stardom." *Policy, Organization and Society*, 22, 1 (2003): 116–36.
Van Dijk, Teun. "Ideological Discourse Analysis." *Courant*, 4 (1996): 135–36.
Van Zoonen, Liesbet. *Feminist Media Studies*. London: Sage Publications, 1994.
Veleva, Violeta. "Interview with Dora Yankova." *Trud* (July 2, 2005): 10–11. Retrieved March 15, 2006, from http://www.trud.bg.
Veleva, Violeta. "Even in Walking Against the Wind, I Always Succeed." Interview with Eleonora Nikolova, *Trud* (July 23, 2005): 15. Retrieved March 15, 2006, from http://www.trud.bg.
Verdery, Katherine. "From Parent-State to Family Patriarchs: Gender and Nation in Contemporary Eastern Europe." *East European Politics and Societies*, 8, 2 (1994): 225–55.
Verdery, Katherine . *What Was Socialism, and What Comes Next?* Princeton: Princeton University Press, 1996.
Vorošilov, Vladimir. *Marketingovye kommunikacii v žurnalistike* [Marketing Commnications and Jouralism]. Saint Petersburg: Izdatel´stvo Mixajlova, 2000.
Walker, Alice. "Coming Apart." In *Take Back the Night: Feminist Papers on Pornography*, edited by Laura Lederer, 95–104. New York: William Morrow and Company, 1980 .
Waters, Elizabeth. "Soviet Beauty Contests." In *Sex and Russian Society*, edited by Igor Kon and James Riordian, 116–35. London: Pluto Press, 1993.
"Who Are They Familiarizing With? With Simeon and Nadezhda." *Trud* (May 29, 2005): 7. Retrieved March 11, 2006, from http://www.trud.bg.
Williams, Raymond. "Advertising: The Magic System". In *Problems in Materialism and Culture*, edited by Raymond Williams, 170–96. London: New Left Books, 1980.
Williamson, Judith . *Decoding Advertisements*. London: Marion Boyars, 1978.
Winship, Janice (1980). Sexuality for sale. In *Culture, Media, Language*, eds Stuart Hall, Dorothy Hobson, Andrew Lowe, & Paul Willis. London, Hutchinson, pp. 217–23.
Winship, Janice. "Women Outdoors: Advertising, Controversy and Disputing Feminism in the 1990s." *International Journal of Cultural Studies*, 3, 1 (2000): 27–55.
Wolf, Naomi. *The Beauty Myth*. New York: Morrow, 1991.
"Women and Journalists First." Report by the Steering Committee for Equality between Women and Men (CDEG). Council of Europe, Strasbourg, December 11, 2011.
Woodcock, Shannon. "Romanian Women's Discourses of Sexual Violence: Othered Ethnicities, Gendered Spaces." In *Living Gender After Communism*, edited by Janet Elise Johnson and Jean C. Robinson, 149–69. Bloomington: Indiana University Press, 2007.
World Trends in Advertising. Published by the World Advertising Research Center (WARC), 2007.
Ziapkova, Nevena. "Children at Play." *Zhenata Dnes* (1969): 21.
Žikić, Biljana. "Dissidents Liked Pretty Girls: Nudity, Pornography and Quality Press in Socialism." *Medij. Istraz*, 16, 1 (2009): 53–71.

Index

advertising, xi, xiii–xiv, xvi, xx, xxii–xxiv, 153–155, 156, 157, 158
 and cultural pedagogy, 153
 and magic system, xi, xxii, xxivn1, xxivn2, xxvn33, 170
aesthetics, xiv, 21, 40, 47, 48, 49, 57, 62, 86, 115, 116
agitation advertising, 50
Agitreklama, 50
alcohol advertising, 114
Amazon warrior, 82, 84, 115
Andrei, 93
aparachiks, 94
April Plenum, 58–59
Atwood, Feona, xxiii

Balkans, the, xvii–xviii, xx, xxiv, xviii, 21, 80, 82, 124, 169
beauty, xiii, xv, xvi, xxi, 9, 17, 18, 19, 20, 22, 23, 26, 36, 40, 42–43, 46n100, 60, 62, 85–86, 87–88, 89, 91, 93, 99, 101, 103–104, 108, 115, 116, 116–117, 118–119, 126–127, 128, 129n12, 132, 136, 137–138, 143, 144, 153, 164, 169, 170; contests, 88, 89, 91, 99, 109n45, 109n48, 110n55; myth, 87, 88, 108; pageants, xv, 88, 89, 91, 121; "sanctioned", 90
body capital, 116–117
Bulgaria, 2, 4–5, 6, 8, 14–15, 17, 18, 19, 21, 26, 27–29, 37, 40, 42, 48, 49, 57, 58–59, 59–61, 67, 70, 77, 86, 91, 96, 98, 99, 103, 114, 116–117, 118–119, 128, 130n32, 131, 132, 136, 140, 142, 152, 153, 155, 157
Burda Moden, 91
byt, 14, 20, 24

capitalism, xi, xii, 1, 23, 29, 32, 40, 50, 55, 69, 70n1, 97, 107, 125, 152, 153, 155–156, 158n13, 159n18, 167, 169
chalga, 118, 126–127, 127, 129n17, 129n18, 130n40, 152, 157, 168
commercial eroticism, 65
commodification, 76, 97, 124–125, 127, 152, 154
communism, xii–xiii, xiv, xvi, xx, xxii, xxiv, 17, 32, 44n13, 44n23, 44n26, 44n35, 47, 48, 69, 70n1, 78, 85, 105, 108n15, 115, 117, 119, 131, 141, 151, 158n6, 158n12, 158n13, 159n14; collapse of, xiv, xxii, 93, 116, 123, 151, 158n6, 165; national, 21
consumption, 18, 20, 23, 44n29, 44n35, 47, 48, 49, 50, 51–52, 53, 54, 54, 55, 56–57, 59, 60–61, 62, 63, 63–64, 65, 67–69, 70, 71n37, 72n61, 72n68, 75–76, 90, 102, 116, 120, 124–125, 151, 154, 155; capitalist, 24, 69; controlled, 50, 63; conspicuous, 62; cultured, 62; gendered, 26, 108n6, 108n15

cosmetics, 18, 19, 86, 100, 101, 129n16, 154, 164
cultural capital, 116

divorce, 9–10, 13, 32, 80, 81
domestic abuse, 9, 91
double burden, 5, 11–12, 13, 42, 162

East Germany, 19, 46n88, 47, 55, 56–57, 90, 97, 109n32. *See* GDR
8th Congress, 60
emancipation, xvii, 1, 6, 24, 31, 42, 77, 78–79, 80–81, 84, 85, 98, 113, 115, 119
empire of seduction, 155, 156
erotica, xv, 34, 77, 86, 91, 92, 93, 96. *See also* commercial eroticism
eugenics, 42

fashion, xv, xxii, 19, 21, 24, 24–30, 40, 40, 48, 61, 62, 65, 87, 89–91, 98, 101, 115, 116, 119

models, 29, 42, 87, 89, 116, 137

. *See also* socialist, fashion
"father" state, 82

feminine mystique, 103, 119
femininity, xv, xx, xxi, xxii, xxiii, 2, 3, 4, 17, 18, 19, 22, 23, 24–25, 30, 76, 85, 86, 87, 90, 91, 94, 100, 102, 107, 109n44, 115, 116, 117, 118, 119, 129n23, 135, 138, 139, 141, 145, 151, 157, 168, 169, 170; post-socialist, 102
framing, 135, 148n34, 162, 168

Gal, Susan and Kligman, Gail, 13, 43n4, 44n17, 44n28, 80, 165
GDR, 56–57, 82, 97
gender status quo, 86
gender stereotypes, xxi, 132, 134, 136
gendered mediation, 135, 136, 143
Ghodsee, Kristen, 18, 44n29, 76, 101, 103, 116, 117, 123, 129n10, 147n3, 155, 158n12, 164
glamour under control, 90

homo consumens, 68
Hungary, xix, 34, 70n1, 77, 86, 90

ideology, xii, xiii, xviii, xii, xiii, xxii, xxiii, 5, 32, 33, 50, 52, 53, 54, 82, 119, 138, 152, 153, 158, 164, 167; communist, xiv, 8–9, 16, 19, 35, 58, 80, 116, 128; gender, 37, 40, 81, 98, 107, 115; market, 55, 152, 158; misogynist, 135; parochial, 106; Soviet, xviii, 3, 7–8, 13, 17, 33, 39, 40, 53, 58, 63, 90, 94, 97, 153, 167
Imre, Aniko, xvi, xx, xxvn17, 76, 111n98

Jhally, Sutt, xii, xxivn4, xxvn11

Kaier, Christina, 20, 22–23, 44n34
Khrushchev, 52
Kipnis, Laura, xxiii, xxvin41

Lepa Brena, 94

macho, 143; culture, 151; liberation, 128
mafia, 117–118, 129n17, 166
magic system, xxii
malestream, 145
Marxist, 1, 10, 23, 29, 48, 53, 55, 113
masculinization, 119, 145, 151
maternity, 36, 113; discourse, 78; pseudo-, 131, 146
matrix of domination, 124
Mayakovski, 51
McNair, Brian, xxiii, xxvn39, 167
McRobbie, Angela, 156, 159n16, 167
modernism, 21, 24, 66
mythical heroine, 115, 116

NEP, 50–51, 72n43, 72n44, 162. *See also* Nepmen
Nepmen, 50, 72n43, 72n44, 162
Neuburger, Mary, 6, 44n10, 58, 156, 159n14, 162, 167
nomenklatura, 90

objectification, 40, 88, 165
Orientalism, xvii, 168

patriarchy, xiv, xviii, xix, 2, 6, 82, 83, 88, 107, 119; domesticated, 5; Muslim, 6; orthodox, 1; precommunist, 1
paternalistic state, 82, 86. *See also* "father" state; socialist, paternalism

planned economy, xii, 30, 48, 55, 57, 67, 76
plural subordination, 124
Poland, xix, 37, 44n8, 142
political economy, 154
of the newsroom, 136

pop folk, 117–118, 126–127. *See also* turbo folk
Popova, Liubov, 24, 24–25
porno-chic, 128, 158
pornographication, xxiii
pornography, xxiii, 77, 92–93, 94, 96, 97, 99, 108n10, 110n60, 124, 154, 165, 167. *See also* porno-chic; pornographication
post-socialism, 107, 125, 129n10, 130n38, 156, 164, 170
propaganda, 11, 36, 39, 48, 48, 54, 55, 58, 62, 66, 67, 75, 113, 125, 144, 145, 151; Communist, 42; commercial, 152; Party, 36; Soviet, 51, 53, 114; state, 39
public hygiene, 18, 35

Reklama, 51, 52, 71n34, 163
Rodchenko, Alexander, 22, 23–24, 25, 51
Roman, Denise, 75, 90, 108n2, 108n4, 110n55, 119, 124, 130n27, 130n37, 135
Romania, xviii, xix, xxii, 20–21, 26, 35, 37, 44n35, 78, 86, 108n2, 108n4, 108n15, 116, 117, 123, 129n9, 129n12, 130n31, 135, 144, 148n22, 148n27, 157, 159n20, 161
Russian constructivism, 22

Said, Edward. *See* Orientalism
Serbia, xviii, xix, 94, 95, 96, 110n70, 110n71, 118, 129n21, 134, 148n23. *See also* Yugoslavia
sex, xi, xiii, xiv, xv, xvi, xx, xxi, xxiii, xxvn11, xxvn31, xxvn39, xxvin40, 18, 22, 24, 25, 32–33, 34, 35, 36–37, 38, 39–40, 42, 45n62, 45n66, 45n76, 45n78, 65, 75, 76, 77, 79, 80–81, 92, 93, 94, 96, 97, 105, 105–106, 108n14, 109n32, 111n98, 121, 123, 126, 127, 133, 144, 145, 146, 152, 154

. *See* also sexism; sexual agency; sexual behavior; sexual complementarity; sexuality; sexualization; sex wave
sexism, 88, 95, 118, 133, 146
sexual agency, 89, 104
sexual behavior, xx, xxiii, 33, 34, 35, 36, 38, 76
sexual complementarity, 106
sexuality, xix, xxiii, xix, xxi–xxii, 18, 22, 24, 31, 32, 32–33, 34, 35, 39, 45n61, 65, 76, 77, 86–87, 92–93, 94, 94–95, 96, 99, 105, 115, 116, 118, 124, 128, 152, 153, 155, 158
sexualization, xv, 118, 119, 120, 121, 123–124, 126, 128, 152, 153, 155, 158
sex wave, 97
socialist, xi

advertising, ix, xix, 22, 24, 54, 56, 61, 66, 67, 68, 70, 89
aesthetics, 47, 48, 57, 116

consumerism, 58
consumption, 21, 58, 60, 72n68, 72n78, 73n90, 73n103, 89, 101, 110n87, 151, 167

fashion, 19, 20, 21–2, 22, 24, 27, 29, 30, 40, 41, 42, 89
feminist discourse, 82

paternalism, 9
propaganda, 2, 48, 68

realism, xi–xii, 21

utopia, 21, 82

socialization, 53, 125, 135
Soviet Burda, 91
Soviet style marketing, 55
spectacle, 143
Stalin, xxivn7, 33, 51, 55, 59, 71n4, 71n40, 164, 168. *See also* Stalinist
Stalinist, 33, 55
Stepanova, Varvara, 22, 24, 25–26

Todorova, Maria, xvii, xviii, xxvn18, 169
turbo folk, 94–95

tyranny of choice, 156, 159n15

Verdery, Katherine, 1, 9, 43n4, 44n12, 76, 108n2, 108n5
vodka, 114, 120–121, 123. *See also* alcohol advertising
VSNKh Advertising Commission, 54
vulgar Marxism, 33. *See also* Marxist

Williams, Raymond. *See* magic system

woman question, the, 13, 14, 16, 31, 78
women's magazines, 2, 11, 18, 21, 26, 30, 31, 42, 77, 78, 82, 86, 91, 107, 125, 129n10, 130n31, 130n38, 156, 164, 170

Yugoslavia, xix, 34, 55–56, 57, 70n1, 76–77, 92, 94, 95

Zhivkov, Todor, 59

About the Author

Elza Ibroscheva is associate professor and director of graduate studies at the Department of Mass Communications, Southern Illinois University Edwardsville. Born and raised in Bulgaria, she witnessed firsthand the exhilarating changes that brought about the end of communism and has closely observed the dramatic changes of the post-socialist transition. Ibroscheva holds a bachelor of arts degree in journalism and mass communication and English from the American University in Bulgaria, a master's degree in journalism and a PhD in mass communications and media arts from Southern Illinois University. She has been the recipient of a number of research and study grants, including awards from ACLS, IREX, University of Oslo, Norway, and Central European University. Ibroscheva is also the author of several book chapters and peer-reviewed articles. Her research interests include women, gender and politics in the media, international and political communication, studies of advertising, and the effects of globalization on culture.